KILIMANJARO

ASCENT PREPARATIONS, PRACTICALITIES AND TREKKING ROUTES TO THE 'ROOF OF AFRICA'

About the Author

Alexander Stewart has been writing guidebooks for 15 years and is the author of six trekking guides around the world. He has a passion for wild places and is particularly interested in mountains. Throughout his adult life he has walked in them, written about them and photographed them. However, he doesn't often find himself on top of them, except on home soil in the UK. Kilimanjaro made a significant impression on him during his first ascent in 1999, and he has subsequently been drawn back repeatedly to the 'Roof of Africa'.

KILIMANJARO

ASCENT PREPARATIONS, PRACTICALITIES AND TREKKING ROUTES TO THE 'ROOF OF AFRICA'

by Alexander Stewart

JUNIPER HOUSE, MURLEY MOSS,
OXENHOLME ROAD, KENDAL, CUMBRIA LA9 7RL
www.cicerone.co.uk

Second edition 2018
ISBN: 978 1 85284 758 6
First edition 2004

Printed in China on behalf of Latitude Press Ltd
A catalogue record for this book is available from the British Library.
All photographs are by the author unless otherwise stated.

For Rory and Merryn and Esme.
And for Katie, of course.

Updates to this Guide

While every effort is made by our authors to ensure the accuracy of guidebooks as they go to print, changes can occur during the lifetime of an edition. Any updates that we know of for this guide will be on the Cicerone website (www.cicerone.co.uk/758/updates), so please check before planning your trip. We also advise that you check information about such things as transport, accommodation and shops locally. Even rights of way can be altered over time.

We are always grateful for information about any discrepancies between a guidebook and the facts on the ground, sent by email to updates@cicerone.co.uk or by post to Cicerone, Juniper House, Murley Moss, Oxenholme Road, Kendal LA9 7RL, United Kingdom.

Register your book: To sign up to receive free updates, special offers and GPX files where available, register your book at www.cicerone.co.uk.

Front cover: Path across the Saddle (Marangu Route) (Martchan/Shutterstock.com)

Back cover (left to right): Resting porter (Machame Route) (photo: Alessandro Zappalorto/Shutterstock.com); Jublilant celebrations at the summit (Summit, Uhuru Peak); Camp on Shira Plateau (Machame Route) (photo: Potifor/Shutterstock.com).

CONTENTS

Warning

All mountain activities contain an element of danger, with a risk of personal injury or death. The treks described in this guidebook are no exception. Under normal conditions wandering the trails of Kilimanjaro will be neither more nor less hazardous than walking among big mountains anywhere in the world, but trekking involves physically demanding exercise in a challenging landscape, where caution is advised and a degree of stamina is often required, and it should be undertaken only by those with a full understanding of the risks, and with the training and experience to evaluate them.

In particular it is important to be aware at all times of the effects of altitude, the need for acclimatisation and the risk of acute mountain sickness.

Trekkers should be properly equipped for the routes undertaken. While every care and effort has been taken in the preparation of this guide, the user should be aware that conditions can be highly variable and change quickly. Rockfall, landslip and crumbling paths can alter the character of a route, and the presence of snow and the possibility of avalanche must be carefully considered, for these can materially affect the seriousness of a trek.

Readers are warned that sometimes a few unfortunate trekkers die of hypothermia or acute mountain sickness, while some simply lose their balance and fall from the trail due to a momentary loss of concentration. Since there is no organised mountain rescue service in Tanzania, such as exists in some mountain regions of Europe, self-help may be your only option if an accident occurs.

Therefore, except for any liability that cannot be excluded by law, neither Cicerone nor the author accepts liability for damage of any nature (including damage to property, personal injury or death) arising directly or indirectly from the information in this guide.

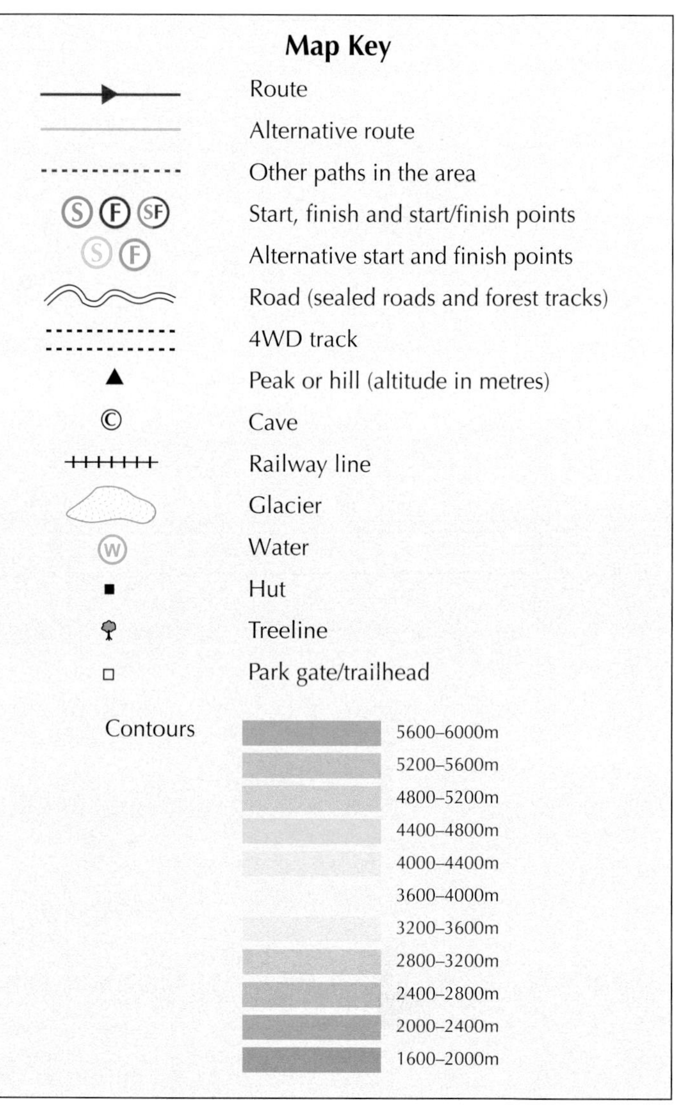
Map Key
Route
Alternative route
Other paths in the area
S F SF
Start, finish and start/finish points
S F
Alternative start and finish points
Road (sealed roads and forest tracks)
4WD track
Peak or hill (altitude in metres)
©
Cave
Railway line
Glacier
W
Water
Hut
Treeline
Park gate/trailhead
Contours
5600–6000m
5200–5600m
4800–5200m
4400–4800m
4000–4400m
3600–4000m
3200–3600m
2800–3200m
2400–2800m
2000–2400m
1600–2000m

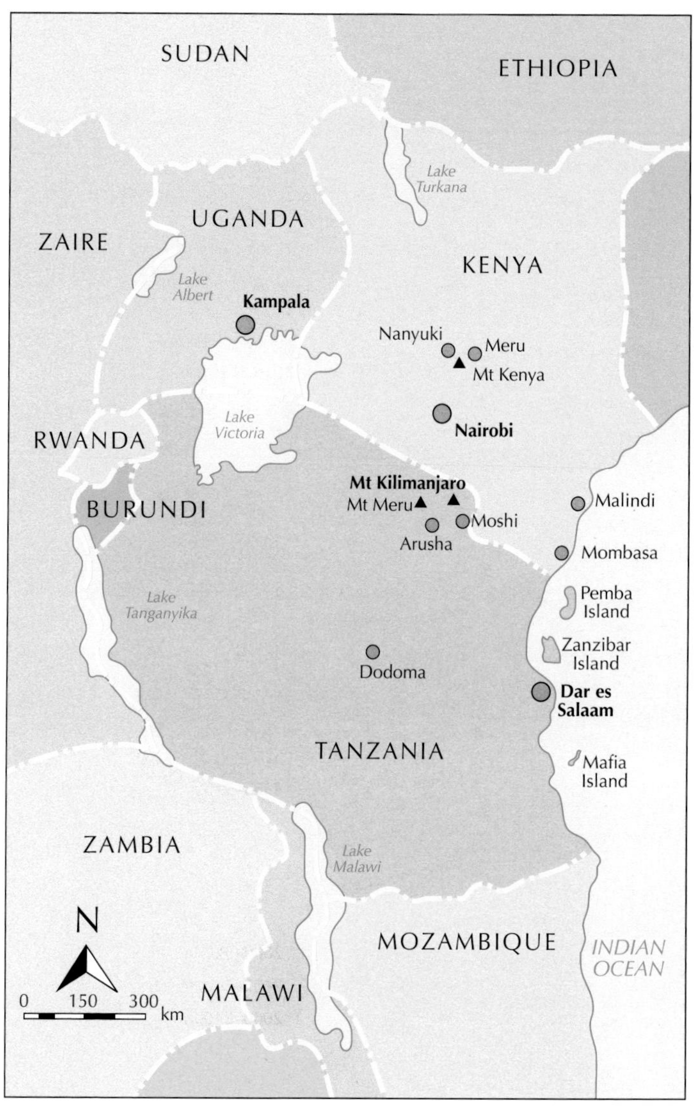

SUDAN
ETHIOPIA
Lake Turkana
UGANDA
ZAIRE
KENYA
Lake Albert
Kampala
Nanyuki
Meru
Mt Kenya
Lake Victoria
Nairobi
RWANDA
Mt Kilimanjaro
Mt Meru
Malindi
BURUNDI
Moshi
Arusha
Mombasa
Pemba Island
Lake Tanganyika
Zanzibar Island
Dodoma
Dar es Salaam
TANZANIA
Mafia Island
ZAMBIA
Lake Malawi
N
MOZAMBIQUE
INDIAN OCEAN
0 150 300 km
MALAWI

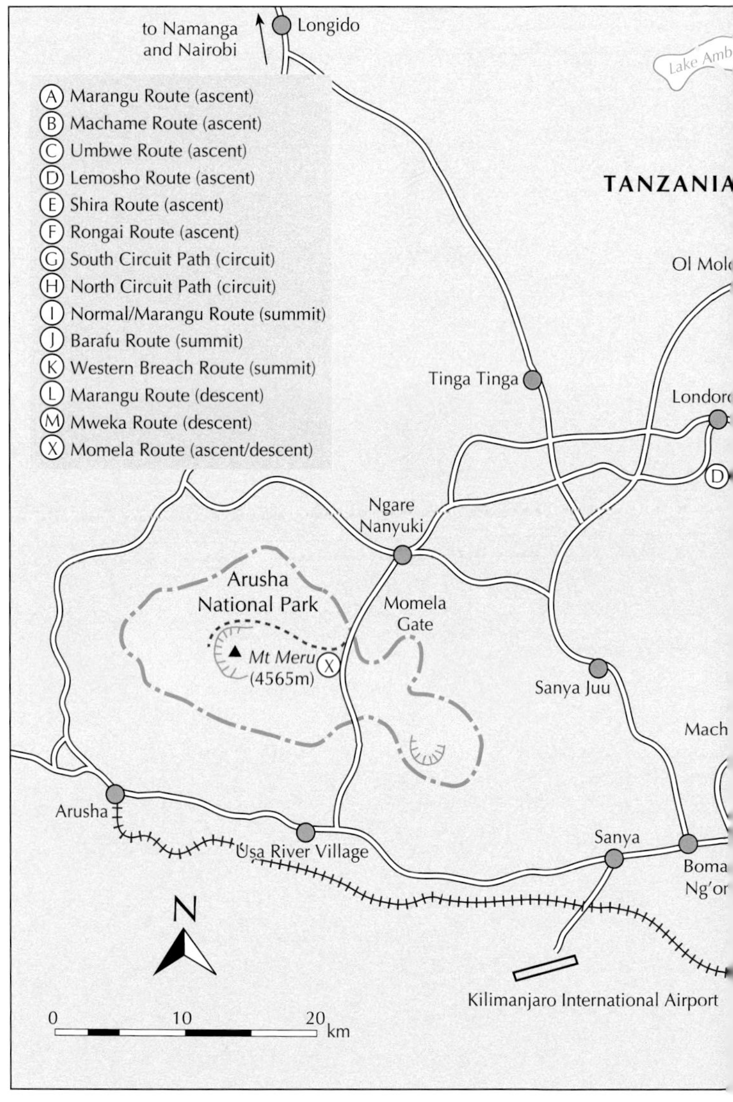
to Namanga
and Nairobi
Longido
Lake Amb
A Marangu Route (ascent)
B Machame Route (ascent)
C Umbwe Route (ascent)
D Lemosho Route (ascent)
E Shira Route (ascent)
F Rongai Route (ascent)
G South Circuit Path (circuit)
H North Circuit Path (circuit)
I Normal/Marangu Route (summit)
J Barafu Route (summit)
K Western Breach Route (summit)
L Marangu Route (descent)
M Mweka Route (descent)
X Momela Route (ascent/descent)
TANZANIA
Ol Mol
Tinga Tinga
Londor
D
Ngare
Nanyuki
Arusha
National Park
Momela
Gate
Mt Meru
(4565m)
X
Sanya Juu
Mach
Arusha
Usa River Village
Sanya
Boma
Ng'or
N
Kilimanjaro International Airport
0
10
20
km

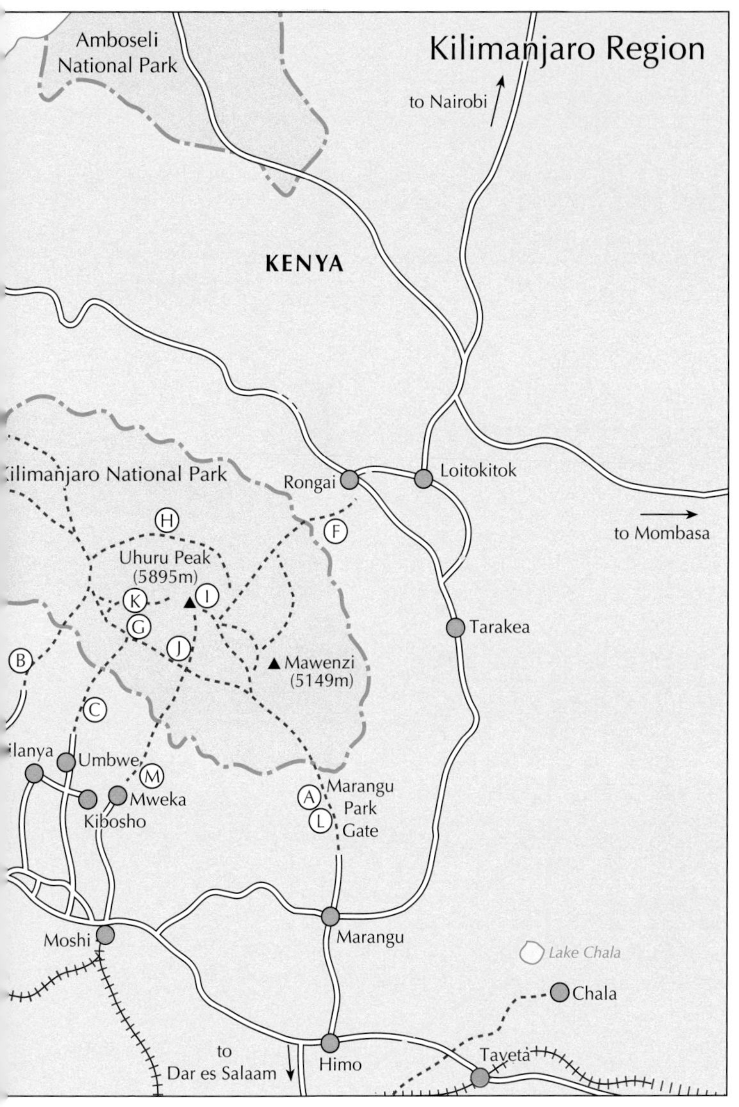

Kilimanjaro Region
Amboseli National Park
to Nairobi
KENYA
Kilimanjaro National Park
Rongai
Loitokitok
to Mombasa
H
F
Uhuru Peak (5895m)
K
I
G
J
B
Mawenzi (5149m)
Tarakea
C
ilanya
Umbwe
M
Mweka
Kibosho
A
L
Marangu Park Gate
Moshi
Marangu
Lake Chala
Chala
to Dar es Salaam
Himo
Taveta

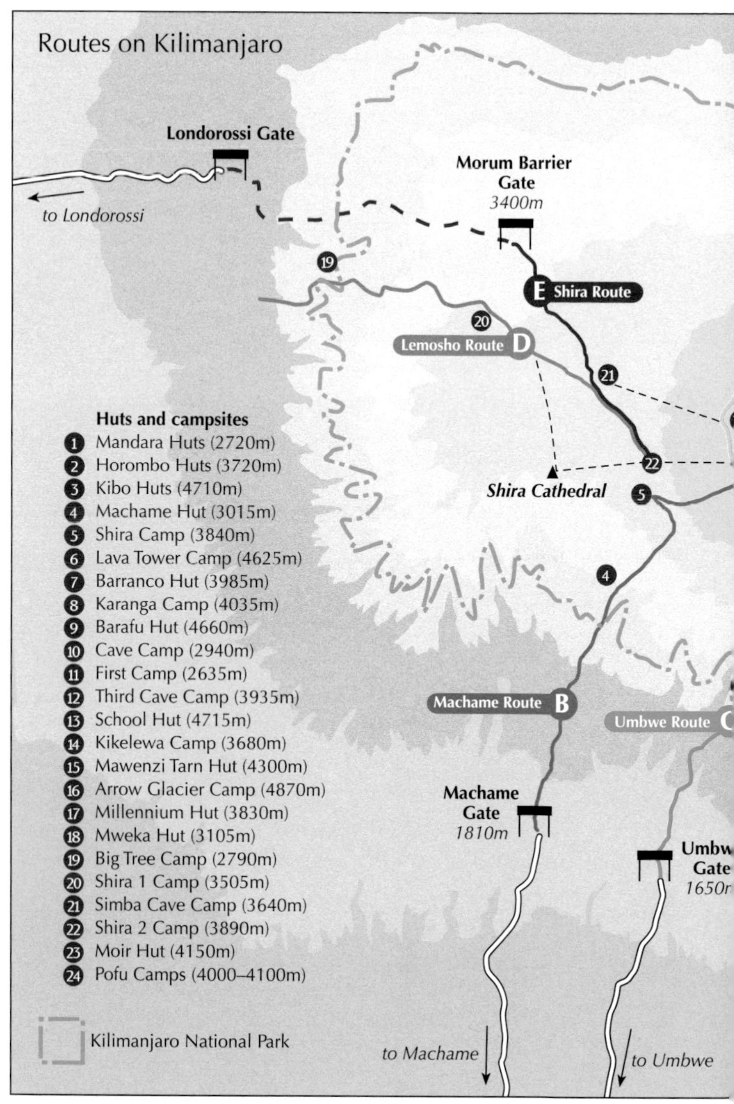
Routes on Kilimanjaro
Londorossi Gate
to Londorossi
Morum Barrier Gate
3400m
E Shira Route
Lemosho Route D
Shira Cathedral
Machame Route B
Umbwe Route C
Machame Gate
1810m
Huts and campsites
1 Mandara Huts (2720m)
2 Horombo Huts (3720m)
3 Kibo Huts (4710m)
4 Machame Hut (3015m)
5 Shira Camp (3840m)
6 Lava Tower Camp (4625m)
7 Barranco Hut (3985m)
8 Karanga Camp (4035m)
9 Barafu Hut (4660m)
10 Cave Camp (2940m)
11 First Camp (2635m)
12 Third Cave Camp (3935m)
13 School Hut (4715m)
14 Kikelewa Camp (3680m)
15 Mawenzi Tarn Hut (4300m)
16 Arrow Glacier Camp (4870m)
17 Millennium Hut (3830m)
18 Mweka Hut (3105m)
19 Big Tree Camp (2790m)
20 Shira 1 Camp (3505m)
21 Simba Cave Camp (3640m)
22 Shira 2 Camp (3890m)
23 Moir Hut (4150m)
24 Pofu Camps (4000–4100m)
Kilimanjaro National Park
to Machame
to Umbwe

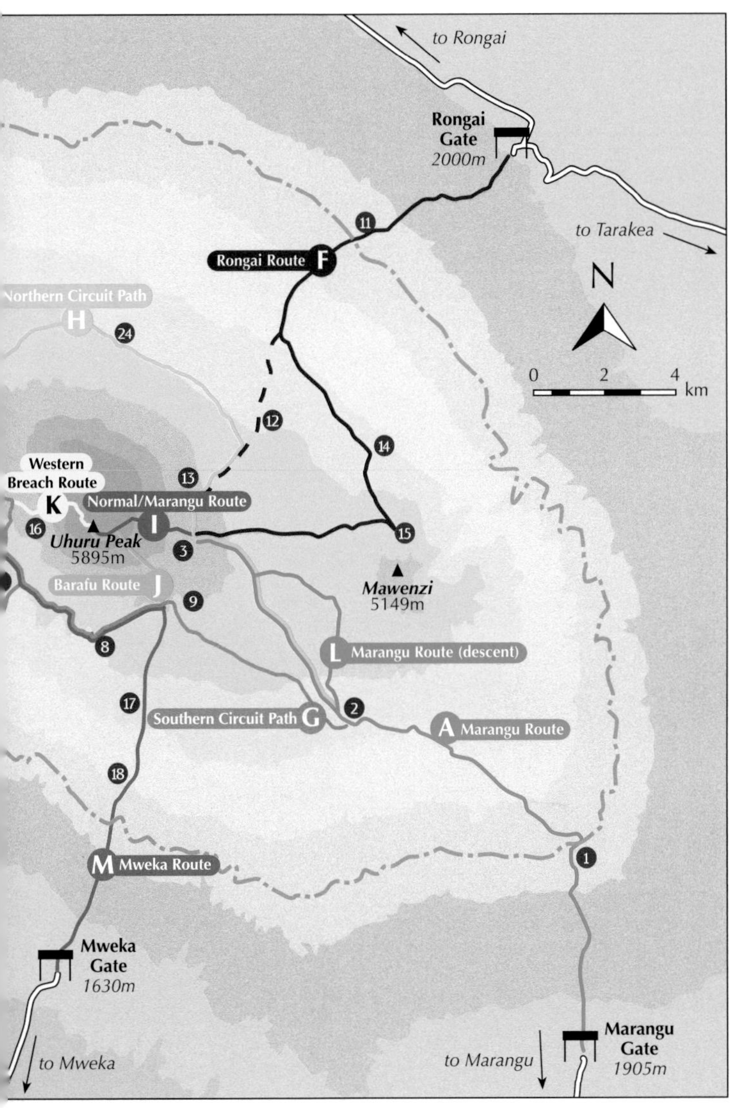
to Rongai
Rongai
Gate
2000m
to Tarakea
Rongai Route F
Northern Circuit Path
H
N
0
2
4
km
Western
Breach Route
K
Normal/Marangu Route
I
Uhuru Peak
5895m
Mawenzi
5149m
Barafu Route J
Marangu Route (descent)
L
Southern Circuit Path G
A Marangu Route
M Mweka Route
Mweka
Gate
1630m
to Mweka
to Marangu
Marangu
Gate
1905m

Ascent route	Marangu	Machame	Umbwe	Lemosho	Shira	Rongai
Length	29km	35km	14km	23km	13.5km	33km
Usual time	3 days	4 days	2 days	3 days	2 days	4 days
Grade	Moderate/hard	Hard	Hard	Moderate/hard	Moderate/hard	Moderate/hard
Vegetation	Good forest sections and moorland sections.	Superb ecological mix. Good forest and moorland sections.	Outstanding forest section. Short moorland section.	Very good forest section. Interesting Shira Plateau section.	No route through forest section on ascent. Interesting moorland section.	Poor lower slopes, deforested and cultivated. Excellent moorland section.
Interest	Lower slopes and forest very interesting. Tedious summit route. Must retrace footsteps on descent route.	Stunning scenery and exceptional views.	Good lower slopes. Excellent views of summit, Barranco Valley and Southern Icefields.	Good forest approach, excellent moorland section and fine traverse of Southern Icefields.	Good Shira Plateau section and fine traverse below Southern Icefields. 4WD access to high trailhead reduces acclimatisation potential.	Good quality route that provides exceptional access to Mawenzi. Tedious summit bid and descent on Marangu Route, which can be crowded.
Summit ascent route	Normal/Marangu	Barafu or Western Breach	Barafu or Western Breach	Barafu or Western Breach	Barafu or Western Breach	Normal/Marangu
Descent route	Marangu	Mweka	Mweka	Mweka	Mweka	Marangu
Total distance	70km	61km	48.5km	67.5km	58km	74km
Total time on mountain (minimum recommended time)	5 days	6 days	4 or 5 days	6 or 7 days	6 days	5 days

ROUTES COMPARISON TABLE

An aerial view of Kilimanjaro reveals a tangle of paths snaking their way across the slopes of the mountain. These paths are interconnected and in the course of a complete climb you will use an ascent route, a summit ascent route and a descent route, with the latter determined by the former. In total, there are six ascent paths that climb across the lower slopes of Kilimanjaro. Working your way clockwise around the mountain from the north-east, these are the Rongai Route (Route F), Marangu Route (Route A), Umbwe Route (Route C), Machame Route (Route B), Lemosho Route (Route D) and Shira Route (Route E). At around 4000m these trails all merge with a circular route that runs around Kibo cone, called either the Northern or Southern Circuit Path (Routes H and G respectively), depending on which side of the mountain you are on. Having joined this circuit path, you are faced with three ascent routes to the crater rim: the Normal/Marangu Route (Route I) from Kibo Huts to Stella Point, the Barafu Route (Route J) from Barafu to Gillman's Point and the Western Breach (Route K) from Arrow Glacier to the crater floor. If you used the Rongai Route or Marangu Route you will climb to the crater via the Normal/Marangu Route. If you used the other paths then you will have a choice of climbing either the longer but easier Barafu Route, or the shorter but more difficult Western Breach. From each arrival point on the crater there is then a short section of trail to the actual summit at Uhuru Peak. Having reached the Roof of Africa, your return journey is pre-determined by the ascent path that you used. If you came up the mountain on the Rongai Route or Marangu Route, you will return via the Marangu Route (Route L). If you ascended by any of the other routes, you will use a dedicated descent path called the Mweka Route (Route M), which falls off the southern side of the mountain below Barafu Hut.

Porter passing through the cloudforest (Machame Route) (photo: Jlwarehouse/Shutterstock)

INTRODUCTION

The aspect presented by this prodigious mountain is one of unparalleled grandeur, sublimity, majesty, and glory. It is doubtful if there be another such sight in this wide world.

Charles New, Life, Wanderings, and Labours in Eastern Africa

East Africa is most often perceived as a flat, arid savannah. Famous for its wildlife safaris and coastal resorts, it is also an extraordinary destination for lovers of mountains, trekking and climbing. Although the history of walking in East Africa is relatively young, the area is rich in potential and the continent's high mountains are among the last secret places of the region.

Africa's mountains stand as solitary peaks above the surrounding plains rather than amid a range of similar mountains. The single greatest attraction is, of course, Mount Kilimanjaro. Although there are many higher mountains in the world, Kilimanjaro is one of the highest volcanoes and the highest free-standing mountain on the planet, making it a powerful visual symbol and a quintessential African image. Rolf Edberg was moved to write that 'Its might is strangely weightless. At a distance, the mountain can seem ethereal. When the sun is low and the clouds light, the mountain with its white shimmering cap seems at times to be floating in space. At such moments, Kilimanjaro seems almost supernatural in its beauty.'

For a lot of trekkers arriving at Kilimanjaro International Airport, the first stop for many on their way to the mountain, it can be quite a shock to be confronted by this new image of Africa. The massive bulk of the country's highest peak dominates the surrounding savannah, looming over it like a colossus. Walking on the high mountains of East Africa banishes the notion that the continent is only covered in stereotypical tawny grasslands. As a result of its tremendous height and its location on the equator, Kilimanjaro's slopes are home to lush tropics, temperate climes and alpine moorland, as well as barren high-alpine desert and permanently snow-capped summits.

The rounded, glacier-clad dome of Kibo (one of the three main volcanic cones that make up Kilimanjaro) is home to Uhuru Peak, the mountain's summit, while the shattered, jagged spires of Mawenzi, Kilimanjaro's second summit, rear up across the blasted, desolate saddle. At 5895m, Uhuru Peak is the highest point on the African continent and, consequently, one of the coveted Seven Summits. Yet it is possible to reach the Roof of Africa without any technical climbing ability. Would-be mountaineers hoping to top one of the Seven Summits naturally gravitate towards Kilimanjaro. With its readily accessible, non-technical slopes, abundance of porters and relatively mild weather, the climb to the summit is considered a moderately easy ascent in mountaineering circles. Climbers with a decent level of fitness, positive attitude and a body that acclimatises to altitude reasonably well have a good chance of success: nowhere else on earth is it possible to scale a mountain of such height without crampons, ice axes and a healthy fear of losing a few fingers to frost bite.

Yet surprisingly large numbers of people fail to make it to the top. Kilimanjaro is a massive personal challenge in defiance of the extreme altitude. Walkers climbing the mountain move through half a dozen environments and climate zones from tropics to polar, and back, typically in the course of only five or six days. By going up so quickly, you break all the rules of mountaineering, yet convention, the types of ascent typically offered by outfitters and the cost of spending each day on the mountain mean that climbers are willing to jeopardise their success by rushing to altitude.

However, the ascent is intensely gratifying and enlightening. Those who visit are amply rewarded by what they encounter: diverse and colourful scenery, stunning natural beauty, endemic flora, warm and friendly locals and a unique sense of isolation. This last impression is reinforced by the knowledge that only a little more than 150 years ago this vast mountain was part of geographers' legend and remained unseen or unclimbed by Europeans. A giant glacier-capped colossus slap up against the earth's hot equator seemed so improbable that in 1849 a German missionary hurried back to Europe with news of his sighting, only to be ridiculed. Verification took another 12 years. It had yet to be conquered by 1886, when Victoria had the border between British and German East Africa redrawn to gift Kilimanjaro to her cousin, the future Kaiser Wilhelm.

There is no independent trekking on Kilimanjaro and every ascent of the mountain must be made in the company of a licensed guide, who will inevitably be accompanied by a team of cooks, assistants and porters. These days it would be a stretch to describe Kilimanjaro as off-the-beaten path. Nonetheless, the mountain wears its celebrity lightly and an ascent of Kilimanjaro remains a gruelling classic trek with magnificent views that are unmatched in Africa. The real magic of the mountain is its stunning beauty and fascinating natural history. To make the most of your trek, walk slowly with your eyes open and you'll come home with something far more important than a summit certificate.

View from Kibo Huts across the Saddle towards Mawenzi (Marangu Route)

CHOOSING A ROUTE

This book is a guide to all of the official trekking routes on Kilimanjaro. It describes in depth the six approach routes through the forest and heath/moorland zones, the Circuit Path (which offers an alternative to ascending to the mountain's top and circumnavigates Kibo at 4000m) and the three summit routes leading to Uhuru Peak. It also details the available descent routes on the mountain. Each of these routes varies in terms of length, difficulty, what you will see along the way and of course cost but each will reward the visitor with stunning panoramas and an incredible variety of scenic wonders. All walkers must follow one of these established paths and note that some routes are ascent or descent only. Trekkers must be accompanied by a licensed guide.

Following the initial trickle of climbers to these slopes, the number of people attempting to reach the highest point in Africa has, according to the latest statistics available from Kilimanjaro National Park authorities, risen to around 60,000 per year, two thirds of whom tackle the Marangu and Machame routes. Such a statistic may horrify you, and conjure images of immense crowds, cramped campsites and litter strewn, eroded trails, but thankfully the reality is very different and every visitor to the slopes ought to strive to ensure that this remains the case.

It is essential to select the route that is most appropriate for you. Be aware of the scenic variety, remoteness and popularity of each route, but most importantly, when choosing your ascent route, be aware of the degree of difficulty

Kibo seen above the camp at Mweka Hut on the Mweka Route

of that route. Don't let a false sense of bravado or an overestimation of your ability allow you to select a route that is beyond your capabilities. If you are inexperienced, less fit, have never been to altitude or have previously struggled at altitude, you should tend towards one of the easier routes and consider the Marangu or Rongai Route with a summit ascent via the Marangu Route from Kibo Huts, or a longer approach such as the Lemosho Route that gives you more time to acclimatise.

If you are fitter, have some experience of walking and being at altitude you may wish to consider the Machame, Shira or Lemosho approach routes coupled with an ascent to the summit via the Barafu Route. If you are very fit and properly acclimatised you might like to consider one of the tougher ascent routes, such as the Umbwe Route, in conjunction with an assault on the Western Breach.

Marangu Route

Historically the most common ascent was via the Marangu Route. This relatively easy five-day trip ascends Kilimanjaro from the south-east. The lower sections provide fine forest and moorland walking. The lunar landscape of the Saddle then leads to the foot of Kibo, from where the final summit bid is undertaken via the Normal/Marangu Route. You descend this route by retracing your steps. This is the only route on which all overnight stops are made in purpose-built huts. Since this is the shortest and cheapest route on the mountain, it is frequently very busy and there is the risk that the facilities along the trail can become stretched. It also has the lowest success rate on the mountain.

Machame Route

These days, the most popular ascent route is the Machame Route. This longer, six-day climb is harder and more spectacular. It climbs Kilimanjaro from the south-west and enjoys some of the finest forest and heath/moorland scenery on the mountain. The final push to the summit is via either the tricky Western Breach or, more usually, the Barafu Route. The stipulated descent route for this path is the Mweka Route. With its new crown as most commonly tackled route on the mountain, this path is no longer the wilderness experience that it once was. Nonetheless it constitutes an exceptional, fully rounded expedition and has a higher success rate in part due to the extra day spent on the mountain.

Rongai Route

Of the more unusual ascent routes, the Rongai Route is the easiest. This minimum-five-day climb, which has grown substantially in popularity over the last decade to become the third most popular ascent, is an excellent alternative to the Marangu Route for those who don't feel capable of undertaking one of the more strenuous climbs. This is the only path that approaches the summit from the north. The path coils across the lower slopes and detours via Mawenzi, allowing you to explore this extraordinary second summit area more fully than on any other route. It then makes the final summit bid via the Normal/Marangu Route. Descent from the mountain is along the Marangu Route. Less heavily used and exceptionally scenic, the Rongai Route is a very fine outing on Kilimanjaro.

Tropical montane cloudforest at an early stage on the Marangu Route

Umbwe Route

The Umbwe Route is the most direct, strenuous ascent route. As little as one percent of climbers on the mountain tackle this ascent, making it far and away the least popular. Climbing stiffly through the thick forest on the southern slopes of the mountain, it rapidly gains height and affords you little time to acclimatise properly. The summit bid is often made via the Western Breach, but is sometimes conducted via the Barafu Route. Regardless, descent is via the Mweka Route. For those who are fit and fully acclimatised, this is probably the most dramatic way to climb Kilimanjaro and experience many of its finest vistas. However, it must not be underestimated, since it poses a very real challenge.

Shira and Lemosho routes

Both the Shira and Lemosho routes approach the mountain from the west. They are variations on the same trail and merge above the forest on the Shira Plateau. The more attractive and enjoyable Lemosho Route is fractionally longer and allows you to ascend to the plateau on foot, whereas the Shira Route begins much higher on the mountain and accesses the plateau by 4WD vehicle. Both paths then either climb to the summit via the Western Breach or, more frequently, traverse the mountain beneath the Southern Icefields to ascend via the Barafu Route. Descent is once more along the Mweka Route. The Lemosho Route is longer than any other route on the mountain, and while being more expensive offers the best opportunity to acclimatise properly ahead of the summit bid and so has grown in popularity over recent years. The isolation and space enjoyed as a result of the remoteness of both trailheads, especially the Lemosho, means that these are still very good ways of escaping the crowds, at least on the early stages of the climb. For those climbers looking to avoid crowds for as long as possible, a variation of the Lemosho Route on the Shira Plateau that joins and detours around the Northern Circuit Path that circumnavigates Kibo at around 4000m, instead of the traditional Southern Circuit Path, allows you to keep well off the most travelled trails and allows a couple more nights of isolation and wild camping before you climb to the summit on a variation of the Normal/Marangu Route.

Circuit paths

While the Northern Circuit Path is very remote and rarely used, other than in conjunction with the Lemosho Route and an ascent to the summit via School Hut, allowing you to enjoy the mountain in peace, the Southern Circuit Path, which connects a number of the ascent routes with the final climbs to the summit, is a busier traverse that provides you with fine panoramas of the Southern

View of Kibo above tents at First Camp (Rongai Route, Naremoru to First Camp)

Porters on path between Horombo Huts and Kibo Huts, Marangu Route (photo: Vadim Petrakov/Shutterstock.com)

Icefields. For those less concerned about claiming the summit's scalp, a complete loop of the Circuit Path is an outstanding way to enjoy the mountain and explore some of its least visited features. However, you will need special permission to trek the full circuit and it isn't tackled as a standard outing on the mountain or regularly offered by outfitters.

COSTS AND BUDGETING

Climbing Kilimanjaro is an expensive business. The Tanzanian government has understandably cashed in on the mountain's popularity and has introduced a series of mandatory fees that must be paid before you can even enter the Kilimanjaro National Park. The charges to climb Kilimanjaro have increased exponentially over the last few years and the combination of park gate fees, camping and hut fees levied by the authorities have now reached well over US$100 per day.

There is no cheap way to climb the mountain. The fees are compulsory. In addition to these, you must also hire and pay for a guide and a team of porters through a licensed outfitter. All food and transport costs need to be factored in as well. On top of all of the unavoidable costs, you must also include the amount of money that you will need to tip the guide and his porters once the climb is completed (see Guides and porters).

The mandatory costs include a conservation fee (formerly the national park daily gate fee), which costs US$70 per day. You must also pay either camping fees of US$50 per night or, on the Marangu Route, hut fees of US$60 per night. There is also a compulsory rescue fee of US$20 per trip. You must also pay US$2 per person per trip as wages for each guide and porter that accompanies you during your ascent. Thus, the basic cost of a five-day Marangu Route ascent using a guide, assistant guide and two porters rapidly escalates to over US$600. By the time that your outfitter includes each member of your team's wages, approximately a further US$150 for a team of four, and the costs for food and transport, you will appreciate how the cost of the expedition very quickly increases. On top of this, you will inevitably be charged another fee by, and for, your outfitter in order to make the business profitable.

When all of these considerations are taken into account, expect to pay an outfitter somewhere in the region of US$1350–1550 for a basic five-day Marangu trek. The Umbwe and Rongai routes will cost somewhere between US$1700–1900, while the Machame Route costs around US$1600–1800. The Shira and Lemosho routes are both slightly more expensive and will set you back at least US$2000. A trek with a top tour operator can cost far more than this and the sky's the limit if you keep adding in extras or expanding your team.

Fresh produce at the start of the trek

It pays to shop around and compare prices offered by each outfitter. Prices are often lower if you walk as part of a group rather than on your own. In most cases it is true that you get what you pay for, and the extra money spent on signing with a more expensive outfitter may pay dividends during your climb. Bear in mind that if you book your climb in the UK the costs will be much higher for each of the routes up the mountain.

Kilimanjaro is fairly unique in that you pay per day spent on the mountain. There is no option to make a one-off payment that would then enable you to make a slow ascent and several attempts on the summit. Every additional day spent on the mountain is an extra cost. This can prove particularly expensive on the longer routes, and consequently groups may be tempted to race up Kilimanjaro in a bid to save money. By charging a daily fee the Tanzanian authorities have created a system that encourages people to climb too quickly, which increases the risks to individuals' health. However, the additional cost is relatively inexpensive when compared to the frustration of having to descend without having made it to the highest point.

Don't let the cost discourage you. The ascent of Kilimanjaro is an exceptional and priceless experience. Nevertheless, do consider spending extra on an additional acclimatisation day to ensure that you maximise your safety on the mountain.

Western Breach and summit viewed from the top of the Lava Tower on the Southern Circuit Path

WHEN TO GO

It is possible to climb Kilimanjaro all year round but there are definitely more preferable times of year to attempt the climb. Ideally you will want to tackle the mountain during one of the two dry seasons that Tanzania enjoys. These last from mid-December to March and then from July to early October. During the dry spell at the start of the year, the weather is generally dry and warm, while during the middle of the year it tends to be dry but cooler. The hottest months are January, February and September. Be aware that even during the preferred months, the weather is erratic and difficult to predict.

The remaining months of the year fall within the two rainy seasons, when climbing Kilimanjaro is less easy or, indeed, enjoyable. The long rains (masika) last from April to June and the short rains (mvuli) occur in November and early December, when thunderstorms are common. During this time, thick cloud shrouds the mountain and there are heavy downpours on the lower slopes, which can turn to snow higher on the mountain.

Temperatures on Kilimanjaro vary wildly. At the foot of the mountain the temperature can exceed 30°C, while on the summit it can plunge to below –20°C. Wind chill and the moisture in the clouds that swirl around the summits during the day can then make it feel even colder than this. While climbing on Kilimanjaro, groups must always be prepared for cold weather and sudden storms. The high winds can mean that weather changes at very short notice and the exposed nature of the climb means that this can be very unpleasant.

At the equator, the sun rises and sets at a fairly consistent time throughout the year. Sunrise tends to occur around 6.30am and sunset takes place 12 hours later, at around 6.30pm.

Porters on the Marangu Route between Mandara Huts and Horombo Huts

As a consequence of these factors, the ideal months to climb Kilimanjaro are January and February, just after the major rains, as the weather improves and becomes relatively settled and the mountain is freshly covered by snow. Alternatively, tackle the ascent from June to October after the short rains; although the forests are frequently encircled by cloud, the summits are often clear. This second set of dates tends to be the most popular time for people to make an ascent of the mountain as it coincides with European summer holidays; escape the crowds by travelling to the mountain from mid-September until the end of October as numbers begin to dwindle.

Having plumped on a season in which to make the climb to the summit, it is also worth trying to coordinate your climb with the full moon since the final push to the summit is conducted in the small hours of the morning. Almost all nights on Kilimanjaro are clear so climbing to the crater rim by moonlight makes the night time ascent more enjoyable and potentially even more beautiful. As a rough guide, a full moon rises at sunset and sets at sunrise, at about the time the sun actually becomes visible in the sky. Strong moonlight to illuminate the path during your ascent makes this the ideal time to tackle the last haul to the crater rim, however, the best conditions are probably a couple of days after the full moon as then the moon begins to set about an hour later each day. This means that at around 5.00am the sky is still lit by the moon and the critical section of the climb can be tackled relatively easily.

In order to coordinate your climb with the full moon and make the most of this period, those embarking on a five-day climb should aim to start the trek

Average monthly temperature and rainfall (Moshi)			
Month	Max temp (°C)	Min temp (°C)	Rainfall (mm)
January	29	10	60
February	29	10	100
March	27	11	170
April	25	13	370
May	22	11	230
June	21	8	50
July	20	9	20
August	22	8	25
September	24	8	25
October	26	11	40
November	27	10	110
December	28	10	100

three days prior to the full moon and those completing the climb in six days should aim to commence their trip four days ahead of the full moon.

As you approach the crater rim, you may also become aware of the morning star, a planet (usually Venus), which becomes visible just before sun rise. The

Silhouetted figures on Mawenzi ridge watching the sunrise (Rongai Route, Mawenzi Tarn Hut to Kibo Huts)

Chagga call this star 'Ngatunyi', which means 'the star that guides nocturnal travellers safely home'.

PRE-DEPARTURE PREPARATION

Kilimanjaro attracts a great number of trekkers who have never undertaken a multi-day walk, and certainly haven't contemplated doing so at altitude. The mountain's environment is regularly underestimated and the result can be fatal. Although many hundreds of people reach the summit without incident, many more don't make it because they fail to prepare and then ascend too quickly and suffer from altitude sickness. It's worth noting that Uhuru Peak is several hundred metres higher than Everest Base Camp, yet climbers in the Himalayas typically take at least two weeks to reach this height on Everest.

Getting to the top of Kilimanjaro demands mental preparation as well as physical fitness. Embarking on an ascent that will take several days and will culminate at almost 6000m is a very different proposition to a walking trip based in one place or predominantly at a single elevation. With a central base, you are able to choose whether or when to go walking. As a member of an organised group on a multi-day ascent, you will have a schedule to maintain and will be expected to walk day after day, rain or shine, whether you fancy it or not. There are few opportunities to escape if you begin to falter, other than to stop and descend.

The most efficient way to get fit for climbing Kilimanjaro is to trek up and down hills. Jogging helps to build stamina and endurance, although there is little you can do to aid acclimatisation, short of spending time at altitude. By walking frequently, at the very least your body is becoming used to the rhythm and rigours of life on the path. When

Mawenzi seen above band of cloud at dusk from Kibo Huts (Rongai Route, Mawenzi Tarn Hut to Kibo Huts)

Path across the barren, hostile Saddle towards Kibo Huts (Marangu Route)

planning your trip, also carefully consider including an extra day for acclimatisation. The additional cost is relatively inexpensive when compared to the frustration of having to descend without having made it to the highest point. Once you arrive on the foothills of the mountain and the path winds away from you into the forest and ever upward, you will be grateful for the preparation and will be able to open your eyes and mind fully to the incredible experience ahead.

Mental preparation will be invaluable when high on the mountain, exhausted and facing potential extended periods of intense cold and discomfort. There will certainly also be times of confusion and times when your western sensibilities are overwhelmed by the sights and smells of life on Kilimanjaro. In order to successfully reach the summit, you must be able to adapt to a whole new range of conditions and circumstances.

If you have significant doubts, forget it. Three or four days into an ascent is no time to discover that you don't enjoy trekking. The financial outlay alone required to undertake an ascent of Kilimanjaro ought to be sufficient to ensure that you do think carefully about going, make suitable preparations and then savour every moment of the trip.

GETTING THERE

Information under this heading is particularly prone to change, especially those details relating to air travel; schedules and times can change and routes can be introduced or cancelled. Make sure to check all of the details with a travel agent or the airline in advance of making a booking.

By air

It is possible to access Kilimanjaro by air from a number of directions, either

Porters on the trail above Machame Hut (Machame Route, Machame Hut to Shira Camp)

flying to Nairobi in Kenya or to Dar es Salaam or, most conveniently, to Kilimanjaro International Airport in Tanzania. Many trekkers fly to Nairobi, taking advantage of the more frequent flights and the cheaper deals. From here there are daily land and air connections to Dar es Salaam and Kilimanjaro Airport. It is in fact far easier to access Arusha or Moshi by road from Nairobi than it is from Dar es Salaam (see 'By land' section).

If you are flying from Europe, it takes 10–14 hours to fly to Tanzania, depending on the route taken and the number of stops made. However, because Tanzania is only three hours ahead of GMT (two hours ahead of British Summer Time), there is minimal jet lag to overcome.

Kilimanjaro International Airport is around 40km west of Moshi and 50km east of Arusha, to the south-west of the mountain. It has a small terminal that can be easily negotiated and all essential facilities including restaurants, cafés, shops, ATMs and a bureau de change. Currently Kilimanjaro International Airport is serviced by KLM (www.klm.com), Ethiopian Airlines (www.ethiopianairlines.com) and Precision Air (www.precisionairtz.com). Precision Air is now partnered with Kenya Airways (www.kenya-airways.com), so you can fly Kenya Airways to Nairobi daily and then onwards to Kilimanjaro with Precision Air. Qatar Airways (www.qatarairways.com) operate a daily service and are a good bet if travelling from Asia. Turkish Airlines (www.turkishairlines.com) offer some of the lowest fares but also some of the most antisocial arrival and departure times. Air Tanzania (www.airtanzania.co.tz) currently aren't operating any flights to Kilimanjaro Airport although they regularly announce that they may start up.

When flying into Kilimanjaro airport from the north, try to sit on the left-hand side of the plane so that when arriving by day (if it's clear) you will be able to have fantastic views of the mountain. If you are unlucky and end up on the right-hand side of the plane, content yourself with views of Lake Turkana in the north of Kenya. Lake Turkana is the world's largest permanent desert lake and is about an hour's flight north of Kilimanjaro.

The cheapest time of year to travel to East Africa is typically between January and May. Flights tend to be heavily booked and occasionally sold out between late June and late August. If you wish to travel during this time, make sure that you book your flights well in advance.

Once you have arrived at Kilimanjaro Airport or Dar es Salaam, there are a number of bus connections that you can take that will shuttle you to Arusha or Moshi, from where you can commence your climb. Alternatively, your outfitter may arrange for you to be collected and transferred to the foot of the mountain. From Kilimanjaro Airport there is a shuttle bus for Precision Air passengers; other arrivals must wait for the shuttle services from Nairobi to Moshi that come via Arusha and the airport, or take a taxi into Moshi, which takes about 45mins (expect to pay around $50). Alternatively, pre-arrange a transfer with your hotel or tour operator. (For information on travelling on from Nairobi to Arusha or Moshi see the 'By land' section.)

If you are flying out of Tanzania, you will be required to pay departure tax. The tax is only levied on flights, not overland departures from the country, and is usually incorporated into the price of your ticket.

Kibo (photo: UbjsP/Shutterstock.com)

A jacaranda tree towering over shacks on a street in Arusha

From the UK

Currently, the only direct flights from the UK to Tanzania are with British Airways (www.ba.com), who fly from Heathrow.

There are however a number of one-stop options that detour via various European, Middle Eastern and African cities. Emirates (www.emiratesairline.com), Ethiopian Airlines (www.ethiopianairlines.com), Kenya Airways (www.kenya-airways.com), Egyptair (www.egyptair.com), South African Airways (www.flysaa.com), Gulf Air (www.gulfair.com) and Swissair (www.swissair.com) are all worth comparing.

The cheapest direct flights to Nairobi are also currently with British Airways. Kenya Airways also run comparably priced direct flights. Alternatively, Emirates, Ethiopian Airlines, Egyptair and Gulf Air offer one-stop flights.

From Ireland

If you are flying from Ireland to Dar es Salaam or Nairobi, British Airways (www.ba.com) will sell you a through ticket from Belfast or Dublin. There are also convenient through-connections from Dublin to Nairobi with KLM (www.klm.com).

From North America

There are currently no direct flights from North America to East Africa. To reach Tanzania from North America you must change planes and possibly even airlines. The quickest route is to fly from New York via London with British Airways (www.ba.com). Otherwise, fly from New York via Amsterdam with North Western (www.nwal.ca) and KLM (www.klm.com). Regardless, the total journey time is still going to be over 20 hours. Fares for these routes are universally expensive.

The alternative to these routes is to fly to a different African destination, such as Addis Ababa (Ethiopian Airlines, www.ethiopianairlines.com) or Cairo (Egyptair, www.egyptair.com), and then continue your journey from there.

From Australia and New Zealand

If travelling from Australia or New Zealand to Tanzania you will have to stop over in Asia, Southern Africa or the Middle East. The best deals are usually to be had either with Gulf Air (www.gulfair.com), who fly via Singapore and Bahrain, Egyptair (www.egyptair.com), who fly via Bangkok and Cairo, or Emirates (www.emiratesairline.com), who fly via Dubai, although none of these options are cheap. It is quicker, but more expensive, to fly with Air Zimbabwe (www.airzimbabwe.aero) via Harare. Alternatively, fly to Johannesburg with Qantas (www.qantas.com) or South African Airways (www.flysaa.com) and pick up a connecting flight to Dar es Salaam from there.

By land

An alternative and easy way of accessing Kilimanjaro is to fly to Nairobi and then travel overland to Arusha or Moshi in Tanzania. The shuttle bus service is cheap and reliable. There are a couple of companies plying the same route, most of them operating 20-seat buses and offering a twice daily service from their offices in the centre of Nairobi. The companies will often offer to collect you from your hotel or from one of the main hotels in town, usually the New Stanley or the Norfolk. The buses cross the border at Namanga and then travel to Arusha, where they pause at the Novotel Hotel and where you may have to change bus, before continuing on to Moshi via Kilimanjaro International Airport. The journey to Arusha takes between five and six hours and the onward trip to Moshi, via the airport, takes a further one and half to two hours – potholes, punctures and breakdowns allowing. A single ticket costs around US$35.

The border crossing at Namanga is straightforward enough, although it is usually slow and time consuming. The crossing has been cleaned up considerably over the years and is now much safer and less hostile to pass through. The large numbers of beggars, sellers, charlatans and thieves that used to congregate here have been dispersed. There are still a number of Maasai that loiter, but generally the crossing is hassle free.

At the border you will need to queue for a visa stamp and to have your baggage checked. You only ever need to pay for the visa. There are no other border fees or payments to be made, no matter what anyone tells you at the time.

In addition to the regular public buses that are run by the bus company Akamba and depart from the hectic River Road area of central Nairobi early in the morning, there are some companies that operate shuttle runs from Nairobi into Tanzania. By using these companies rather than the public buses, you are forced to pay a little extra, but are then able to board the buses in the comparative safety of downtown Nairobi. The best known and most established is Riverside, although another operator, Impala, is also a good bet. There are services provided by smaller companies too including AA Luxury Shuttle Bus, East Africa Shuttles, Nairobi Arusha Shuttle Transport Company and

A view of the Western Breach and summit amid cloud as seen on the Southern Circuit Path

Kilimanjaro's summit seen at sunset

Regional Luxury Shuttle. Most of the company websites have booking facilities, timetables, prices and information about where to meet the buses. See Appendix B for a list of outfitters.

PERMITS AND VISAS

Tanzanian visas

Most nationalities require a visa to enter Tanzania. The UK is no exception. Kenyans, Ugandans and the Irish are exempt. The visa should be obtained in advance of your arrival. This can be done in person or by post from any Tanzanian embassy, consulate or High Commission. It is possible to download the application form in advance from the High Commission website, http://tanzaniahighcomm.co.uk (see Appendix B for contact details). The visa application desks are generally open from 10.00am to 12.30pm Monday to Friday. The visa request takes 24 hours to process and requires two passport photos and a passport that is valid for at least six months. A three-month single entry visa costs £40; £50 for a next day service or £60 for a same day service. A multiple entry visa costs roughly double that.

It is possible to get a visa on arrival in Tanzania, but only at a couple of entry points. You may also have to explain why you didn't get one in advance if there is a Tanzanian High Commission in your home country. The immigration points at Tanzania's three international airports (Dar es Salaam, Kilimanjaro and Zanzibar) and several of the major land border crossing points, including Namanga, are authorised to issue visas. If you are applying for a visa upon entry to Tanzania, US dollars are the most readily accepted currency, although sterling is usually accepted as well. Your passport will then be stamped to show how long you are allowed to remain in Tanzania.

YELLOW FEVER VACCINATION CERTIFICATES

Officially, Tanzania has stopped checking yellow fever vaccination certificates upon arrival in the country. While this is probably fine for the airports, it may be advisable to get the jab anyway and have the certificate handy if you are travelling overland into the country. Try to ensure that you have the inoculation done in advance of departure, in your home country.

As long as your Tanzanian visa remains valid, you can visit Kenya or Uganda and then return to Tanzania without having to reapply for another visa. You will still need to have your passport and visa stamp checked.

Should you wish to extend your visa, you may apply at the immigration office in any major town: there's an Immigration department on Afrika Mashariki Road in Arusha (tel 027 250 3569) and Boma Road in Moshi (tel 027 275 1557). There is no extra charge, you do not require any extra photos and the extension is usually issued the same day. If you have already spent three months in Tanzania, you will need an acceptable reason to stay on. The alternative is to quit the country and reapply for a fresh visa. If you are intending to stay in Tanzania longer than three months, you may be as well to apply for a residency permit from the Tanzanian High Commission in your home country in advance of your trip.

Kenyan visas

If you choose to fly into Nairobi and then transfer overland to Tanzania, you will also require a Kenyan visa, http://kenyahighcomm.org.uk. Most western and European nationalities, including the UK, need to obtain a visa in order to enter Kenya. This can be done in advance at any Kenyan embassy or high commission, where it generally takes 24–48 hours to process and requires two passport photos and an air ticket that confirms your departure from the country. A single entry visa costs £30 and is valid for three months. A multiple entry visa costs twice as much. It is possible to secure a visa upon arrival at the airport in Kenya. This process is usually trouble free, but is very slow and time consuming.

Your visa allows you to re-enter Kenya after visits to Uganda or Tanzania, assuming that your Kenyan visa is still valid. This is particularly useful for those people who have a return ticket to Nairobi and are planning to use the shuttle services to access and return from Kilimanjaro.

If you wish to apply for a visa extension, you must present yourself at the immigration offices in either Nairobi, Mombasa, Lamu or Kisumu. It is only possible to extend the visa for a further three months.

ACCOMMODATION

There is no shortage of accommodation at the foot of Kilimanjaro. Most groups base themselves in Moshi before the climb. This is a small town that has benefited considerably from its proximity to

Main A-frame communal dining and bunkroom at Mandara Huts on the Marangu Route

the mountain. Set at just over 800m, it has grown to become a bustling, cosmopolitan place and is now the capital of the Kilimanjaro region. It is the home of the Chagga people and the centre of the region's successful coffee production industry.

The town itself is open and relatively spacious. The central streets are wide and the general pace of life is slow, making it an attractive and relaxing place to spend time. There are a number of hotel options in town to suit all budgets (see Appendix A), making this an ideal base for the climb up Kilimanjaro.

All overnight stays on the mountain are arranged by the outfitter – as a climber you don't have to book or notify anyone of anything. Once you begin your ascent, your accommodation options are affected by the route that you have chosen to ascend. If you are going to climb the Marangu Route, then you will most likely take advantage of the huts constructed along the path. These are relatively basic structures that provide bunks and mattresses for their overnight guests. There are also communal dining areas, long-drop toilets, and, at the two lower huts, running water and solar powered lighting. More detailed descriptions of the huts and their facilities are provided in the description of the Marangu Route.

If you choose to climb Kilimanjaro by any other route, you will need to camp throughout your trip. There are designated campsites on each of the paths. These are usually situated close to water sources, frequently streams or pools and adjacent to an old metal uniport cabin. Outline details relating to these sites are given in the text wherever they can be found on the mountain. Each campsite has long-drop toilets in the vicinity.

Karanga Camp on the Machame Route (photo: Wallix/Shutterstock.com)

It is worth bearing in mind that the final hut or campsite on the ascent will be dry, and water will have to be carried here from the last water points lower on the mountain.

MONEY AND CURRENCIES

The national currency in Tanzania is the Tanzanian shilling (Tsh). It is a relatively stable currency: for latest exchange rates see www.xe.com. When travelling in Tanzania you are best using a credit/debit card to withdraw money as this is the lightest, easiest and safest way to carry money. Most bank ATMs in Tanzania accept foreign cards, especially Visa, making getting hold of shillings easy. In case your card is lost, rejected by the machine or swallowed, it's worth having a second card as a back up method of withdrawing money. Certain purchases can technically only be bought with US dollars, the preferred international currency in Tanzania, including plane tickets and top end hotel rooms but in the main you'll find Tanzanian shillings easiest to carry and welcome in most places. When travelling throughout Tanzania, make sure to have a number of small denomination notes available as lots of shops struggle to break larger notes and sometimes don't have sufficient change. On Kilimanjaro, there are limited opportunities to spend money but you might find a drink stop or entrepreneurial individual selling souvenirs at the gates, so have a number of small shilling notes to hand. You'll need dollars to tip the team after the climb is complete.

LANGUAGE

The official languages of Tanzania are Swahili and English. Swahili, or Kiswahili, has played a major role in uniting the people and solidifying the country's sense of self. Swahili was adopted as the country's national language after Tanzania secured independence. It has become the most widely spoken language used by Tanzania's ethnic groups and provides a degree of commonality. English is widely spoken in the main towns and tourist areas, but is much less common in rural or smaller towns. It is the official language of commerce, administration and higher education.

Swahili is technically a Bantu language, although it has assimilated a number of Arabic, Persian, Hindi, Portuguese and English words. Trade and immigration have influenced and moulded it, and it is now the lingua franca of central and eastern Africa. It is surprisingly easy to learn and is pronounced as it is written, with the stress nearly always on the penultimate syllable. Local people are often delighted if you make the effort to try and speak a little Swahili, even if it is just to say 'Hello'. Your guides will undoubtedly introduce you to a handful of phrases and essential words, most usefully the Kilimanjaro mantra, 'pole, pole', which means 'slowly, slowly'. A glossary of useful words is provided at the back of this book in Appendix D.

Besides Swahili, there are a host of local languages that can be categorised in four groups: Bantu, Nilotic, Coshitic and Khoisan. The vast majority of Tanzanians speak one of the Bantu languages as their first language. The Maasai are the main speakers of the Nilotic languages.

MAPS

There are a number of maps of Kilimanjaro itself available, both in Tanzania and abroad. Specialist map

View across the barren Saddle to the Kibo massif (Rongai Route, Mawenzi Tarn Hut to Kibo Huts)

shops in the UK, such as Stanfords (branches in London and Bristol, www.stanfords.co.uk), carry a range of the best trekking maps available. Some of these are also available at the national park headquarters at the Marangu Gate or in the towns of Moshi or Arusha. Most of the maps that are available are general overview maps of the entire mountain and are not really of sufficient detail to be used as trekking maps. Nonetheless, they help to put the mountain and the various routes into context, as well as providing some useful and interesting details.

A revised edition of the ITMB (International Travel Maps) Kilimanjaro map was published in 2006. Drawn at 1:62,500 scale, it shows all of the main trekking routes, campsites, huts and water points. Colour shading to show altitude is combined with 100m contours and spot heights. There is a comprehensive index that lists many of the caves, glaciers, mountain features and surrounding villages, as well as some short text providing additional information about the routes.

You will also come across the Kilimanjaro Map and Guide by Andrew Wielochowski and published by West Col Productions. This double-sided sheet features a 1:75,000 scale topographic trekking map of Kilimanjaro. While similar to the ITMB map, the physical features such as scree slopes, glaciers and cliffs are more clearly shown here. On the reverse there are also more detailed maps of Kibo (1:30,000 scale) and Mawenzi (1:20,000 scale), in addition to text on the routes, climate, flora, fauna and suggestions for essential equipment.

The map of Kilimanjaro-Kibo by Sandra Greulich and Sacha Wettstein was published by Climbing Map in 2008. It is an excellent 1:80,000 map that combines topographic coverage of the mountain with an enlargement for the Kibo crater, a list of GPS waypoints, profiles of the main routes and street plans of Arusha and Moshi.

German publisher Harms Verlag produces a map of Kilimanjaro National Park and the surrounding area at 1:100,000 scale, with Kibo shown as an inset at 1:50,000. Ascent and descent routes are clearly marked, with huts and camps indicated along with altitude.

The Ordnance Survey produced an attractive map of Kilimanjaro at 1:100,000 scale in the early 1990s, although the overlaid route maps are not entirely reliable. Unavailable in the UK since the end of the 1990s, this map can still be found in Moshi and at the park gates.

One of the most readily available maps is the attractive, hand-drawn New Map of the Kilimanjaro National Park, drawn at a scale of 1:125,000, produced by Giovanni Tombazzi and published by Maco Editions in 1998. Although it provides a good overview of the mountain and the routes, it is not so useful as a topographic map.

If you are simply in Tanzania to climb Kilimanjaro, then you will have little need of a general road map of the country. Your outfitter will transport you to the trailhead and ensure that you are collected from the end of the track as well.

EQUIPMENT

'We will trek over fifty miles, going from a few thousand feet to over nineteen thousand feet. During the course of our journey temperatures will range from 100 degrees plus at the jungle base to minus 20 degrees at Kilimanjaro's summit, and we must carry the gear and supplies essential for survival in both extremes. Every ounce must be counted, every square inch of space put to utmost use. To take too much will weigh us down and wear us out on the approach.'

Rob Taylor

Climbing Kilimanjaro is in no way technical and no mountaineering skills or equipment are required to make the ascent. In addition, a team of porters will carry the majority of your kit and supplies, leaving you to simply transport yourselves and a day pack to the next camp. Porters usually carry more than one person's gear, bound together with string or rope. Several outfitters now supply their charges with kitbags for the climb, so that the bags can be transported and identified more easily. Nonetheless, it is essential that you are properly equipped for all of the different stages on the mountain and that you recognise the need to restrict the size and weight of your rucksack to a manageable limit. There is a very real tendency for people to take far too much clothing and equipment on the climb. Just because you won't be carrying it is no reason to overload your pack. Besides which, the porters are restricted to carrying 15kg, and if your gear comes to more than they can legitimately carry, you will be forced to hire additional porters at additional cost.

Your choice of equipment is important and can influence your chances of succeeding on the mountain. You must be prepared for all eventualities and have sufficient resources to combat extremes of temperature, exposure and weather. While shorts and t-shirts may be appropriate on the lower slopes, they are not adequate clothing at higher elevations and anything short of a full cold kit on the summit is potentially life threatening. It is worth remembering that while the daytime temperatures can be very high, at night the mountain gets very cold.

A warm sleeping bag, and if camping a good ground mat, can drastically improve your chances of getting a reasonable night's sleep when camping at altitude. You should also expect rainfall at some stage. Waterproof clothing is essential to prevent the disruption of, or even early termination of, your climb: good waterproofs are an indispensable part of any Kilimanjaro climber's clothing. They are essential for protection against rain or snowfall, but also double up as a windproof outer layer. Jacket and trousers made from waterproof, breathable fabric are ideal for this purpose.

The type of boot that you wear can be critical to your enjoyment and success. Your boots should be comfortable, medium to heavyweight and of a good fit. It is essential that they are well broken in before your departure, in order to minimise the likelihood of you developing blisters during the trek. The boots must provide good ankle support and have thick lug soles that give a degree of cushioning and excellent grip. Leather

Porters with their full packs walking through the forest to Mandara Huts (Marangu Route, Marangu Gate to Mandara Huts)

walking boots or indeed any other type of waterproof boot are ideal, since some of the ascent is through damp, wet forest or heath and the possibility of heavy rain can not be discounted. Make sure that there is enough room to prevent your toes hitting the front of the boot when descending a steep slope. You should also carry sandals or other lightweight footwear to change into at the hut or campsite.

Gaiters are a very sound investment prior to your ascent. The early stages in the forest can be exceptionally muddy and the use of gaiters helps to keep your feet dry and thus prevents potential blisters. On the heath/moorland, highland desert and summit ascent there are large quantities of scree and gravel to be negotiated. Gaiters worn on these sections will stop the small shards of lava or rock from getting inside your footwear. The descent from the crater rim is on loose scree and the passage of feet tends to result in quantities of fine, penetrating dust being kicked up. Gaiters will once again prevent this material from getting into your boots.

A lot of walkers now use telescopic trekking poles. These are very useful when ascending or more particularly descending, steep or scree slopes. They provide extra balance and help to support your weight, taking the pressure off your knees. Use one or two poles, depending on your own personal preference.

All climbers should also take a fleece or insulated jacket to wear in the evenings or on the upper slopes of the mountain. In order to combat the fluctuating temperatures on the mountain, adopt a layering policy when dressing. It is always easier to take something off than it is to put it on. A woollen hat or balaclava, scarf and gloves are also a good idea.

In addition to protective gear that combats the cold and wet, you should also have sufficient equipment to be able to endure extremes of sunshine and heat. The sun on the equator and at altitude is very strong. A brimmed hat, sun cream (factor 15+), lip salve and sunglasses are vital.

In addition to these items of clothing and kit, a first aid kit should be carried so that you can patch up minor injuries, such as blisters, cuts and grazes, or trail ailments (see Health considerations). A water bottle with at least a two-litre capacity is also essential. For the final ascent to the crater rim you will require a headtorch, which is also useful when moving about inside your tent or around the campsite. Make sure to bring spare batteries and a spare bulb with you. Additionally, a whistle is useful for attracting attention if you are lost or separated from your group. A small amount of emergency, high energy food, such as chocolate or nuts, ought to be carried as well. A penknife is also a handy tool to have. Plastic bags to store your rubbish in are also a good idea.

While on the mountain, secure all of your valuable or important possessions in waterproof bags. This will ensure that they remain dry in the eventuality of rain or your pack leaking. At short notice a dustbin bag will double up as a pack liner.

Although you won't be carrying your full size pack, try to ensure that it is in good condition and is waterproof. The porters may or may not choose to carry it in the conventional manner. A sturdy day pack is essential. Make sure that it

EQUIPMENT CHECKLIST

Clothing: boots and spare laces, light shoes or sandals, down jacket, fleece or jumper, shirts (t-shirts and long-sleeved collared shirts), socks, trekking trousers, waterproof jacket and overtrousers, underwear (including thermals), gloves, woollen hat or balaclava, wide-brimmed hat.

Essential items: passport, rucksack, day pack, trekking poles, gaiters, sleeping bag (3 season+), floor mat, water bottle (2 litre+), water purifying tablets, head-torch, batteries, bulbs, first aid kit, penknife, lighter, sunglasses, sun cream (factor 15+), lip salve, towel and wash bag, money belt, map, whistle, toilet paper, plastic bags.

Optional items: camera, binoculars, altimeter, compass, notebook and pen, ear plugs, waterproof pack cover, spare pair of prescription glasses.

fits comfortably and is easily adjustable. It need not be especially large, 30 to 40-litre capacity is sufficient, but do make sure that it can contain all of your cameras, maps, water supplies, some food, additional clothing, waterproofs and sun cream.

Second Cave sign with packs and poles (Rongai Route, First Camp to Kikelewa Cave)

INSURANCE

It is wise to take out a good insurance policy. When researching insurance policies, make sure that you mention that you are going to climb Kilimanjaro. Although this may result in an increase in your premium, it will at least ensure that you are covered in case of an accident on the mountain. Make sure that you take a copy of the policy and that it is accessible to a friend or family member.

HEALTH CONSIDERATIONS

'We were turning into geezers. Ratty beards sprouted. Fingers swelled. Faces grew puffy and wrinkled. Our rest steps slowed to funereal pace. We got gaseous ... Why do people put themselves through this wringer?'

Tom Dunkel

First-time visitors to Africa can easily become obsessed with concerns regarding their health. While the potential dangers of trekking in a developing country can seem overwhelming it is important

FIRST AID KIT

- Plasters
- Blister kit
- Bandages (both cotton gauze and elastic)
- Knee supports
- Antiseptic cream
- Aspirin or paracetamol
- Throat lozenges
- Imodium
- Iodine tablets
- Sun cream
- Lip salve
- Safety pins
- Scissors
- Wet wipes
- Insect repellent
- Sterile needles
- Any prescription medicines that you would usually take in your home country

to prevent these worries from becoming obsessive. In reality, Tanzania isn't a particularly dangerous country and very few travellers experience anything more than an upset stomach. In order to minimise the risks of becoming sick, have the requisite inoculations before leaving home, make sure that you carry a first aid kit and adopt a sensible attitude to food and hygiene while on the trek.

Pre-trek health

It would be sensible to safeguard against the following:

- **Diptheria and tetanus** – usually a combined vaccination that is initially administered in three injections and is then topped up every 10 years.
- **Polio** – usually administered during childhood, requires a booster every 10 years.
- **Hepatitis A** – Havrix injection lasts for 10 years if you have a second booster shot after six months. Short term administration of gamma globulin provides immediate protection for up to six months.
- **Typhoid** – recommended for most parts of Africa. Available as an injection or as capsules to be taken orally.
- **Tuberculosis** – usually administered during childhood. The risk to travellers is low in Tanzania.
- **Rabies** – although there is a low risk of contracting the disease, it should be considered if you plan to spend more than a month in Tanzania, particularly if you propose to work with animals. It is a three-part injection that requires two booster injections upon being bitten.
- **Yellow fever** – recommended for travel in areas where the disease is endemic, including Tanzania. Only becomes effective 10 days after it has been administered. It is a good idea to carry proof of your vaccination, especially if you are entering the country overland.
- **Meningococcal meningitis** – recommended for travel to parts of Africa, including Tanzania, particularly if you intend to stay for several months or work among the local population. Not necessary for short stays in the country.
- **Malaria** – the risk on Kilimanjaro itself is low since much of the mountain is too high and cold to support mosquitoes. However, there is a risk

Porters descending towards the Saddle to approach Kibo (Rongai Route, Mawenzi Tarn Hut to Kibo Huts)

of contracting malaria elsewhere in Tanzania and you should consult a GP or medical professional to gauge the risk posed to you. Your medical history, age and destination will all influence the advice given to you. Some anti-malarial medication is reported to have unpleasant side effects. Regardless, when on the mountain, especially in the forest and on the lower slopes, take precautions to avoid being bitten by mosquitoes. Cover exposed skin and use a repellent spray in the evenings to decrease the chances of being bitten.

There are a number of steps that you can take before you even leave your home country to improve your chances of remaining healthy. For fully up-to-date health advice and for information as to which inoculations are necessary, contact the Department of Health Helpline (tel 0800 555 777). Alternatively contact the Medical Advisory Service for Travellers Abroad (MASTA) (tel 01276 685 040, www.masta-travel-health.com) or the World Health Organisation (WHO) (www.who.int). If you would prefer to talk to someone face to face, approach your GP or try visiting the Nomad Travellers store and medical centre in STA Travel in London or the British Airways Travel Clinic, also in London (see Appendix B for contact details).

Remember to plan ahead when getting vaccinations. Some vaccinations need more than one injection and others can not be administered together. Currently, Tanzania makes no requirements for visitors to show proof of immunisation, although in the past travellers have had to show a certificate of vaccination against yellow fever (this practice has officially been stopped

– although you may still wish to have the vaccination).

On-trek health and safety

The majority of individuals who set off to climb Kilimanjaro complete their trip without any undue mishap. With the application of a bit of common sense and care, the mountain shouldn't pose an undue threat and the worst that will happen to you is that you have to deal with a blister. However, Kilimanjaro must not be underestimated and its very real dangers should be taken seriously. In 1884 Harry Johnston prematurely wrote that on Kilimanjaro '... the most serious obstacles arise from mist and cold which would scarcely deter a cockney from ascending Snowdon'. He later noted on his climb to around 4850m that at one point he felt 'as if I would never more regain the force to move, and must remain and die amid this horrid solitude of stones and snow'.

Although the path is generally well trodden and you are accompanied by a guide, the route to the summit passes through some wild and forbidding terrain. An accident here can have serious consequences. The national park authorities are understandably cagey about the exact death toll on Kilimanjaro, but it is likely that 10–15 people die on the mountain every year.

At the start of each day, talk through your itinerary with your guide. Pay particular attention to the amount of height to be gained and how quickly. Don't over-estimate your own physical ability or that of your group; it is far better to be realistic than optimistic in these circumstances. Make an allowance for delays, bad weather and innumerable photo stops to ensure that you have sufficient time to enjoy the day.

When trekking it is essential to remain hydrated. This is even more true at altitude, where the regular consumption of water helps to combat the effects of AMS (Acute Mountain Sickness). Drink water regularly and continually throughout the day. Although mountain water and runoff is generally okay to drink, it is well worth treating all drinking water before you consume it. Boil the water for three minutes, treat it with

Crossing the Saddle from Horombo Huts to Kibo Huts on the Marangu Route (photo: Vadim Petrakov/Shutterstock.com)

iodine or filter it using a portable filter to ensure that it is free from contamination by bacteria. Bottled water should come with an unbroken seal (equally true for water drunk in the towns). A host of organisms are active in the waterways of Tanzania that could lay you low with a variety of ailments. The same precautions should be borne in mind with regards to ice or water used for cleaning your teeth.

A good standard of personal hygiene throughout the trek will also minimise the risk of you becoming ill or suffering from gastro-intestinal problems. Try to clean your hands and fingers before you eat. Carry a pack of baby wipes for this purpose.

Carry a few emergency, high energy foodstuffs and a first aid kit with you on the trek. Keep an eye on the weather and be aware of the sudden build up of cloud or a rapid drop in temperature that may herald the onset of bad weather.

While following the routes up the mountain, stick to the approved paths. Try not to leave the clearly marked track and resist the urge to take a shortcut. At higher elevations don't try to venture onto the glaciers unless you are properly equipped and experienced enough to do so safely. Make sure that you keep an eye on all of the members of your group and watch out for anyone flagging or showing signs of distress.

In the unlikely event that you become separated from your group or have an accident, stay calm and try to draw attention to yourself. The international distress signal is six blasts on a whistle or flashes of a torch after dark, spaced evenly for one minute. Wait for a minute and then repeat the sequence. Continue to do so until you are spotted. The appropriate response to the signal from someone who recognises what it means is three whistles or flashes evenly spaced throughout a minute,

Various pieces of rescue equipment at Kibo Huts

Camp on the Shira Plateau (Machame Route) (photo: Potifor/Shutterstock.com)

followed by a minute's pause and a second set of three.

While climbing Kilimanjaro you will be subjected to extremes of temperature. Consequently, you must be conscious of the dangers of sunburn and hypothermia. Sunburn occurs quickly, particularly in the rarefied air and deceptive coolness of the mountain. Make sure that you wear the appropriate clothing and use sufficiently strong sun cream to protect yourself. Sunglasses can also protect your eyes from damage when walking on or near snow or ice. If you do get burnt, aloe vera or calamine lotion will soothe the burn. Continued exposure to high temperatures coupled with a low water intake can sometimes result in heatstroke. At the other end of the temperature gauge, hypothermia occurs when the body loses heat faster than it can produce it and the person's core temperature drops. A combination of wind, wet clothing, fatigue and hunger usually bring on the condition. To combat mild hypothermia, retreat out of the wind, put on dry, warm clothing and drink warm fluids. Do not rub the casualty, allow them to warm up slowly instead.

Mountain Sickness (AMS)

'Haraka haraka haina baraka'
'Hurry hurry has no blessings'
Swahili proverb

One of the main fears that people have when climbing Kilimanjaro is that they will succumb to Acute Mountain Sickness (AMS). This is a very serious condition that can affect anyone. However, it is alright to get AMS in its mild form, and by being aware of the symptoms and by adhering to the rules of acclimatisation you can significantly reduce the likelihood of suffering adversely. Other forms of varying severity of this condition, which are described later, include High Altitude Cerebral Edema (HACE) and High Altitude Pulmonary Edema (HAPE).

As you gain altitude, the air gets thinner, the pressure drops and less oxygen is available in the atmosphere. The drop in oxygen is noticeable above 2500m. 'High altitude' extends to 3700m and 'very high altitude' extends to 5500m, at which point there is only half the oxygen in each breath. 'Extreme altitude' is defined as being above 5500m. Consequently, as you gain altitude your heart and lungs have to work harder to oxygenate the body. Unfortunately, as you climb, this coincides with an increased requirement for oxygen in the tissues, resulting in a deficit. If you ascend slowly and carefully, your body adapts to the rarefied atmosphere and continues to deliver the necessary amount of oxygen to the blood cells. Most people have the ability to adapt to altitude, if they expose themselves to it sufficiently slowly. However, acclimatization takes different lengths of times for each individual and there is no hard or fast rule as to how long it ought to take to ascend a mountain. It is impossible to predict who will suffer from AMS. Neither youthfulness or physical fitness are guarantees that you won't be affected. In fact, those young trekkers who forge ahead are the most likely to succumb to the debilitating effects of altitude. Generally though, effective acclimatization to any given altitude takes about a week while full acclimatization can take up to six weeks.

Another vital consideration is water intake. When climbing at altitude, you must consume three to four litres of water per day in order to avoid dehydration. A lot of moisture is lost as you breathe or sweat during the climb. Thirst is not a reliable indicator that you are suffering from dehydration. Instead, look out for signs that include peeing infrequently, in small amounts and the urine being darker and stronger smelling.

A failure to allow sufficient time to acclimatise is almost certain to bring on AMS. The best way to avoid it is to ascend slowly. In this respect, the Kilimanjaro mantra, 'pole, pole' meaning 'slowly, slowly', is wholly appropriate and accurate. However, there is no optimum period for acclimatisation. A conservative recommendation for climbing high is that above 3200m (10,000ft) you should ideally only increase the sleeping altitude by around 350m (1200ft) per day. It is also recommended that while ascending you take a break every two or three days by sleeping at the same altitude as the previous day. To maximise the benefit of this, you should climb higher during the day, exposing your body to greater altitude, before returning to sleep at the lower elevation. In this way, an ideal ascent of Kilimanjaro should take seven to 10 days to acclimatise properly.

Most ascent routes on Kilimanjaro give you a fraction of that time to reach the top. The ascent is generally far too rapid and side effects of this are inevitable. The summit bid on the standard Marangu Route begins after three days. This is almost three times as fast as the recommendation.

At altitude, it is best to assume that any illness is AMS, until proven otherwise. Early indicators that something is amiss include extreme fatigue, persistent headache, dizziness, a loss of appetite and disturbed sleep caused by irregular breathing. In its mildest form it feels akin to a hangover. A tendency to run out of breath after minimal exertion is also an indication. If any of these symptoms become apparent, the trekker should pause until they have passed. As long as the symptoms remain mild, ascent at a modest rate can continue. If they persist after a day or two, descent to a lower elevation should be strongly considered. If possible, strong painkillers should be avoided as they will mask these early symptoms meaning a potentially serious problem could pass unnoticed.

If the condition continues to deteriorate, the casualty will become even more lethargic, confused, disorientated and out of breath. They may have wet, bubbly breath. The headache will become severe and they may start to cough harshly, sometimes producing pinkish or rust coloured sputum. They may vomit as well. They will also suffer a loss of co-ordination, known as ataxia, and will be unable to walk in a straight line or complete simple tasks. At this stage, the victim is enduring the onset of either pulmonary or cerebral oedema, both of which can result in unconsciousness and death within 12 hours. AMS has been fatal as low as 3000m (9850ft), but most commonly occurs above 3500m (11500ft).

High Altitude Cerebral Edema (HACE)

HACE is a very severe condition. The brain swells and ceases to function properly. This can result in death very quickly. The hallmark of HACE is a change in the ability of the victim to think. They may become confused, disorientated or very lethargic. There is a characteristic loss of co-ordination, called ataxia, that most often manifests

To camp in the crater adjacent to the Furtwangler Glacier (Summit Route) you must ascend slowly and steadily and acclimatise properly

itself as a staggering walk. If the victim can't walk in a straight line, even when not carrying a pack and on level ground, they should be presumed to have HACE.

The treatment is to descend immediately, even if that means doing so in the dark. Delay, even until the following morning, could be fatal. The casualty should be accompanied down at least as far as the last elevation at which they felt no symptoms of the condition. If uncertain, dropping 1000m is a good start. People with HACE usually survive if they descend sufficiently quickly and often recover completely.

High Altitude Pulmonary Edema (HAPE)

HAPE, another form of severe altitude sickness, is caused by a build up of fluid in the lungs. In addition to the usual symptoms of AMS, the victim may make a gurgling or rattling breathing sound. They may also feel a tightness around their chest. HAPE frequently occurs at night and may worsen with exertion. It is also common for HAPE to develop into HACE due to the extremely low levels of oxygen in the victim's blood.

The treatment for HAPE is the same as for AMS and HACE. Immediate descent to a lower altitude is the optimal solution – even a descent of 500m and the associated increase in oxygen content of the air is often sufficient to reduce the symptoms to a manageable level. People suffering from serious altitude illness should be accompanied off the mountain – at no time should they be allowed to set off on their own. HAPE resolves itself rapidly upon descent and a couple of days' rest at a lower elevation should ensure a complete recovery.

If, when on your trek, you or a companion begins to suffer HAPE symptoms, it is important to descend at once. If the casualty improves sufficiently, they may be able to continue. However, more

Trekkers on the Marangu Route often spend an extra day at Horombo Huts to aid acclimatisation and reduce the risk of AMS (Kibo in background)

DIAMOX (ACETAZOLAMIDE)

Diamox can aid acclimatisation. However, it is not a substitute for a slow and appropriate ascent and should not be taken as a matter of course. Most people with a reasonable rate of ascent will not need it. You must seek guidance from a GP before taking Diamox. The dosage required is based on your body weight, although 125mg (half a tablet) two or three times a day is usually enough to have an effect. Diamox re-acidifies the blood, balancing the effects of the hyperventilation that occurs at altitude in an attempt to get sufficient oxygen. This in turn acts as a respiratory stimulant, whose end effect is to accelerate acclimatisation.

It is not a magic cure, however. Diamox doesn't cover up the symptoms of AMS. Neither does it protect you from worsening AMS if you continue to ascend after symptoms have been diagnosed. Although it may reduce the time it takes for you to acclimatise, it will not totally prevent you from suffering from AMS. If you still feel sick after taking Diamox, you must descend.

If you take Diamox remember to increase your level of fluid intake as the drug is a diuretic and you may become more prone to dehydration. There are also several other side effects of using the drug. You may feel a numbness or tingling sensation in your hands, feet and lips. These may be accompanied by a ringing sound in your ears. These side effects cease once you stop taking the drug.

than likely, once the descent has begun, the affected person will not be allowed to continue up the mountain. Do not let this prospect cloud anyone's judgement. Be willing to admit that you or your companion has altitude sickness. As soon as feelings of illness arise the symptoms should be recognised and acted upon.

Remember, the golden rules for avoiding AMS are: ascend slowly. If you start to feel the onset of symptoms of AMS go no higher. If the symptoms persist, descend at once.

Porters and AMS

While on the mountain it is important to remember that the porters can be affected by AMS just as readily as you. Although most of them have been to altitude before and are likely to be better acclimatised than their charges, they may still suffer from the condition. The fact that they are unlikely to know much about AMS, have a communication barrier that prevents them from explaining in detail how they feel and may actively conceal their symptoms so as not to lose their jobs makes them susceptible to the more extreme versions of the condition.

SELECTING AN OUTFITTER

All walkers on Kilimanjaro must make the ascent with a licensed outfitter as independent trekking on the mountain was banned by the park authorities in 1991. There is now no independent trekking on the mountain at all. At the very least you must take a guide supplied by the outfitter, and the guide will require a porter to help carry all of the equipment

Porters climbing above the Machame Hut on the Machame Route, with Mount Meru in the distance

and food supplies. Bigger groups will require much larger teams of porters, cooks and assistant guides.

Trekking on Kilimanjaro with a group is the norm for most people. It is always easier to undertake this sort of trip in the company of friends and is a very sociable way to climb the mountain. The companionship and camaraderie are highly desirable and can act as a positive incentive to succeed.

It is possible to organise a trip on your own, and use the services of an outfitter to obtain a guide. That way you can plan the trek that you want, without having to incorporate the wishes of others. Most outfitters will try to introduce you to a larger group and will encourage you to trek in the company of other individuals. Even if you do opt to attempt the mountain on your own, you will never feel completely alone. Campsites are communal and lively places and there is a great deal of interaction between groups.

There are a great number of outfitters that organise treks on the mountain, based both in the UK and in Tanzania. They are responsible for ensuring the success and safety of your trip. It is important that you choose one that you think is best suited to your needs. Climbing Kilimanjaro is an expensive expedition, so it is worth spending some time comparing and contrasting the various organisations out there before parting with your money.

The vast majority of people book their climb on Kilimanjaro before they leave their home country. This is the easiest, least hassled way of organising the trip, since nearly all agencies will sell you a complete package, including airport pick up and transfers, accommodation and the ingredients for the climb itself. They may also be able to sell you flights as well. This is the least time consuming option and means that you can make all of the arrangements well in advance. Inevitably this does cost a little more than booking direct with an outfitter in Tanzania, but the additional money buys you peace of mind.

Most of the outfitters and agencies in Tanzania are found at the foot of the mountain, in either Arusha or Moshi. The larger and more established agencies now have online booking facilities as well, which mean that you can arrange your trek from outside Tanzania. Arusha tends to be a little more expensive than its neighbour, Moshi, not least because many of the agents in Arusha are working on behalf of outfitters in Moshi and need to take their cut. There are also higher transport costs to the trailhead from Arusha as it is further away from the mountain. Moshi has the largest number of outfitters (see Appendix B for a selection of the better outfitters in Moshi). Many of these are affiliated to agencies in the UK. Booking directly with an outfitter in Moshi represents the best value in terms of how much you will pay and what your money will buy. As a result of the sheer mass of competition in the town and the fact that you have removed all of the middlemen, you are also likely to pay less than if you book your trip elsewhere.

The most important thing to bear in mind when booking your trip is that the agency must be licensed. Ask to see the licence and make sure that it is in date. A good way of comparing the different agencies is to ask other people about their experiences on the mountain.

Porters with supplies at Naremoru trailhead before leading on to the Rongai Route

Check the visitors' books and read the various comments. Shop around and consult several outfitters in order to get a feel for the types of service and price ranges on offer. Check the day-to-day itineraries proposed by the outfitters and, if possible, ask to see the standard of equipment that they propose to use. Make sure that you establish exactly what is and isn't included in the price. All national park fees, rescue fees, hut or camping fees for both you, the guide and all of the porters that will accompany you should be included. Food and drinks for the entire trip should also be part of the proposed deal, as should all equipment hire costs and the price of being transported to and from the trailhead by the outfitter. Most of the established reputable outfitters will have standard contracts that stipulate all of this information, so that you know what you are signing yourself up for.

GUIDES AND PORTERS

The outlawing of independent trekking on Kilimanjaro ensured that groups were no longer allowed to pitch up at the foot of the mountain and just start climbing. Nowadays, all ascents must be conducted with a guide and usually with a team of porters who carry all of the team's equipment and food up the mountain on their heads and backs. Trekkers only shoulder a modest day pack and yet there are times on the mountain when even that will seem like a Sisyphean burden. Kilimanjaro National Park recommends that each individual making an ascent of the mountain does so with at least one or two porters. The guide will stay with you throughout the climb, accompanying you right to the summit should you be fortunate enough to make it that far. The porters will climb as far as the top camp, then wait for you to return from the summit bid before descending with you.

Climbing the mountain with a guide and porters is nothing new. In 1889, Hans Meyer was accompanied by a team of porters and guides. The group was led by 18-year-old Yohana Kinyala Lauwo, supported by an assistant, Jonathan Mtui, and several porters: Elia Minja, Tom Mosha, Makalio Lyimo and Mamba Kowera. Their names are commemorated on a plaque at the Marangu Gate. Lauwo went on to guide people up the mountain for most of his life. He was present at the centennial celebrations when he was honoured in recognition of his role in the first ever ascent of the mountain. He died, allegedly aged 125, in 1996. The first Chagga to actually stand on the summit were the guides Oforo and Jonathan, who did so in 1925 and have been credited with the 11th and 12th ascents.

The guides and porters are often interesting and entertaining companions, whose easy humour, ready laugh and knowledge of the mountain and the area can enhance your trip. Most are affiliated to one or other of the outfitters at the foot of the mountain. All guides must be registered with the national park authorities and will have a permit which confirms that. They are drawn from all walks of life and represent a broad spectrum of ages, tribes and backgrounds. That said, most of the porters are members of the Chagga tribe. Many are youngsters in their late teens and early twenties. Others have worked on the mountain for a decade or more.

Many porters volunteer to climb Kilimanjaro to supplement the income they generate from farming. Others are freelancers who have no other job. The role of porter is by no means a demeaning one and has long been a major source of employment in the Kilimanjaro region. In an area where the unemployment rate is around 80%, it is a respectable and comparatively well paid job

Porters gathered at the foot of the mountain

and money earned in tips supplements pay. Porters usually receive US$5–7 per day, although the official rate of pay is US$10. Cooks and assistant guides earn US$6–8 (official rate: US$15) and guides can expect to be paid US$8–9 per day (official rate: US$20). There have been attempts to enforce the official wages but the likelihood of the official salaries being standardised and applied across the board is very slim.

Porters are also often open to exploitation. Hopefully you'll be slightly more considerate towards your team than HW Tilman, who noted on his return to Gillman's Point from higher on the crater rim: 'We picked up the patient Solomon, now the colour of a mottled and overripe Victoria plum, and at twelve o'clock started down.' There is never enough work on the mountain to go round and competition to become a porter is fierce. Only by serving an apprenticeship as a porter will they become an assistant guide and have a chance to progress to the level of guide. Although there are regulations in place to try to preserve porters' rights, these are sometimes flouted by unscrupulous outfitters or guides.

Tourism Concern (www.tourism concern.org.uk), a UK-based organisation that lobbies on behalf of porters' rights, noted 'There have been reports of guides bribing the rangers who weigh the porters' loads, for example, so that the porters end up carrying huge weights, and of guides choosing porters on the basis of payments and bribes. Porters who complain fear that they will be threatened by the guide and told that they will not climb again.' Porter conditions and standards vary considerably from one group to another. The lack of standardised rates of pay can mean that it is often the outfitters that get rich while the porters put in the hard graft.

Other organisations working for improved conditions for porters include the International Porter Protection Group (www.ippg.net) and the Kilimanjaro Porters Assistance Project (www.kiliporters.org). The latter lends out equipment and clothing, donated by trekkers, to porters for free, teaches the porters English and first aid, and generally tries to raise the issue of porter exploitation in the public mind by arranging for people to spend a day with a porter and see what his life is really like. KPAP estimates that a fair wage for a porter's work done properly is 28,000 Tsh per day. They have also set up a 'Partner' scheme for trekking agencies, and there are lists online of those agencies which have signed up to it. To qualify as a partner, one of the criteria is paying porters at least US$7, assistant guides US$10 and guides US$14.

The level of equipment given to porters has improved considerably over recent years. That said, in the main, the porters are still woefully kitted out for mountain climbing and often make do with whatever they can scrounge or cobble together. Outfitters are now obliged to provide tents for their teams since the porters have been banned from sleeping in caves along the routes.

Nonetheless, the porters are still at very high risk on the mountain. Although they appear superhuman, carrying massive loads, seemingly unaffected by altitude and surviving in the harsh conditions without the benefit of modern equipment or clothing, many of them are inexperienced, unsure of what to expect on the mountain and lack the proper equipment and clothing. They are still susceptible to appalling accidents, frostbite, altitude sickness and death. In bad weather it is not uncommon for a porter to die of exposure or hypothermia, most often because of a lack of appropriate mountain clothing.

Although extreme, this issue is symptomatic of a major problem of exploitation by unprincipled outfitters. There are a number of things that you can do as an individual to try and address this problem. Before booking your trek ask the tour operator or outfitter what policies they have in regard to porters' working conditions, and make sure that they know that it is important to you that your trip does not exploit its team of porters. If booking in the UK, only travel with an operator that has policies on porters' rights. Tourism Concern has a list of over 35 registered tour operators in the UK who have written policies on working conditions for porters. Before you set off, try to make sure that adequate clothing is available for the porters. While on the climb check to see how the porters are being treated, noting the standard of kit they have, the amount that they have to carry and where they sleep at night. Once you have descended from the mountain, tell the outfitter if you thought they were mistreated and report this to Tourism Concern. Equally, make sure that you tell the outfitter if you thought that the porters were treated fairly and make it clear that this was very important to you and your enjoyment of the climb. This sort of interest and concern will compel the trekking industry to improve itself and sharpen its practices.

TIPPING

In addition to the fee agreed with the outfitter for your climb on Kilimanjaro, you must include in your budget an amount

Porters watching the sunrise illuminate clouds below Mawenzi Tarn Hut (Rongai Route, Mawenzi Tarn Hut to Kibo Huts)

to be allocated as tips for the guide and porters. While it is not mandatory to tip those who accompany you on your climb, a situation has developed whereby the local people depend upon the tips to supplement their meagre income. To this end, tipping is no longer strictly discretionary and has become more-or-less obligatory. Nonetheless, do not let yourself be bullied into tipping excessively and make the team aware of the fact that the tip is for work well done. In fairness, once you see how much effort goes into making your climb a safe and successful one you will not begrudge the guide and porters the extra money.

When it comes to distributing the tips, you can either hand the money to the guide and allow him to share it among his team, or you may choose to give it to the individuals yourself. The second option is more personal and allows you to say thank you. It also ensures that each member of the group actually receives what is meant for them. If you do hand the money to the guide, make sure that you write down what each member is to receive so that they can see that they have been treated fairly and haven't been swindled by an unscrupulous leader.

Bear in mind that tips can be sought quite aggressively and that there are a host of tricks designed to help you part with additional cash, but equally also keep in mind that what is a fairly small amount by western standards means an awful lot to the guides and porters on the mountain.

- The play-acting and aggrieved faces are designed to prick your conscience and open your wallet.
- Make sure that you are only tipping members of your own team.
- Ascertain how many people are associated with your group and make sure that you actually see them working on your behalf during the course of your climb.
- Don't let the guide persuade you that there was an additional porter accompanying the group that you simply didn't see. Be especially sceptical if this mysterious individual fails to appear to collect his tip and the others volunteer to take it on his behalf.

What to tip?

There are several ways of determining how much to tip the team. In the case of large groups, it has become common practice for each member of the group to contribute 10% of the cost of the climb to a tip kitty. The total amount is then shared between all of the porters and guides associated with that group. If there are only a few members in the group you should consider increasing the percentage donated to the kitty.

Alternatively, you might like to consider allocating a set amount to each individual in the team. Although there are no hard or fast rules, a general guideline for the Marangu Route would be to tip the porters US$20–25, the cook US$30–35, and the assistant guides US$35–45. The guide ought to have made the most effort on your behalf and accompanied you to the summit, and so should be tipped US$55–65. On each of the other routes, which are all slightly longer and more arduous, you should consider being slightly more generous. Thus for the Machame Route, the porters

Kibo cone seen from Shira Plateau on the Machame Route (photo: Steve Lagreca/Shutterstock.com)

might earn US$20–30, the cook US$30–40, the assistant guide US$40–50 and the guide US$60–70.

If the team accompanying you worked especially hard or did additional work, you may wish to recognise this by increasing their tip. Almost all of the local people will be very grateful for any shoes or clothes that you may wish to give them after the climb, but these should be gifts and not offered as an alternative to a cash tip.

ENVIRONMENTAL AND CULTURAL CONSIDERATIONS

Kilimanjaro is a very important area of biodiversity and it has a very high value to local people. The slopes of the mountain support high density populations, whose numbers have increased fivefold over the last century. These people rely on the mountain to provide them with water for drinking and irrigation and a pleasant and relatively disease-free environment. Consequently, in order to preserve this situation, the Tanzanian national parks' authorities have declared that Kilimanjaro should be at the centre of a substantial area of wilderness, where the evidence of man and man's activities are minimal. Thus, all land above 2700m constitutes Kilimanjaro National Park.

The Tanzanian policy for park management is to conserve the natural environment with as little interference as possible. This involves the national parks' authorities taking responsibility for providing and maintaining facilities and routes on the mountain. Funds and manpower are scarce, and they rely on trekkers adhering to the various regulations and making a conscious effort not to damage the mountain in the course of their visit.

Every trekker on Kilimanjaro will have an impact on the mountain and the region simply by virtue of being there. On its own, this may be minimal; but with up to 60,000 people visiting Kilimanjaro every year the effect on the environment and the people that live in the area is greatly magnified. Each visitor has the potential to make their impact a positive one. By being aware of this and following the requests below, you will secure the future of the mountain.

Remove all litter

Sadly, although steps have been taken to improve the state of the mountain and instill in trekkers the need to collect and remove from the mountain all of the rubbish that they generate in the course of their climb, the slopes are increasingly littered. This can pose a health risk and is dangerous to animals.

You must pack-out everything that you carry in, including empty food packaging and detritus. Neither burning the rubbish nor burying it is acceptable – metal cans and many modern plastics do not burn completely, and buried rubbish will take years to break down and will, in the meantime, disturb the soil and promote erosion. The rubbish that you collect must be weighed by the park rangers at the end of your trek. If there is a suspicion that any has been dumped, the guide runs the risk of losing his license or being fined.

Toilet paper should be carefully burnt after use, in order to prevent it later becoming strewn across the mountain slopes. Carry a lighter for this purpose. If you are in the forest or heath/moorland zones and think that this will constitute a fire hazard then pack the paper out with you.

Don't pollute water sources

Water is a valuable resource on the mountain and should be treated as such.

Crossing the Saddle on ascent to Kibo Huts (Machame Route) (photo: Mountaintreks/Shutterstock.com)

At the campsite use the long-drop toilets provided. If there are no toilet facilities to hand, select a spot that is at least 30m from any water source and the path, dig a shallow hole and bury the faeces. At the very least, make sure that you cover everything with stones.

Be careful when gathering water from streams and make sure that you leave the source uncontaminated. Also take care when washing not to pollute the water. Soaps, detergents and toothpaste can have a very negative impact on the flora and fauna. Even biodegradable soaps can harm wildlife. Your guide will make sure that, when in the campsite, you are brought warmed water several times a day for you to use to clean up. Dispose of the used water carefully, pouring it onto the ground away from other water sources.

Don't use bottled water

Abandoned water bottles are unsightly and can quickly build up. They aren't biodegradable and do not break down. Now that the huts along the Marangu Route have started to sell bottled water, there is a very real potential of littering. Instead, use water collected from the mountain and boil, filter or treat it before consumption (see Health considerations above).

Fires

Fires are capable of destroying enormous areas of forest and heath/moorland vegetation, particularly in the dry seasons. The inaccessible nature of many of the slopes mean that if a fire does break out it is very hard to control or extinguish. The farmers below the national park boundaries use fires to remove dry grass from cropland. These are meant to be controlled but there is evidence to suggest that they have previously contributed to forest fires. Inside the national park, fires can start as a result of carelessness – dropped cigarettes and roaring campfires are the worst culprits.

All of your meals should be prepared on kerosene stoves rather than on wood fires. Fires should not be lit at the hut or campsite areas either. The reason for this is twofold: it prevents the removal and destruction of timber along the routes and ensures that the risks of accidental forest fires are minimal. Huge forest fires have ravaged the heath/moorland slopes of the mountain above Horombo Huts in the past; the charred remains of these events are still evident beneath the regenerating vegetation. If you are cold in the evenings, resist the urge to light a fire and simply put on another layer of clothing.

Stay on the trail

In order to minimise the destruction of the flora and reduce the erosion of the mountain, you should stick to the clearly visible paths. Do not take short cuts across the slopes. Be especially careful in areas where the ground is boggy. These ecosystems are very fragile and can suffer irreparable damage if you trample over them. When descending from the crater rim, try to follow the switchbacks. It is very tempting to simply run down the scree in a straight line, but this dislodges enormous amounts of soil and gravel, shunting it off the slopes and hastening their deterioration.

Flora and fauna

It is illegal to remove any plants or animals from the mountain. Many of the

View of Mawenzi and Kibo across the heath above Mandara Huts (Marangu Route)

flora species found on Kilimanjaro are unique or vulnerable. Do not pick any of the flowers that you find on the mountain and do not disturb any wildlife that you come across. Everything should be left on the mountain for others to enjoy. Illegal hunting does occur in the forest zone. Poachers set snares and traps for duikers, hyraxes and monkeys. If you see any suspicious activity or find any evidence of poaching, report it to the park warden.

Cultural interaction

A lot of people who climb Kilimanjaro discover that the interaction that they enjoy with their guide and porters is one of the highlights of their trip. By rising above cultural prejudices and engaging with your hosts and companions on the mountain, you will become more sensitive to their ways of living and beliefs. To not do so will reduce the value of your trip and contribute to the cultural erosion of the country. Be patient, friendly and open when meeting people and the courtesy will usually be returned. Try to learn a few words of Swahili; the endeavour will be appreciated by the porters and guides, if only because your attempts to pronounce their language are so risible. A glossary of useful words and phrases can be found in Appendix D. If you hang on to your sense of humour and maintain a sense of perspective, then your time on the mountain will be enriched. With a bit of effort, you will cease to be the 'Mzungu Kichaa', or 'crazy European', and become a friend instead.

USING THIS GUIDE

The purpose of this guide is to add something to the experience of climbing this remarkable mountain by helping you to prepare for and then undertake the trek. By forewarning you of the nature of the climb and the potential seriousness of some of the routes, it is hoped that you will be properly prepared for the challenge. By adding a history of the area and of the early exploration and attempted ascents of Kilimanjaro, you will also get a sense of the mountain's place in local life and its importance in a wider context, ensuring that you come away with a far better and broader appreciation of what it means both to live on and around the slopes, as well as to summit, Kilimanjaro.

The following sections include descriptions of an acclimatisation trek, all the ascent routes, circuit paths, summit ascent routes and then the descent routes. In the course of a complete climb you will use an ascent route, a summit ascent route and a descent route, with the latter determined by the former. The Circuit Path encircles the summit massif at around 4000m and connects the ascent and summit ascent routes. Although a detailed route guide to climbing Kilimanjaro is hardly necessary – the majority of the routes up the mountain are so well travelled that it's almost impossible to become lost – it is useful to know the nature of the paths, the distance you will be walking and the time it will take you to complete the different stages; and these details are included here in the route descriptions. In the following pages, all of the main routes up and down the mountain are described on a day-by-day basis, and are accompanied by a series of sketch maps showing the route and key features of the landscape. Places and features in the text that also appear on the maps are marked in the route descriptions in **bold**.

The introduction to each route includes a box summarising the route. The ascent route summaries show both the time spent on the ascent route and the minimum total number of days you will spend on the mountain (ie cumulative time spent on the ascent, summit ascent and descent routes) if you choose to take that particular ascent route. The

Work to be done at First Camp on the Rongai Route, Mawenzi in the distance

Route finding is not a problem in this neck of the woods (Machame Route)

time shown in the summit ascent and descent route summaries reflects only the time spent on that route.

An indication of how long each daily section takes is found in the summary of the daily schedule. The times quoted are average walking times only and will not correspond to everyone's experiences, but are intended as a rough guide. These approximations refer to the actual time spent walking and do not take into account breaks, photographic opportunities or any other delays.

The altitude gain and loss figures refer to the difference between the start and finish points. The altitudes noted are taken from as reliable a set of sources as possible. There are wildly differing estimates of the height of each feature, and even of the summit, and the altitudes quoted here may not be in accordance with each map or every guide. The distances mentioned are also at best estimates that will provide as accurate an impression of the ascent of the mountain as possible.

PEOPLE OF THE REGION

Mount Kilimanjaro erupted from the savannah approximately one million years ago as the result of a series of cataclysmic earth movements associated with the formation of the Rift Valley. Geologically speaking, this is recent and means that the volcano is one of the youngest in Africa and would have been formed during the time that hominids were on the earth. In fact, Kilimanjaro is likely to have been seen by at least four different *Homo* species including *H. erectus* and *H. ergaster*, the forerunners of the Neanderthals. Once Kilimanjaro's slopes had become safe to inhabit, they would have supported early hunter-gatherer tribes. The extensive network of springs and streams, in conjunction with the temperate climate and bountiful supplies of food and wood, would have made this a highly desirable location for early man.

However, little of great anthropological or archaeological antiquity has been found on the mountain itself. Primitive stone bowls fashioned from lava have been discovered on the lower western slopes of the mountain, leading archaeologists to conclude that hunter-gatherer tribes based themselves here from around 1000BC onwards. However, there is little evidence available to conclusively prove what sort of life these tribes may have enjoyed.

Waves of people migrated across Africa. First Cushites entered the region from the southern highlands of Ethiopia and spread across and settled on the plains and highlands of Tanzania. It is thought that these early agriculturalists may have been responsible for some of the irrigation channels found on Kilimanjaro. Within the last few thousand years, Bantu people from West Africa and Nilotic people from the Nile Basin migrated to this region. These groups are represented around Kilimanjaro today by two tribes: the Chagga and the Maasai.

The Chagga

The Chagga live around the southern slopes of Kilimanjaro, right up to the national park boundary. They currently constitute the third largest tribal group in Tanzania, numbering over 800,000 people. They are also known as the Chaga or Shaka, and sometimes the tribe is referred to as the Wachagga (the prefix 'wa' meaning 'the people of').

The Chagga are descended from a variety of groups who migrated to the foothills of Kilimanjaro and took possession of the fertile mountain slopes several hundred years ago. The tribe was composed of around 400 main clans, most of which were descended from the Kamba, a Bantu-speaking people. They have since intermingled with the Taita, Maasai and other peoples.

The new homeland, Chaggaland, was divided into a number of politically independent chiefdoms, defined by natural barriers. However, each of these rulers constantly strove for supremacy and control over the whole tribe. The tribe was almost united by the

View across the exposed Saddle to the Kibo massif (Rongai Route)

great chief Horombo in the mid-18th century. Nicknamed 'Kilimia', meaning 'the Conqueror', Horombo inspired respect and command throughout the Kilimanjaro region and was close to becoming the paramount chief of the Chagga. He would probably have succeeded too had he not been slain by Maasai warriors. The policy of unification died with him and the tribe returned to fighting among itself.

The internal rivalry between chiefs vying to be the most powerful reached its peak in the late 19th century. The dominant chiefs of Moshi and of Marangu, called Mandara (or sometimes Rindi) and Sina respectively, were at this stage at the height of their powers. Kathleen Stahl, an authority on the Chagga, has credited both leaders, describing Mandara as 'The most illustrious ruler of Moshi, and the ablest diplomatist on Kilimanjaro', and Sina as 'the greatest warrior chief that Kilimanjaro has ever known'.

As colonials began to arrive in Tanzania the chiefs each realised the potential benefits to be gleaned from this influx and attempted to play one off against the other. The German colonials took advantage of this and in turn exploited the Chagga. They encouraged the spats and directed the tribe to attack the German's enemies. While Sina ruled by virtue of his powerful and ferocious army, Mandara proved to be the more astute and made a number of treaties with the wealthy foreigners. In 1885, Mandara held negotiations with the German colonists and agreed to allow them to use Moshi as their central base in this part of East Africa. The result was that Moshi became an important staging post for the slave and ivory trade, and consequently prospered.

A number of years later, an overall chief of the Chagga did emerge, although it had little to do with the internal unification of the tribe and was in fact the work of the then colonial administration. Marealle, from Marangu, was nominated the paramount chief in 1893; one of his descendants is still the foremost chief of the Chagga, although the position has lost much of its official power.

Today, the Chagga have a reputation as being among the most organised and successful tribes in East Africa. The fertile nature of their land and the high-altitude climate of the region have contributed to their continued success. The creation of ingenious water irrigation channels with little more than wooden hoes is a marvel of primitive engineering. In addition to the advantageous location of their lands, they were also one of the first groups to have sustained contact with the European missionaries, in particular those from the Roman Catholic and Lutheran churches. The initial provision of education in the region led to them being more advanced than many of the other tribes at that time.

As the population of the tribe has increased, so the Chagga have developed new intensive farming methods to sustain their numbers. This has resulted in the use of agricultural irrigation, fertilisers and crop rotation in the Kilimanjaro region, ensuring that the lower slopes can be cultivated all year round. The Chagga, who have proved to be diligent, industrious farmers, have realised the benefits of producing cash crops such as coffee and bananas, and now grow these alongside more traditional staple foods. They also brew beer from bananas and a small seed known as eleusine. The Kilimanjaro region is so clement and fertile that, with sufficient water, almost anything can be produced there. However, the rains are erratic and the threat of drought is very real.

The Chagga are also fairly open-minded towards new ideas and developments. Consequently, they consistently participate in community activities and are involved in the cooperative production and marketing of coffee. They are now responsible for producing the largest amount of arabica coffee in the Kilimanjaro region, selling the product worldwide. Their relatively high level of education and the ability to take advantage of cash crops has also meant that the Chagga enjoy a comparatively high level of income.

Their location at the foot of Kilimanjaro means that they are also ideally placed to take advantage of the region's boom in tourism. From the initial interaction with colonials onwards they have had sustained contact with visitors to the region over the centuries: European missionaries, colonisers, mountaineers, geographers, botanists and, now, streams of trekkers from around the world.

The majority of guides and porters that accompany trekkers are Chagga. Despite having lived so close to Kilimanjaro for centuries, the Chagga formerly had no cause to climb the mountain, believing that it was full of evil spirits and djinns. Although there is evidence to suggest that the Chagga may have ventured as far as the snowline, it is thought that they considered the mountain too high to climb to the top. Charles Dundas wrote in his book, *Kilimanjaro and its People*, that 'It is inconceivable that natives can ever have ascended to the crater rim, for apart from cold, altitude and superstitious fears, it is sheer impossibility that they could have negotiated the ice. Nor is there any tradition amongst the natives that anyone went up as high.'

Nonetheless, the tribe have always venerated Kilimanjaro. It gives them a very visible focal point and inspires a sense of identity and unity. It is also a provider of essential water and rainfall. Such is their reverence for the mountain that traditionally their dead are buried facing Kibo.

The Chagga traditionally worship a god known as Ruwa, who lives in the sky. He is the most important and powerful of all their deities and, although not responsible for earth's creation, did provide man with plants and fruit. The Chagga consider that all men are descended from him and that he is their great protector. Animal sacrifices used to be made to Ruwa in times of drought, famine or if the tribe was affected by an epidemic.

Sacrifices would also be made to the spirits of the dead, who the Chagga hold in high regard. They maintain that when a person dies they move across to live in a different world in a different form. They also consider that the spirits of the dead are able to return to earth in order to demand from their relatives what is rightly theirs. These spirits only appear in dreams or visions but can communicate using animal noises.

However, there are also a number of modern Chagga who have converted to

Christianity and are receptive to the various teachings of the different denominations of missionaries in the region. It is also worth noting that as a result of their increased involvement with the modern world, a great many of the Chagga's traditional practices have died out.

Today, land shortages have altered their economic structure and many Chagga are now wage earners in large cities. They are also prominent in politics and hold a number of important positions. As such, they are important contributors to the country's economy and direction. However, the success of the Chagga is not universally applauded and in some cases it is actively resented. Some Chagga businessmen and entrepreneurs find themselves affected by adverse discrimination and are the victims of anti-Chagga sentiments born of jealousy.

The Maasai

The Maasai (sometimes spelt 'Masai') are one of the best-known tribes in Africa. Although mythology surrounds their origins (see box), the mundane reality is that the Maasai are descended from Nilotic pastoralists who migrated to Tanzania from further north, following the course of the Nile from southern Sudan.

Initial reports from the missionaries and early explorers in the region cemented the Maasai's reputation as fierce, war-like people; Ludwig Krapf recorded that throughout the mid-19th

Kilimanjaro Lager label – making the most of the tourist numbers

MYTH OF THE ORIGIN OF THE MAASAI

The myth of the origin of the Maasai is described in Joseph Thomson's account of his travels, *Through Masai Land*. He recorded that: 'The primal ancestor of the Masai was one Kidenoi, who lived at Donyo Egere [Mount Kenya], was hairy, and had a tail. Filled with the spirit of exploration, he left his home and wandered south. The people of the country, seeing him shaking something in a calabash, were so struck with admiration at the wonderful performance that they brought him women as a present. By these he had children who, strangely enough, were not hairy, and had no tails, and these were the progenitors of the Masai.'

century the Maasai were engaged in a 'useless and savage civil war', while Charles New described them as 'congenital killers of the Dark Interior'. In reality, they are proud semi-nomadic pastoralists, whose wealth and well-being is largely dependent on their herds of cattle.

The Maasai have a deep, almost sacred relationship with cattle. They are guided by a strong belief that their god, Engai, created cattle especially for them and that they are the sole custodians of all the cattle on Earth. This bond has led them to follow a nomadic way of life, following the seasons and rainfall over vast tracts of land in search of food and water for their large herds.

The warrior remains of great importance to the Maasai culture, however – to be a Maasai is to be born into one of the world's last great warrior cultures. From boyhood to adulthood, young Maasai still learn the cultural practices, customary laws and responsibilities of being a man and a warrior. Today, there are 12 distinct groups of Maasai, the largest of which lives in Tanzania. This biggest group is known as Otunlanyana loo Ngishu, which literally translates as 'people of the cattle'.

The Maasai adhere to a strict social structure. Their society is heavily regulated and maintained by the highest-ranking member of the tribe, the Olaibou – unlike many tribes, the Maasai do not have a paramount chief. The Olaibou is an important tribal figure and these men, since Maasai society is very much male orientated, are accorded a great deal of respect. He has the greatest wisdom and the most knowledge regarding the use of plant remedies (used as medicines). He also mediates between the people of his tribe and their ancestral spirits.

There are strict rites of passage to be endured by members of the tribe. They have to pass through several age divisions, each lasting seven years (apart from the Sokolyo which lasts three months): the Engayok are children who are too young to leave their home; the Layooni are uncircumcised boys who are taught to herd the cattle; newly circumcised boys awaiting the ceremony that formally makes them a Maasai Moran warrior are the Sokoliyo. These youths spend up to three months as Sokoliyo, during which time they must dress in black and paint their faces with white chalk and soot. They are also required to hunt and kill birds on the savannah in order to make their own headdress. Once they become Moran, they must spend seven more years protecting the community. After this they can marry (frequently more than one woman) and become Orpaiyan, after which they may have children. Finally, they become an Ilmoruak, an elder responsible for making the important decisions that affect the group's future.

A set of traditional beliefs based on the teachings of the god Engai, and his messiah, Kindong'oi (from whom Maasai priests are believed to descend), govern the daily lives of the Maasai. All forms of worship are conducted either beneath fig trees, which are considered holy, or at Ol Doinyo Lengai, the 'mountain of god'. The Maasai do not believe in any form of afterlife.

The strict tribal regulations and the emphasis on a traditional way of life have made the transition to modern living particularly tough for the Maasai. The modern Maasai retain their original language, Maa. Although some still attempt to maintain a pastoral, nomadic existence, their population numbers are increasing and they are facing the enforcement of tight boundaries. As a consequence, some Maasai have switched to cultivation rather than animal husbandry. Regardless, the rural Maasai continue to exist on a traditional diet of milk, meat and occasionally cow's blood. They are easily recognised by their proud, upright stance, large hooped earlobes and their red, frequently checked cloth robes, known as a *shuka*.

The impact of modern civilisation, education and western influence have not completely spared this traditional tribe and some of the Maasai's deep-rooted culture is being eroded as younger members move to urban environments and secure jobs. That said, many of the Maasai are highly educated

View of Kibo and the cloud cap at sunrise from Shira Plateau (Machame Route)

and have very strong leadership abilities. They are respected and frequently secure important positions in the country's government.

ORIGIN OF THE MOUNTAIN'S NAME

Few names have such a powerful resonance as Kilimanjaro. It echoes like a spell, evoking awesome images on a par with Xanadu, Timbuktu or Machu Picchu. It signifies somewhere special. Yet there is no consensus as to how the mountain came to be known as this or even as to what it means.

The origin of the name remains uncertain, but it probably evolved during the explorations of the 19th century. The missionary Johannes Rebmann reported that in the 1840s the Chagga referred to the two summits separately, calling them Kibo (or Kipoo), meaning 'snow', and Kimawenzi, meaning 'broken top'. Interestingly, they didn't have a name for the massif as a whole.

The coastal traders and local tribes had several versions of the name for Kilimanjaro, calling it Kilima Njaro or Kilimanscharo. In 1848 Rebmann surmised that the most probable definition of this name was 'mountain of greatness'. He then undermined his theory by considering an alternative interpretation of the name, suggesting that if 'njaro' was a corruption of the Chagga word 'jaro', the name would translate as 'mountain of caravans', which he took to be a veiled reference to the traders and trade routes that used Kilimanjaro as a landmark. However, there is no philological explanation for either of these theories. It is also highly unlikely that the name is a composite of two languages. Consequently, these theories have largely been disregarded.

Swahili, the majority language in Tanzania, offers the most likely derivation of the name. The name 'Kilimanjaro' comprises two root words, 'kilima', which is a corruption of the Swahili word 'mlima' (meaning 'mountain'), and 'njaro', which is the Swahili name for a type of devil that was reputed to be responsible for creating coldness. This particular rendition of the name seems most likely and appropriate, and also ties in with Chagga folklore, which is full of accounts of such devils.

The prefix 'ki' in Swahili is often applied to make the noun diminutive or to reduce it in size. Thus the great mountain becomes a hill. The suggestion is that this is a term of affection for Kilimanjaro, or an ironic reference to its vast size. In Swahili there is also a word, 'njara', that means shining. This potential interpretation of the name seems an equally valid and apt reference to the mountain.

There are also a handful of local variations of the name, which have most likely come about as a consequence of it being called Kilimanjaro, rather than as forerunners of the current name. Thus, you may hear the mountain referred to as Kilimoroyoo, or Kilemakyaro, which when translated literally means 'something that is impossible to climb'.

EXPLORATION

Early references

It is unclear exactly when people outside of the Kilimanjaro region became aware of the giant peak. There are several allusions to such a mountain, but no specific references to it by name. In the fifth century BC scholars believed that the Nile sprang from snow clad mountains in equatorial Africa. This misfounded belief can be traced back to the writings of Aeschylus, who believed that Egypt was 'nourished by melting snows'. The Greek historian Herodotus propagated this myth by wrongly depicting the sources of the Nile as three great fountains astride the equator amid what he called the 'Mountains of the Moon'. In the fourth century BC, the Greek philosopher Aristotle referred to 'the so-called silver mountain' southwest of the Nile. The legend of a summit strewn with silver persisted among Swahili coastal people until the middle of the 19th century.

By the onset of the first century AD, merchants from the Mediterranean were trading along the East African coastline. A Greek merchant, Diogenes, is alleged to have ventured inland from 'Rhapta' for 25 days and reached two great lakes and a snowy range of mountains, 'whence the Nile draws its twin sources'. (Rhapta's exact location is unknown, but it is probably modern day Pangani.) In AD45 a book entitled *The Periplus of the Erythraeu Sea* was published, which described the town of Rhapta as 'the very last market town of the continent of Azania'. Although there is no mention of Kilimanjaro in this particular text, in view of the distance travelled by Diogenes, it is possible that the 'snowy range of mountains' he described may be Kilimanjaro.

The Alexandrian astronomer and geographer Ptolemy incorporated the 'Montes Lunae' into his great *Geography*, which became the standard geographical textbook until the discoveries of the 15th century. Although the information Ptolemy recorded was most likely gleaned from hearsay, it is possible that this is the first written description of the mountain.

Potential references to Kilimanjaro continue to appear in Chinese and Arabic texts during the 12th and 13th centuries. Traders passing through the region probably used the mountain as a landmark since it is such a dominant feature in an otherwise geographically unremarkable landscape. In addition to being an invaluable navigational tool, the mountain would also have been an excellent source of water and firewood for caravan troops.

During the 16th century, as colonial interests replaced commercial ones, the world's interest in the region shifted focus. In 1507 the Spanish scholar and astronomer Fernandez de Encisco visited Mombasa and gained information from traders relating to the interior of the country. He reported that west of Mombasa lay 'the Ethiopian Olympus, which is very high, and further off are the mountains of the moon, in which are the sources of the Nile', echoing the theory circulated by Ptolemy almost 1400 years earlier. The 'Ethiopian Olympus' is thought to be Kilimanjaro and the 'mountains of the moon', the Ruwenzoris, the range bordering Uganda and Congo. In 1519 *Suma de Geographia*, a book based on Fernandez de Encisco's trip reports, was published in Seville and subsequently the 'Ethiopian Olympus' began to appear on maps of the region. By the 19th century, Arab slave traders regularly referred to a high snow mountain in Chagga country that had heavily populated, fertile slopes.

Rebmann was the first European to lay eyes on Kilimanjaro's glaciers and icefields

19th-century European interest

The British Royal Geographical Society, founded in 1830 with the intention of promoting geographical research, centred its interest on Africa in trying to pinpoint the source of the Nile; it seemed unthinkable to the Victorians that the Nile could rise from snow-capped peaks astride the equator. Remarkably, the society was uninterested in confirming the actual existence of Kilimanjaro or indeed the existence of snow on the equator, which it resolutely refused to acknowledge.

Interest in the region did increase, however, when in 1834 the then ruler of East Africa sent his envoy, Khamis bin Uthman, to Europe. He met a number of dignitaries and academics, including the English armchair geographer William Desborough Cooley, who later wrote that 'The most famous mountain of East Africa is Kirimanjara, which we suppose, from a number of circumstances to be the highest ridge crossed on the road to Monomoezi'. Although the world was aware of other snow-capped mountains near the equator, Cooley was convinced that 'Kirimanjara' was only a fifth of the height required to sustain perennial snow in Africa. However, Bin Uthman's visit led to a flurry of academic interest in East Africa and inspired further exploration.

At this time, missionaries were also focusing their attention on East Africa. In 1846 the Swiss-German missionary Johannes Rebmann joined the Protestant mission in Mombasa, originally founded by Ludwig Krapf. Krapf had arrived in Africa nurturing an ambition to create a chain of mission stations across the continent, which would spread the gospel and combat the perfidious slave trade. Rebmann enthusiastically embarked on a series of reconnaissance trips, journeying first to Kasigau to establish the first link in the chain, before relocating to the Jagga (now Chagga) region.

From the outset, Rebmann was captivated by the myth of Kilimanjaro.

He had heard rumours that Jagga suffered from extreme cold; Rebmann's caravan leader, Bwana Kheri, confirmed this and described a giant mountain, which he called 'Kilimansharo', which was allegedly crowned with a strange white substance that glittered like silver. The locals simply called this substance 'cold'. Bwana Kheri reported that the local people believed the mountain was protected by djinns and evil spirits, who were capable of killing a man.

On 11 May 1848 Rebmann, the first European to recognise Kilimanjaro, had his first tantalising glimpse of Kilimanjaro from a distance of about 25 miles (40km). Two days later he saw the mountain again. Captivated by the apparition, he made a second expedition to the region in November 1848. On this trip he reached Machame village and was able to obtain fine views of the mountain that enabled him to describe the two main peaks and the saddle-shaped depression that separated them: 'There are two principal summits placed upon a basis some ten leagues long and as many broad, so that the space between them forms as it were a saddle ... The eastern summit is lower, and pointed, while the western and higher one presents a fine crown, which, even in the hot season, when its eastern and lowlier neighbour can no longer support its snowy roof, remains covered by a mass of snow', he wrote in a report for the April 1849 edition of the *Church Missionary Intelligencer* (a monthly periodical that was set up to raise funds for overseas endeavours). Rebmann was able to explain a number of the legends and stories that he had heard. 'All the strange stories we had so often heard about the gold and silver mountain Kilimandjaro in Jagga, supposed to be inaccessible on account of evil spirits, which had killed a great many of those who had attempted to ascend it, were now at once rendered intelligible to me, as of course the extreme cold to which poor natives are perfect strangers, would soon chill and kill the half-naked visitors', he wrote. Initially he believed that the members of his party had no word for snow, but subsequently learnt that the locals called the mountain Kibo, which also meant 'snow'. It transpired that it was only the coastal people who couldn't comprehend the concept of snow. Rebmann recorded a story told to him by Bwana Kheri concerning Kilimanjaro and the 'Madjame' tribe. The powerful king of Madjame, Rungua, was so intrigued by the substance that capped Kilimanjaro that he sent a selection of his retinue to determine the exact nature of this unusual matter. Only one of this group, a man named Sabaya who Bwana Kheri claimed to have spoken to, was to return from the mountain, his hands and feet hideously crippled. Rebmann reported the story in his piece for the *Church Missionary Intelligencer* in 1849 and surmised that the man had suffered severe frostbite and that his group had either frozen to death or fled and died on the mountain.

Scepticism over snow-clad peaks

The article in the *Church Missionary Intelligencer* caused a great deal of consternation in the western world. Geographers universally scoffed at the reports of a snow-capped peak. William Desborough Cooley was especially outspoken in his denial of the existence of such a mountain. Cooley was devising a map of Africa from the comfort of his study in England, based on his interpretations of classical and Arab reports. Although he had never been to East Africa, Cooley had written major essays on the region's geography in 1835 and 1845. His reputation as an Africa expert lent extra weight to his denunciation of the existence of snow on the equator. 'I deny altogether the existence of snow on Mount Kilimanjaro. It rests entirely on the testimony of Mr Rebmann ... and he ascertained it not with his eyes but by inference and in the visions of his imagination', Cooley wrote in the May 1849 edition of *Athanaeum*.

Cooley wasn't alone in ridiculing Rebmann's findings. Rebmann was no scientist and had no real geographical aptitude. His reports were vague and the references to latitude, longitude, altitude, direction and distances in them were incomplete. His extravagant writing style and lack of reliable observations further caused people to doubt the validity of his claims.

In order to press inland and establish the third link of the proposed chain of mission stations, Rebmann returned to the region in April 1849, ahead of the publication of his article. Consequently, he was unaware of the widespread scepticism that greeted his announcements. Although this expedition was much more organised than his previous efforts, Rebmann did away with Bwana Kheris' services and guidance. As he approached Machame village once more he declared that he seemed 'so close to the snow line that, supposing no impassable abyss to intervene, I could have reached it in three to four hours'. This would have been a wildly optimistic and inaccurate assessment (being at least three or four days away from the snowline). Rebmann's expedition later fell foul of the powerful local king in Machame, Mamkinga. Mamkinga extorted all of Rebmann's possessions and eventually the missionary fled from the greedy tyrant, a dispirited, humiliated, sick man. Thoroughly broken, he abandoned the project and refrained from further exploration.

Rebmann's missionary co-worker, Ludwig Krapf, continued to practice in the region, however. Krapf visited the Wakamba district to the north of Kilimanjaro in November 1849, and sighted the mountain twice, first on 10 November and again on 16 November. Krapf reported these sightings, only to be faced with the same scepticism that Rebmann's earlier descriptions had met. Cooley insisted that he had been hallucinating. However, it was harder for people to dismiss two independent European sightings of the snow-capped mountain. Doubts began to surface as to the accuracy of Cooley's rebuttals. In 1852 Cooley published his thoughts in the book *Inner Africa Laid Open*, reiterating his belief that Rebmann's sightings were 'a most delightful mental recognition only, not supported by the evidence of his senses'. Cooley gained support from a number of powerful public figures including the president of the Royal Geographical Society, Sir Roderick Murchison, and esteemed explorer, Richard Burton, who declared that Rebmann's stories reminded him of 'a de Lunatico'. Burton, who was to cross Tanzania with John Hanning Speke in 1857, was cruelly dismissive of Rebmann, noting that although

Path across the Saddle (Marangu Route) (photo: Martchan/Shutterstock.com)

he was 'an honest and conscientious man, he had yet all the qualities which secure unsuccess'. David Livingstone further undermined the reports by describing mountains topped by 'glittering whiteness' in the Zambezi valley as actually being topped by 'masses of white rock, somewhat like quartz', insinuating that this was the case in Jagga.

The first serious attempt to climb the mountain was made in August 1861 by the Hanoverian naturalist and traveller Baron Carl Claus von der Decken. Supported by a team of 50 porters, von der Decken claimed to have reached 13,900ft only to be forced back by atrocious weather. He described the mountain rising from the savannah and the shapes of the two summits, portraying Kibo as a 'mighty dome, rising to a height of about 20,000ft of which the last 3000ft are covered in snow'. Both of these figures were exaggerations and it is likely that the group actually only reached 8200ft (2500m). However, his companion, the English surveyor and explorer Richard Thornton, correctly deduced that the mountain was in fact a volcano. His scientific background lent credence to his reports and carried extra weight in Britain. In December 1862, von der Decken returned to the mountain with Dr Otto Kersten and climbed as high as 14,000ft before becoming caught in a snowstorm. Von der Decken reported that 'During the night it snowed heavily and next morning the ground lay white all around us'. He finished his report by boldly declaring, 'Surely the obstinate Cooley will be satisfied now'. Cooley responded by calling this latest report a 'traveller's tale' and poured scorn on its contents and 'so opportune a fall of snow', announcing that the whole thing had been cooked up to support Rebmann and Krapf.

Nonetheless, Cooley began to lose support. The Royal Geographical Society withdrew its backing for him and formally announced that it now recognised that Rebmann, who first declared that there was snow on the equator 14 years earlier, may have been correct. In 1863 the society awarded its Gold Medal to von der Decken for his contributions to the sum of the world's geographical knowledge of Africa. There were however no retrospective awards for Rebmann or Krapf. Despite all of the evidence to the contrary, Cooley maintained his disbelief to the day he died.

Reduced interest in the mountain

Once geographers had solved the mystery of where the source of the Nile lay, they lost interest in the topography of East Africa and exploration abated. Von der Decken was the only European to travel to Kilimanjaro in the 1860s, and during the 1870s only the English missionary Charles New explored the region. In 1871 New climbed Kilimanjaro from the south-east, at a point where the snowline dipped almost to the foot of Kibo. He recorded seeing 'mountains upon mountains of dark forest; loftier still, height upon heights of grassy hills' and ultimately 'barren, rocky steeps' beneath permanent snowfields, and became the first European to actually cross the snowline in equatorial Africa. New published his book, *Life, Wanderings and Labours in Eastern Africa*, in 1873, writing that 'Of Kilimanjaro we have little more to say: its leading characteristics have been pointed out, and its "eternal snows" must be regarded now as "eternal verities"'. In 1874 New returned to the village of Moshi with the intention of continuing his exploration. Unfortunately, he fell foul of the fearsome Chagga chieftain, Mandara, who claimed to have met every European explorer on Kilimanjaro and appropriated gifts from them in return for safe passage through his land; New, in turn, was robbed of all of his possessions, including a gold watch that had been given to him by the Royal Geographical Society. Finding his path to the mountain blocked, New was forced to retreat from the region. Dispirited, he decided to return to Mombasa but during the journey fell sick and died before arriving back at the coast.

Arrival of the European colonialists

For several years explorers steered clear of the mountain and its hostile, greedy inhabitants. But in 1883 Dr Gustave Fischer passed to the south of Kilimanjaro on his way to Lake Naivasha and observed that the region seemed 'well adapted to European settlement'. This statement heightened interest in the area as a possible colonial possession. Later the same year, the Scottish geologist Joseph Thomson journeyed to the north of Kilimanjaro, recording his expedition in his account, *Through Masai Land*. He was awestruck by the mountain and rhapsodised 'There is the grand dome or crater of Kibo, with its snow cap glancing and scintillating like burnished silver ... on its eastern flank, rise the jagged outlines of the craggy peak of Kimawenzi. What words can adequately describe this glimpse of majestic grandeur and godlike repose?' Thomson crossed the lower slopes of the mountain and was in turn robbed by Mandara. Undeterred, he went on to climb to 9000ft (2750m) in order to collect flora specimens. Having allowed only a day for the summit attempt, it is not surprising that he barely made it above the treeline. He was, however, the first European to see the northern slopes up close, and virtually completed a circuit of the mountain as part of his travels.

A year later, in 1884, Harry Johnston fronted an expedition funded by a number of eminent British scientific societies, including the Royal Geographic Society. His mission was to collect flora and fauna specimens on Kilimanjaro for the herbarium at Kew Gardens. Johnston spent five months on the mountain, working out of a number of self-supporting base camps and gathered 600 species of new and rare plants, as well as six new species of bird, a new species of colobus monkey and various new butterfly and beetle specimens. He was responsible for collecting and naming the first specimen of the endemic *Impatiens kilimanjari* and described the unusual heath and moorlands, detailing the strange *senecios* and *lobelia* found there. Johnston made an attempt to climb Kibo, but abandoned the ascent on the Saddle, as the summit was blanketed by cloud, which he likened to 'a kind of London fog, very depressing in character'.

Johnston was able to reassure other travellers that the region was safe and exhorted the British government to colonise the country. 'I am on the spot, the first in the field, and able to make Kilima-njaro as completely English as Ceylon', Johnston wrote in his report 'The Kilima-njaro Expedition'. In his memoirs, Johnston claimed to be a secret agent, tasked with assessing colonial prospects in East Africa on behalf of the British government. There is, however, no evidence to support this flight of fancy. Previously the British government

Porters today ascending to the Saddle through cloud (Marangu Route)

had dragged its feet when considering its future role in East Africa. The Prime Minister William Gladstone was unable to imagine why anyone should be interested in that 'mountain country behind Zanzibar with the unrememberable name', and was astounded when his advisors suggested making Kilimanjaro a British protectorate.

Germany was also being urged to take control of the region by the fervent empire builder Dr Karl Peters, the founder of the GDK (Gessellschaft fur Deutsche Kolonisation). The Society for German Colonisation was a political party whose ultimate aim was to colonise East Africa on behalf of the German nation. Peters hoped that by acting independently of the German government, he would be able to establish German influence in the region and provoke the government into backing his policy of expansion. To this end, Peters travelled to East Africa to secure treaties with 12 local chiefs that granted Germany exclusive rights, at least on paper, to vast tracts of land in the Kilimanjaro region. He persuaded the local chiefs to reject the rule of the Sultan of Zanzibar, who was guided by the British, and throw in their lot with Germany. This direct action sparked a contest for land rights between the two great East African colonisers, Germany and Britain.

Britain's immediate response was to force twice as many chiefs, including some of the rogue leaders who had sided with Germany, to restate their allegiance to the Sultan of Zanzibar. By swearing this allegiance, they indirectly aligned themselves with Britain. The situation in East Africa became increasingly unstable and war between the two countries appeared inevitable.

In order to prevent hostilities, the two countries agreed the Berlin Treaty in November 1886, which delineated their spheres of influence in the region. The result was the creation of German East Africa and a British administered East Africa Protectorate, with Kilimanjaro falling inside German East Africa. Stories abound as to why the border drawn up between the two new regions kinks to pass Kilimanjaro. The account of Queen Victoria gifting Kilimanjaro to her grandson Wilhelm II because he lacked a snow-capped mountain in his territory and Britain already boasted Mount Kenya in hers is appealing but fanciful. The border was kinked in order to ensure that Mombasa remained in Britain's East African territory, providing her with a port on the Indian Ocean; German East Africa had Dar es Salaam as its access port.

Karl Peters was given the task of administering German East Africa. The first period of German rule was considered to be very harsh: Peters has been described as 'short on ethics and long on cruelty', and even some of his contemporaries felt uneasy about the excesses of their leader. This draconian approach to governing the new territory led to the locals' burgeoning hatred of the colonists.

With the cessation of hostilities between Germany and Britain, English and American 'tourists' began to flock to the region to take advantage of the hunting opportunities. As a result of this explosion in interest, there was widespread and appalling slaughter of wildlife in the name of sport. The exploration of Kilimanjaro also resumed. The son of the king of Hungary, Crown Prince Rudolph, persuaded the Hungarian geographer, Count Teleki, and Lt Von Hohnel to lead an expedition to explore the Meru area in 1887. Teleki made a serious attempt on Kilimanjaro, following Johnston's route to the Saddle. He reached 15,800ft (4815m) before exhaustion, bleeding lips and a 'rushing noise' in his head brought on by the altitude checked his progress. During the ascent, Von Hohnel made a series of astute observations and consequently a new map of the mountain was drawn-up, which included the northern flank of Kilimanjaro.

Plaque at Marangu Gate commemorating Hans Meyer's first successful ascent

The race for the summit: Hans Meyer's expeditions

Motivated by Count Teleki's colourful tales, Hans Meyer, a geology professor from Leipzig, made the first of three visits to Kilimanjaro in 1887. He made good progress on the mountain, following Teleki's advice and ascending from the village of Marangu. Abandoning the majority of his entourage, Meyer led a small group swiftly through the forest zone and onto the heath/moorland. It took the group five days to gain the Saddle, where they rested for a day before pushing on. As the weather worsened and snow began to fall, the group's morale deteriorated and their resolve weakened. Meyer pushed on alone until he came up against a solid wall of ice that marked the lower edge of the Kibo ice cap. Recognising that this obstacle could only be tackled with the proper equipment, and lacking crampons or an ice axe, Meyer retreated to rejoin the rest of his group.

The Alpine Journal of November 1887 mistakenly wrote this trip up as a first ascent and Meyer was forced to correct them, pointing out that he was probably 1500ft (460m) shy of the summit, having only reached 17,800ft (5425m). He did manage to collect a large number of flora specimens, take a number of photographs and make a series of useful measurements. The failure to reach the peak merely fired his determination to conquer Kilimanjaro and he resolved to return.

Before Meyer could return to the mountain, Dr Abbott, an American naturalist who had spent a year and a half in the region making natural history notes, and the German Otto Ehlers made an attempt to reach the summit in the autumn of 1888. Dr Abbott abandoned the ascent at 17,000ft (5180m) as a result of altitude sickness, but

Little Penck Glacier seen at sunset from Lava Tower Camp (Western Breach Route)

Ehlers persevered. He later claimed to have reached the 'north-western side of the summit' at a height that 'could not have been less than 19,680ft'. Ehlers' claims are widely doubted, not least because he alleges he stood on a point considerably higher than Kilimanjaro's actual summit. Meyer and others disputed the claims at the time and Ehlers conceded that he might have been mistaken.

Later the same year, Meyer tried to return to Kilimanjaro with Dr Oscar Bauman. Unfortunately, their expedition became caught up in an organised insurrection against the German rulers of the region. Meyer and Bauman were taken prisoner by Chief Bushiri and ransomed. The chief was paid off and the pair released, although they forfeited all of their equipment and supplies. As a result they, unsurprisingly, called off the expedition. Bushiri was later executed by the Germans.

By early 1889, Meyer calculated that 49 Europeans had battled their way to Kilimanjaro. He realised that if he wanted to be the first to summit the mountain, he couldn't afford to wait much longer before making a concerted effort on the peak. In the second half of the year he returned to the mountain with the celebrated Austrian climber Ludwig Purtscheller, for a third attempt. His climbing team included two local headmen, nine porters, a cook and a guide. Meyer stayed with Dr Abbott in Moshi. Having questioned him at length about the mountain, he recognised that the biggest problem in conquering the summit was the lack of food supplies at the top of the mountain, so established a series of camps along the route he proposed to follow. By stocking camps at 13,970ft (4260m) and 15,020ft (4580m), Meyer ensured that he didn't have to quit the mountain after every attempt on the summit.

Beginning from the Marangu village on 28 September 1889, Meyer trekked through the forest zone for two days, climbing to the west of where modern-day Mandara Huts is situated. He then contoured across the mountainside and camped in the vicinity of today's Rau Campsite. From here he climbed north onto the Saddle and stopped at a campsite previously established by Dr Abbott at 12,770ft (3894m). Meyer then launched himself directly at Kibo. From a base camp at the foot of the slope, Meyer and Purtscheller began to climb towards the Ratzel Glacier. Once they encountered the permanent ice, they began to carve out a series of steps, taking up to 20 strokes with an ice axe to chip out a small foothold in the ice cap. Reaching the crater rim on 3 October, Meyer realised that the pair were too exhausted and the weather too inclement to push on to the summit. The climbers retreated to the foot of Kibo and spent a day recuperating and taking essential readings and measurements before advancing to a higher bivouac site and making a final assault on the summit.

Beginning at 3am on 6 October, Purtscheller's 40th birthday, the pair approached the summit. By dawn they had reached the foot of the glacier and located the steps in the ice that they had cut previously. They climbed the glacier and traversed a deep crevasse to crest the crater rim, becoming the first people to see into the crater, which Meyer declared 'burst upon us with such unexpected suddenness that, for a moment, it quite took away our breath'. He went on to note that '... the earth opened up there before us, revealing the secret of Kibo: Taking in the whole upper part of Kibo there opened up a great crater with precipitous sides ...' The two climbers then trekked around the southern rim of the crater, climbing three hillocks that they encountered to arrive at the highest point at 10.30am on the morning of 6 October. Meyer soberly recorded in his account *Across East African Glaciers*: 'In virtue of my right as its first discoverer (I) christened this hitherto unknown and unnamed mountain peak – the loftiest spot in Africa and in the German Empire – Kaiser Wilhelm Spitze. Then we gave three cheers more for the Emperor, and shook hands in mutual congratulation.' He then commented that 'Njaro, the guardian spirit of the mountain, seemed to take his conquest with a good grace, for neither snow nor tempest marred our triumphal invasion of his sanctuary.'

Meyer and Purtscheller then descended to the Saddle and attempted to climb Mawenzi. They reached the lower summit of Klute Peak but illness prevented them from attempting the highest point on Kilimanjaro's second peak. For good measure they returned to Kibo's crater rim on 18 October via a similar route to that now ascended from Kibo Huts, and crested the rim at Hans Meyer Notch. Although they failed to reach the inner cone, they were able to confirm that it was made of mud and ash. In total, Meyer and Purtscheller spent an incredible 16 days above 15,000ft on Kilimanjaro and made four forays to the crater rim, reaching the summit on one of these occasions, in addition to making a number of sorties on Mawenzi.

Once the peak had been claimed, interest in Kilimanjaro waned and fewer expeditions were undertaken to explore the mountain. In fact, the summit was not revisited for 20 years. In 1898, Hans Meyer returned to Kilimanjaro once more, to study the glaciers on the mountain. He was amazed and appalled to observe that the glaciers had retreated about 100 metres since 1889. The ice in the crater had all but disappeared and there were visible flows of meltwater at the snout of many of the glaciers. This process continues unabated today.

Advances of the early 20th century

At the onset of the 20th century, Kilimanjaro was declared a wildlife reservation by the German colonial government. The early years of the century were then dominated by private scientific explorations which, although undertaken in the name of science, frequently turned out to be nothing more than glorified hunting sprees. The specimen collecting phase reached its peak in 1908, with many of the western world's premier scientific institutions sourcing specimens from the mountain.

These trips in the early 20th century were not without a human cost. The region's natives were still held in low regard and were considered expendable; on several expeditions inadequately equipped porters died as a result of exposure and hypothermia. In 1908 the Americans Peter MacQueen and Peter Dutkewich mounted an ascent that was beset with problems. Abandoned by their guides at the snowline, the pair began to retreat only for Dutkewich to fall and fracture several ribs. As the temperatures plummeted and the weather deteriorated, the porters attempted to assist the evacuation. Some reports suggest that while each of the Americans had four blankets, the porters were only given one each. Inevitably, three of the porters died from hypothermia on the descent. MacQueen wrote in his diaries, *In Wildest Africa*, 'Poor Mapandi, a carrier whom I had noticed shivering with fever for the last day or two, stiffened, grew cold and died beside me in the mud.' Realising the hopelessness of the situation, he left his injured partner and went to fetch help alone. MacQueen reached a German mission station and raised the alarm. Dr Ahlboy and a colleague scrambled up the mountain and retrieved Dutkewich and the single porter that remained with him.

The following year, in 1909, the surveyor M Lange and his assistant Weigele became the next people to make the summit. They went on to escape from Kilimanjaro without mishap.

Summiting Mawenzi

Kilimanjaro's second summit, Mawenzi, remained unclimbed for a further three years until, in 1912, the Germans Edward Oehler and Fritz Klute reached the highest point, which they christened Hans Meyer Peak, in tribute to their countryman. The pair then skirted Kibo and tackled the Drygalski Glacier. They reached the crater rim and descended via the Western Breach, becoming the first people to use this route.

As Kilimanjaro's reputation grew, and the number of people attempting to climb the now popularised Marangu Route increased, an enterprising German planter and hotelkeeper, Dr E Forster, set up two huts along the track on behalf of the German Kilimanjaro Mountain Club. The Bismarck Hut (now

Mandara Huts) and the Peters Hut (now Horombo Huts) have been used ever since, although they have been modified and refurbished over the years.

In December 1912 Dr Walter Furtwangler and Siegfried Konig became the fourth group to summit Kibo, and the first to descend the mountain on skis. Kibo was conquered twice more before the onset of World War I, one of these ascents was the first full ascent by an Englishman, WC West. During the same era, the German Fran Von Ruckteschell became the first woman to reach the crater rim at Gillman's Point.

World War I

With the outbreak of World War I in 1914, climbing and exploration took a back seat. The Kilimanjaro region became the scene of sustained, ferocious fighting as German and Allied troops contested the border. Both sides relied heavily on recruiting local people to bolster their armies and these divisions inevitably bore the brunt of the fiercest fighting. African deaths as a result of the East African campaigns have been put as high as 100,000. The German army led by Paul von Lettow-Vorbeck adopted guerrilla-style tactics to tie down the numerically superior Allied army. Cut off behind enemy lines, one German patrol dug in on Kilimanjaro's slopes and held out for eight months, before eventually surrendering at Hans Meyer Cave.

Post-war Kilimanjaro

In 1920, following the defeat of Germany in 1918, German East Africa became Tanganyika, a 'mandated territory' under the protection of Britain, and the region ostensibly reverted to British control. British rule was relatively benign in comparison to the regime that had existed before. Positive measures were enacted and the precious wooded lower slopes on and around Kilimanjaro were made into a forest and game reserve.

After some hesitation, climbers and explorers returned to the slopes, and in 1921 C Gillman led a group to Kibo's crater rim, becoming the first climber to crest the crater since Kilimanjaro fell under British protection. Although Gillman didn't cover any fresh ground, he did provide much needed first-hand reports in English. Previously the only information had come from translations of material such as Meyer's reports. The first significant climb since the war occurred in 1924, when the South African George Londt became the first man to summit Mawenzi's south peak, albeit by mistake since he was aiming for the highest point, Hans Meyer Peak, but became lost on the ascent.

Kilimanjaro's local climbers

At this stage it was still only the European climbers who received any recognition for their achievements on the mountain; but in 1925 East Africans were at last depicted as climbers on the mountain, when the Berlin film studio, UFA, made a film at high altitude. The resulting film showed local Chagga guides, including Msameri (who had accompanied Hans Meyer) and his son Oforo, ascending the mountain. Oforo, who accompanied many of the European explorers at this time (including Londt, Reusch and West), was to later become the first Chagga known to reach the summit.

LEOPARD POINT

In 1926 an unusual sight was shown to the world. An English mountaineer, Dr Donald Latham, discovered the mummified corpse of a leopard on the crater rim, at a place that became known as Leopard Point. Latham took photographs of the leopard on a pile of rocks and being held triumphantly by a porter. He recorded his extraordinary find in an article entitled 'Kilimanjaro' for the *Geographical Journal* of December 1926, saying: 'A remarkable discovery was the remains of a leopard, sun-dried and frozen, right at the crater rim. The beast must have wandered there and died of exposure.' The leopard was later to become immortalised by Ernest Hemmingway, who wrote in the prologue to his classic short story, *The Snows of Kilimanjaro,* that 'Close to the western summit there is the dried and frozen carcass of a leopard. No one has explained what the leopard was seeking at that altitude.' The leopard carcass remained on the crater rim until the early 1930s, when it disappeared.

Kilimanjaro's continuing popularity

The Lutheran missionary Dr Richard Reusch made several ascents of Kilimanjaro between 1925 and 1927. On one such climb he came across the leopard that Latham had found and cut one of its ears off as a souvenir. In 1927 Reusch became the first climber to gaze down into the inner crater having forged a path across the inner cone. The ash pit at the centre of the crater was later named after him in recognition of his discoveries. During the same year, WC West, who summited Kilimanjaro in 1914, returned to the mountain and scaled Mawenzi and Kibo with Sheila MacDonald, who became the first woman to reach both of the two highest points on the mountain.

Plaque honouring the porters that accompanied Meyer on his first ascent

The slopes of Kilimanjaro were also graced by some of the celebrated climbers more usually associated with the Himalayas. The English mountaineers, HW Tilman and Eric Shipton, trudged up Kibo from Marangu in 1930 and reached Gillman's Point despite deteriorating weather. From here they circled to Stella Point in an impenetrable mist and abandoned the final push to the summit. By then Tilman was suffering from altitude sickness and vomiting regularly. Both of the climbers were also becoming snow-blind. Tilman wrote that his and Shipton's, 'eyes began to smart, then to hurt, until by evening they were firmly closed and exceedingly painful. We were completely snow-blind.' Despite this set back, they rested at Peters Hut (now Horombo Huts) and then tackled Mawenzi, becoming the first climbers to scale Nordecke Peak, having become disorientated on the way up to Hans Meyer Peak. They promptly descended and repeated the climb, this time successfully negotiating the way to the highest point.

In the same year, the rest of the world was also able to see exactly what lay at the top of the giant volcano, when the Swiss pilots, Walter Mittelholzer and Alfred Kunzler, became the first to fly over Kilimanjaro. The photographs taken from their 200Hp Fokker airplane offered the first comprehensive views of the Reusch Crater and provided a unique perspective of Kilimanjaro.

Three years later, in 1933, Tilman returned to make a solo ascent of Kibo, summiting the mountain and camping in the crater. He made some unusual observations and reported fumarole (vent through which hot steam and sulphurous gases emerge) activity in the Reusch Crater. In his account of both his climbs, *Snow on the Equator*, he described the inner crater and reported that 'At the top the diameter was about 400 yards across, at the bottom 200 yards. Sulphurous fumes rose from the lip and pieces of Sulphur lay about'. The report caused a great deal of concern among scientists and locals, who had previously thought that Kilimanjaro was extinct. Reusch immediately climbed to the summit again in search of the fumaroles. Failing to find them, he blithely and incorrectly announced that Tilman must have been mistaken and had allowed himself to be convinced that a 'certain kind of whirling little cloud' had resembled sulphurous steam.

During the 20th century, climbing on Kilimanjaro had become a much more popular pastime. Indicative of this was the creation of the Mountain Club of East Africa in Moshi in July 1929, which later became the Kilimanjaro Mountain Club. To supplement the Peters and Bismarck huts, Kibo Huts was built in 1932.

Tanzanian Independence

The outbreak of World War II inevitably resulted in the cessation of climbing activity on Kilimanjaro and the end of the war in 1945 marked a major turning point in the history of Tanzania. Opposition to colonial rule was now widespread across Africa and the European powers realised that change was unavoidable. Recognising that, the United Nations appointed Tanganyika a trust territory, under British Guardianship, and vowed to secure self-government and independence for the people.

The independence movement was led by the Tanganyika African National Union (TANU), which chose Julius Nyere as its president in 1953. Nyere won the begrudging respect of the British, who saw him as a trustworthy, peaceful man. In a speech to the Tanganyika Legislative Assembly in 1959, Nyere pronounced: 'We, the people of Tanganyika, would like to light a candle and put it on the top of Mount Kilimanjaro, which would shine beyond our borders, giving hope where there was despair, love where there was hate, and dignity where before there was only humiliation.'

Mounting tension in the wake of a series of rigged elections forced the holding of free elections in August 1960. TANU won 70 out of 71 seats in the Tanganyika Legislative Council and Nyere duly became chief minister. In this role, he spearheaded the drive to independence, which was officially proclaimed on 9 December 1961. In a move that echoed Nyere's speech in 1959, the nation's new flag was raised on the top of Kilimanjaro. Unfortunately, exceptionally bad weather and heavy snow prevented the flag bearers from reaching the summit, and the flag was eventually hoisted at Gillman's Point. Exactly a year later, on Republic Day, Lt Alex Nyirenda planted the flag on the summit, which was renamed Uhuru Peak, meaning 'Freedom'. Two years later, in April 1964, Nyere persuaded the Sultan of Zanzibar to sign an Act of Union that merged Tanganyika and Zanzibar, and Tanzania was formed.

Measuring Kilimanjaro

During Tanzania's evolution from European colony to republic, climbing and scientific expeditions on Kilimanjaro continued. A great deal of geological survey work was also done. In 1952 the British Ordnance Survey mounted an expedition to determine the exact height of the mountain by taking a number of readings from predetermined triangulation points. Hans Meyer had claimed to reach a height of 19,720ft (6010m) in 1889. This figure had been revised by the German colonial regime five years later and set at 19,330ft (5892m). The OS calculations resulted in Kilimanjaro being officially accorded an altitude of 19,340ft (5895m). Since then, in 1999, a new survey of the mountain conducted with the latest Global Positioning System (GPS) and satellite technology by a joint German and Tanzanian geological expedition, concluded that Kilimanjaro was in fact only 19,330ft (5892.55m) high. This figure is some 10ft (2.5m) lower than the one long held to be correct. This figure has subsequently been challenged as well and the debate as to the exact height of Africa's highest peak and the cause of the discrepancies still rages. Despite these new claims, the official height remains 5895m and it is this figure that is still displayed on the summit board that marks Uhuru Peak.

A year after the OS calculation, in 1953, a team from Sheffield University, working in tandem with the then Tanganyikan government, became the first outfit to descend into Mawenzi's Great Barranco, the cavernous ravine on the north-eastern side of the peak. The audacious descent was part of a geological reconnaissance trip. In the course of the climb, the group found a plug of diorite at 14,000ft (4265m) whose diameter measured approximately 300ft (90 metres). After further investigation, Professor C Downie and Peter Wilkinson declared that this had been Mawenzi's main volcanic vent. The implication of this discovery was that the whole of Mawenzi's crater had been eroded over the years by the river gorges that now form the Little and Great Barrancos. After studying information gathered during the trip, the group later declared that Kilimanjaro was in fact a dormant volcano, which in all likelihood was

View around the crater rim to Stella Point and Gillman's Point

virtually extinct. Their report contained the comforting pronouncement that 'it seems highly unlikely that Kilimanjaro will erupt destructively in the foreseeable future'.

Opening the mountain to others

Success on Kilimanjaro became more commonplace during the second half of the 20th century. In 1955 an Outward Bound Centre was established at Loitokitok in Kenya, just to the north of the border with Tanzania. From here groups made regular ascents of the mountain as the culmination of their course.

These successes were tainted by the occasional tragedy. On 18 May 1955, an East African Airways Dakota became disorientated in thick cloud and flew straight into the south-eastern face of Mawenzi. Everyone on board was killed. Tragically, the plane was only about 35ft (10m) lower than it needed to be in order to scrape over the summit ridge.

Since the glory of reaching the summit for the first time had been captured by Hans Meyer, climbers felt obligated to undertake new and more challenging routes to the top of the mountain. One by one, the glaciers were climbed and Kilimanjaro's plum routes plucked. The Heim Glacier was broached in 1957, the Great Penck Glacier in 1960 and in 1962 a difficult Grade 6 route was pioneered on the steep Kersten Glacier. Additionally, disinclined to reach the summit by walking or climbing, three French parachutists broke the world record for a high altitude landing by dropping into Kibo's crater. But the most fantastic was yet to come. In February 1964, Barry Clift and Rusty Baillie successfully climbed both Kilimanjaro and Mount Kenya within 24 hours. Beginning from the third cave on the then Loitokitok Route (now Rongai), they raced to the summit by 2pm. Using Outward Bound instructors as pace setters, they hurtled off the mountain and jogged to their car, which drove non-stop to Mount Kenya. Beginning at 2am they ascended the peak, crossing the Lewis Glacier at 8am before climbing and reaching the summit, Batian, at 11.40am, an incredible 21 hours and 40 minutes after they began the challenge. Perhaps unsurprisingly, this feat has never been repeated.

New routes were also being secured on Mawenzi. Two RAF climbers, John Edwards and William Thomson, made the first ascent of Mawenzi's grim, complex East Face in 1964. The face drops almost 9845ft (3000m) into two gorges, the Little and Great Barrancos. During the climb up innumerable dead-end chimneys and gullies that led to sheer cliffs of solid ice, the pair found the wreck of the Dakota that crashed on Mawenzi in 1955. They also came across the skeleton of a buffalo, improbably lying on a narrow ledge at almost 15750ft (4800m). Four years later, Ian Howell and Roger 'Fred' Higgins forged a separate route up the stupendous East Face. The pair called off their first approach to the East Face when they realised that the Great Barranco they intended to follow had far too many waterfalls cascading down its sheer sides, causing Higgins to comment that 'If it rained on the mountain we could expect to be flushed from the Barranco like rats from a sewer'. Their second, successful attempt approached the East Face via

View of the entire Western Breach, which was caused by a massive landslide

the Downie Ridge that separated the Little and Great Barrancos, before eventually merging with the East Face.

Using a more conventional route, a group of seven blind African climbers were led to the summit in 1969 in an effort to alert the rest of the world to the plight of blind people in Africa.

In a deliberate bid to prevent people approaching Kilimanjaro from Kenya, and in order to channel the tourists onto the Marangu Route, the Tanzanian government closed the border between Loitokitok in Kenya and the mountain in 1970. Since then it has only been possible to start your climb from within Tanzania. Realising the potential revenue to be garnered from tourism in the area, the government also began the construction of Kilimanjaro International Airport during the same year.

During the 1970s, the massive Breach Wall on Kibo's western flank became the primary objective for talented mountaineers. After his tricky traverse of Mawenzi's eastern slopes at the end of 1969, the Swiss climber Fritz Lortscher was especially keen to secure the first ascent of this epic obstacle and tackled the Breach Wall in the early 1970s. Although he managed to ascend an inner section of the Wall, the main section resolutely defied his advances.

Through the middle of the decade the stakes were raised as first John Temple and Tony Charlton forced a spectacular route at the eastern end of the Breach Wall and then Temple and Dave Cheesmond pioneered a new line up the Balleto Icefield and the series of gullies above it. A magazine published Temple's description of the breathtaking Breach Icicle that linked the Balleto and Diamond Glaciers in August 1976, fuelling the interest already shown in the Breach Wall. Elsewhere on the mountain, talented climbers (including Ian Howell, Bill O'Connor, John Cleare, Iain

Allen and Mark Savage) were completing dramatic first ascents. Following his inspiring direct ascent of the precipitous Kersten Glacier in 1975, John Cleare wrote: 'We were level with the upper tier of the Great Breach Wall itself ... draped with fantastic icicles; one, a slim pillar linking the snow band to the tiny Diamond Glacier overhanging the Wall, was 500ft long! That was the line! But it would wait for the next generation.'

In 1978 the highly talented Americans Rob Taylor and Henry Barber approached the Breach Wall via the Umbwe Route. Bypassing the park authorities, they quickly trekked to the foot of the Wall and began to climb the face via the Window Buttress. Once on the icicle, Taylor realised the enormity of the climb ahead, later writing 'The ice on the icicle is the worst I have ever encountered ... I quickly find myself fully extended just trying to stay in contact with the decomposed vertical sludge'. Twenty feet into the climb, an ice pedestal Taylor was clutching snapped off and he fell heavily, smashing feet first into a sloping ledge at the base of the icicle and badly breaking his ankle. A broken ankle at this altitude, in such an isolated area, is often tantamount to a death sentence. Barber managed to manoeuvre and lower Taylor off the face and down the Heim Glacier in a remarkable display of skill. At the foot of the glacier he left the fading Taylor and

KILIMANJARO, A CHALLENGING CLIMB

On August 13 2014, Swiss-Ecuadorian mountain guide and altitude runner Karl Egloff set a new record for the fastest ascent of Kilimanjaro; having guided a group to the summit several days earlier, he ran up the Umbwe Route, reaching Uhuru Peak in just 4 hours and 56 minutes, fuelled mainly by a handful of energy bars and gels. In so doing he beat the previous record set four years earlier by renowned Spanish mountain runner Kilian Jornet. Before the climb, guides on the mountain had scoffed at Egloff's attempt to break the record, believing that Jornet's impressive record would stand unchallenged for some time. After catching his breath at the top, Egloff hustled back down the mountain as well, completing the ascent and descent in only 6 hours, 42 minutes (and 24 seconds), shaving just over half an hour off Jornet's round-trip time of 7 hours and 14 minutes.

While racing up and down Kilimanjaro is in no way recommended and contravenes every climbing principle on a big mountain, there are two challenges that you might want to take up: the Kilimanjaro Marathon (www.kilimanjaromarathon.com), an impressive 16-mile (26km) loop from and to Moshi that doesn't actually climb the mountain; and the Kiliman Challenge (www.kilimanjaroman.com), which includes an ascent of the Machame Route, a circumnavigation of the mountain on bicycle and a quick lap of the Kilimanjaro marathon circuit. Only the last two elements are actually races as the organisers do not want to encourage people to race up the mountain itself. It should go without saying that these challenges are, of course, only for very fit, fully acclimatised individuals.

Kilimanjaro Park sign at the Marangu Gate

hacked across the mountainside to find help. Five days after the accident, the alarm was raised and after a further two days Taylor was found and evacuated from the mountain. Emergency surgery saved his gangrenous foot from amputation. After an horrific two months of hospitalisation in Tanzania, Taylor was flown back to America to eventually regain the use of his leg eight months later. Controversy followed the publication of Taylor's version of events in the Breach, as each climber blamed the other for the accident.

Despite its atrocious condition that year, the Breach Wall did eventually fall. The legendary South Tyrolean climber Reinhold Messner and his companion Konrad Renzler completed the first full direct ascent of the Breach Wall, including the ascent of the 300ft (90m) icicle, on 31 January 1978. The pair free-climbed the route in an incredible 12 hours. The mountaineer Iain Allen, in the Mountain Club of Kenya's guide to Kilimanjaro, advises 'Future parties should allow at least 2 days'. The Wall was not climbed again for five years, until Wes Krause and Scott Fischer succeeded in 1983.

KILIMANJARO NATIONAL PARK

Although the wooded lower slopes of Kilimanjaro had been made into a forest reserve by the British after World War I, and the Tanganyikan National Parks Authority had proposed that the mountain become a national park in 1957, it wasn't until 1973 that the Kilimanjaro National Park (KINAPA) was actually set up. The national park was designed to incorporate all land above 8860ft (2700m) and preserve the flora and fauna found there. A major hut-building programme was launched, with a group of Norwegians lending development assistance and expertise; Mandara and Horombo huts were constructed on the site of the old Bismarck and Peters huts. Despite this pre-emptive step having been taken, the park was not officially opened until 1977 by President Julius Nyere. After much consideration, UNESCO declared Kilimanjaro National Park a World Heritage Site in 1989, in recognition of its extraordinary beauty and unique features. Since then, botanists and biogeographers have conducted extensive fieldwork on Kilimanjaro that has greatly added to the scientific knowledge of mountain ecology.

Sign at Uhuru Peak, on the Roof of Africa, the goal of many

People have continued to climb Kilimanjaro in large numbers and in increasingly bizarre ways. In 1985 cousins Richard and Nicholas Crane mountain biked to the summit along the Marangu Route. By this time, cycling, motorbiking, paragliding and hangliding on Kilimanjaro had become an almost regular occurrence, frequently in conjunction with sponsored charity events. In 1995 the national park took the unprecedented step of banning all high-risk stunts on the mountain to reduce the danger that these events posed to the public and to minimise the detrimental impact of such exploits on the mountain itself. Nonetheless, Kilimanjaro remains an enormous lure for people wishing to challenge themselves and is still the scene of innumerable charity climbs.

Kilimanjaro's popularity soared at the close of the 20th century, culminating in a mammoth, mass climb of the mountain to see in the new millennium. Some 7000 people tackled the mountain in that week, with 1000 of them on the slopes of Kilimanjaro on New Year's Eve alone. However, a third of all attempts failed to reach the summit during this period, with dozens having to be rescued in the course of the week and three fatalities underlining just how tough the challenge remains. The number of people who harbour a desire to reach the Roof of Africa shows no sign in letting up and the millennium celebrations should have been the perfect justification for the authorities to give the mountain infrastructure a much needed boost by ploughing funds generated by the large number of climbers into upgrading and maintaining the routes and campsites, particularly if Kilimanjaro is to survive the immediate future unscarred by human activity, let alone see out the next 1000 years intact.

GEOLOGY AND VOLCANOLOGY

'The enormous base detracts from the apparent height, and this detraction is accentuated by the squat, pudding-like dome of Kibo, the highest summit. In fine weather Kibo can be seen from Nairobi, when the haze rising from the hot intervening plains blots out the lower slope, leaving the white dome suspended in mid-air like a cloud.'

HW Tilman

Mount Kilimanjaro is the highest mountain in Africa and one of the largest volcanoes in the world. The enormous volcanic massif rises 4876m above the surrounding savannah to a height of 5895m. Aligned in an east-south-east direction, it is situated 80km east of the Rift Valley. It is roughly 80km by 40km and covers an area of some 388,500ha.

This extraordinary apparition, which rises from the level plains unhindered by any adjoining mountain range, was born as a consequence of the cataclysmic movements of the earth's crust that formed the Rift Valley over one million years ago. Kilimanjaro itself is probably over 750,000 years old, making it a relative infant in geological terms.

In the course of the last two million years, the African plate, Arabian plate and the Somalian sub plate began to move against each other, rupturing and slumping as they did so. As the plates shifted, the Rift Valley was created, stretching 10,000km from the Middle East to Southern Africa. The deep fractures in the earth's crust allowed magma to surge along lines of weakness and erupt from beneath the surface of the buckled plains. The resulting volcanic activity was greatest where the original Rift Valley was deepest. The result was the eventual formation of a string of large volcanoes along the 100km stretch of the Rift Valley. These included Ngorongoro on the Rift Valley itself and to the east, Mount Kenya, Meru and Kilimanjaro.

Kilimanjaro is technically a giant stratovolcano comprising three independent vents. The cones of Shira, Mawenzi and Kibo grew for thousands of years. The oldest peak, Shira, ceased to be active about 500,000 years ago, having reached a height of around 5000m: although the cone has since collapsed in on itself to form a caldera, it is still possible to make out the broad outline of the cone on the Shira Plateau. Mawenzi and Kibo remained active and continued to grow beyond this. Mawenzi became the second vent to become inactive, and was rapidly and dramatically eroded, not least by the subsequent eruptions of Kibo, whose growth continued unabated.

Kilimanjaro reached its most lofty point some 450,000 years ago when it probably grazed 5900m. Since then it has been in decline. Eruptions continued to occur sporadically; the most explosive was 350,000 years ago when vast quantities of black lava spewed forth from the earth and filled the collapsed Shira cone as well as creating the Saddle linking Kibo and Mawenzi before fanning far down the northern and southern slopes. These prodigious extrusions of black rhomb porphyry lava are still clearly visible on the mountain, most noticeably on the Shira Plateau.

During periods of dormancy, erosion sculpted the mountain's surface. Shira became a gentle, rolling plateau; Mawenzi was almost completely eroded to leave just the hard core visible and Kibo was flattened and rounded.

Glaciers repeatedly covered and uncovered the peak, grinding the summit down and wearing it into its present shape. At one stage, an ice cap 100m deep covered Kibo, its fingers reaching far down the flank of the mountain.

As volcanic activity became more and more intermittent, a rash of parasitic, ash and cinder cones developed, running across the mountain in a north-west/south-east direction. A final burst of activity saw the formation of the flows in the inner crater and the creation of the Ash Pit. It is believed that this unusual volcanic feature was created within the last 300 years.

Sightings of volcanic activity by geologists and mountaineers and scientific studies have since led people to conclude that Kilimanjaro is currently dormant. Although virtually extinct, small fumaroles in the Reusch Crater continue to emit sulphurous steam, hinting at the enormous energy that once raged here.

Shira

The Shira volcano is the oldest part of the Kilimanjaro massif. It was the first to erupt and the first to become extinct. Consequently, from a height of over 4900m, Shira has been eroded and reduced to create a much lower caldera. The western and southern rims of the volcano are all that remain of what was probably a cone 3km in diameter. The Shira Ridge, which includes Johnsell

A view across the Shira Plateau to Shira Needle, Shira Cathedral and East Shira Hill (Machame Route)

Point and Klute Peak, and the steep-sided cliffs below the Shira Needle, Cathedral and East Shira Hill mark the western and eastern extremities of the caldera respectively. The Shira Plateau is now an expansive, rumpled plateau that peaks at Johnsell Point (3962m).

As the erosion progressed and the cone collapsed, smaller lava extrusions welled out onto the surface of the mountain. Streams have subsequently worn creases into the surface of the plateau and weathering continues to shape and mould the region.

There are a large number of rock types in the Shira area. A final eruption on Kibo caused the caldera to infill with black rhomb porphyry lava, a dark lava that is easily recognisable by the crystals of rhombic or occasionally diamond-shaped cross-section that stud its surface. There are also fragments of the green crystal olivine, which was forced to the earth's surface from a depth of almost 80km.

Mawenzi

The vertiginous, erosion-worn peaks of Mawenzi are the most visually impressive of Kilimanjaro's three cones. The blasted, shattered slopes rise to a high point, Hans Meyer Peak, at 5149m, making Mawenzi the third highest peak in Africa, behind Kibo and Mount Kenya.

The western face of Mawenzi, which is the one most commonly seen, is steep and rises over 600m from the Saddle. The face is craggy and has numerous pinnacles and gullies etched into it. However, the rarely seen East Face is substantially more dramatic. The face is sheer for over 1000m and the maze of gullies and chutes here has only partially been explored. The East Face drops into two deep gorges; the Little and Great Barrancos are sheer-sided gouges in the mountainside. A lake used to be held here by a rock wall; when it duly collapsed water flooded out and spread volcanic debris over an area of 1000sq km to the north and east of the mountain. The collapse of the wall resulted in the creation of the gorges and hastened the erosion of Mawenzi.

A local Chagga folk tale goes some way to explaining Mawenzi's broken, shattered appearance. Many years ago, while Kibo and Mawenzi were sat by their respective hearths, Mawenzi allowed his fire to go out. He approached his younger, but larger brother in order to beg a few embers in order to relight his fire. Kibo complied, but on his return journey across the Saddle, Mawenzi let the embers go out once again. He asked for a second set of coals and was in turn given them. These too he let grow cold. In a rage, Kibo attacked his younger sibling and battered him with such force that all of his features were scarred and damaged. The myth suggests (although there is no geological evidence to support this) that there has been volcanic activity on Mawenzi since the last phase of the ice age, during the time that the Chagga have lived on the lower slopes.

Erosion on Mawenzi is highly pronounced, and the peak is in an advanced state of decay. Erosion is responsible for wearing away the main part of the cone and for producing the current shape of the peak. During the various volcanic eruptions, liquid lava was forced into gaps on the face of the cone where it cooled and set. The hardened lava is less

A view back across the Saddle to Mawenzi (Rongai Route)

prone to erosion than the surrounding rock and so remains after the rock has been worn away. These dykes are thus left as prominent pinnacles on the slopes of the peak; a host of dyke swarms make up about half the summit area of Mawenzi.

Mawenzi has a number of dramatically fluted rock faces. The rock that makes up these cliffs is brittle and prone to shattering, making it very difficult to climb. Since Mawenzi is strictly a technical climb, the peak is attempted far less frequently than Kibo. Only exceptionally experienced, talented climbers tackle the ascent to Hans Meyer Peak. Nonetheless, it is a very enticing proposition and represents a substantial prize. The mountaineer, HW Tilman, who was determined to conquer Mawenzi while tackling Kilimanjaro in the 1930s, described Mawenzi as 'a fantastically weathered peak of red volcanic rock, 17,000ft high, separated from the higher but less interesting Kibo by a wide, flat saddle of shale'. In preparing to tackle the climb he noted that 'It looked difficult, and if the climbing of Kibo was a duty, that of Mawenzi promised to be a pleasure'.

In addition, the technical difficulties are further complicated by the altitude, making the ascent of Kilimanjaro's second summit a real challenge. In his book *Kilimanjaro*, the photojournalist John Reader included the grisly story of two climbers who died on Mawenzi. Having successfully reached the summit, the two experienced climbers decided to try and pioneer a new descent route. Something went wrong on the descent and, having detached himself from the rope for some reason, one of the climbers fell to the foot of the slopes and was killed. In turn, the second climber fell and died as he tried to complete the descent. His rope snagged on an overhang as he plummeted and jerked him to a halt on the cliff face. Because of the extreme nature of the ascent, it wasn't feasible to try and collect the body by climbing the face and so a drastic alternative solution was devised. Reader recorded: 'The body hung in such an inaccessible place that to retrieve it a marksman severed the rope with a bullet.'

Kibo

Kibo is the most recently formed of the three volcanic cones that comprise Kilimanjaro. Although now dormant, it is thought that Kibo may have been active as recently as a few hundred years ago.

As a result of this relative youthfulness, Kibo retains a more perfectly preserved shape. The upper part of Kibo is largely intact, but the crater wall has collapsed to create a caldera that measures 2km by 2.25km wide. On the southern side, this caldera is up to 180m deep. The summit has been flattened and rounded by erosion so that its upper slopes now incline at approximately a 30° angle.

Inside the caldera is a resurgent dome, an inner cone, which stands 150m higher than Gillman's Point but is currently still 60m lower than the actual summit of the mountain. Uhuru Peak (5895m) lies to the south-west of the cone on the crater rim.

In turn, the inner cone contains the Reusch Crater, which is over 800 metres wide. An ash cone containing a central ash pit made of shale and up to 130m deep and 360 metres wide is set within the Reusch Crater. The ash pit on Kilimanjaro is considered to be one of the most perfectly formed examples of this feature in the world.

The final eruptions on Kilimanjaro filled the caldera here with lava, which overflowed and ran down Kibo's north-eastern slopes. A smaller flow also followed the Western Breach and penetrated into the Weru Weru River Valley. The predominant rock types on Kibo, as on Mawenzi, are trachybasalts.

The jagged north ridge on the lower slopes of Mawenzi (Rongai Route)

However, the different flows have produced a variety of different rock types.

There are still frequent reports of fumarole activity in the Reusch Crater which suggest that the mountain is still only dormant and not yet extinct. However, these may represent the final death throes of the volcano. The fumaroles do however provide a unique microclimate for lichens in an otherwise inhospitable environment.

Around 100,000 years ago, an enormous landslip broke away a chunk of the crater rim. The gash in the uniformity of the summit is slightly less steep than the surrounding cliffs and now forms the Western Breach. The landslip proceeded to gouge a giant wound in the side of the mountain and created Kibo's Great Barranco Valley.

Kibo was once completely covered by an ice cap that would have stood 100m high and the glaciers extended far down the slopes. The brilliant white of the ice reflects the heat from the sun and enables the glaciers to survive at this latitude. Although Kibo still supports glaciers and permanent snow, these are much diminished and definitely in retreat. The only remnants of the glaciers at lower elevations are the numerous moraine ridges that are visible on the southern slopes around 4000m. The remaining glaciers are a shadow of the giant floes that dominated the summit previously and display little of the power that their predecessors must have shown.

GLACIAL RECESSION

At the height of the glaciated period, both Kibo and Mawenzi were completely covered by ice. The glaciers generally flowed down from the peaks to around 4000m, although some fingers reached as low as 3000m. The heavy, powerful ice moulded and shaped the

Cloud and high winds over Kibo summit

Little Penck Glacier, on the western flank of Kibo, was once connected to the Northern Icefields

mountain and was responsible for levelling a number of the parasitic cones that had formed on the lower slopes.

In the 19th century, Hans Meyer encountered a glacial wall at 5500m on his first ascent. The glacial wall at that time encircled the summit and covered an area approximately 10 times as great as today. When Meyer returned to Kilimanjaro in 1898, nine years after his first ascent, he was horrified to discover that the glaciers had retreated considerably on all sides. Furthermore, the crater floor was now more or less free of ice. At that time, Meyer speculated that all of Kilimanjaro's glaciers would have melted within 20 or 30 years.

When first scientifically examined in 1912, the Northern Icefields and the Eastern Icefields were connected to the Southern Icefields and formed part of a continuous body of glacial ice atop Mount Kilimanjaro. Ice flowing off the Northern Icefields still fed numerous glaciers, including, north to south, the Credner, Drygalski, Great Penck and Little Penck glaciers.

By comparing photographs taken over the course of the last couple of decades, it is possible to readily determine the extent to which the glaciers have retreated. Views of the Southern Icefields and the Heim Glacier in particular as seen from Barranco Hut are markedly different in appearance. In the 15 years between 1984 and 1999 for instance, the glacier was seen to lose 300 vertical metres of ice.

However, while it is possible to detect that this is happening, it is harder to say why, since there isn't a simple, conclusive explanation. The fact that Meyer first recorded glacial recession at the end of the 19th century suggests that global warming, while a significant factor, is not simply or solely to blame, and that recession is in fact part of a longer-term cycle of climatic change.

Studies of Kilimanjaro's icefields by Sheffield University during the 1950s concluded that there has been a long history of glacial advance and retreat on Kilimanjaro. The current glaciers date from around 9700BC and have remained on the summit due to repeated ice ages during which time the glaciers were able to recover from melting. There have been eight separate glaciations. The current glaciers are thought to be the remnant of the ice cap that formed as a result of the worldwide drop in temperatures that occurred between AD1400 and 1700.

However, the rate of retreat has accelerated rapidly over recent years as a direct consequence of a general increase in the earth's temperature. Lonnie Thompson of Ohio State University made an aerial survey of Kilimanjaro reporting 'comparisons with previous mapping showed 332 of Mt Kilimanjaro's ice had disappeared in the last two decades – 82% had gone since 1912'. There is less than 2.6sq km of ice left on the summit. Although the warnings of the disappearing ice aren't new, the current rate of reduction is abnormally high. Separate ice tongues that used to exist have lost their definition and shrunk to form a continuous body of ice. Similarly, glaciers such as the Arrow Glacier or the Ratzel Glacier have ceased to be imposing landmarks and now remain only as vestigial ice floes.

Although the glaciers reflect much of the sunlight and consequently don't warm up and thereby melt, the dark coloured lava does heat up and this undermines the ice. As the ground's temperature increases, the ice begins to melt from beneath the glacier; eventually the weight of the overhanging ice becomes too much and a chunk sheers off, exposing more of the glacier to the same phenomenon.

A view of the Southern Icefields showing pools of melting slush

A porter collecting water is dwarfed by the snout of Arrow Glacier

The melting glaciers are usually replenished by snowfall, but recently there has been a dearth of heavy snow on the mountain. This has been the case since the 19th century. Meyer wrote: 'It may have caused some surprise that all along I have continued to speak of ice, and not of snow, as might have been expected. But, as a matter of fact, at this season of the year there was hardly any snow on Kibo worth mentioning.' He continued: 'In the great snowfields, which in July partially covered the slopes of Kibo from the ice-cap to the saddle plateau, the snow near the base was soft and slushy, whilst higher up it was dry and granular. In October, when all the snowfields had disappeared, there was likewise comparatively little snow to be met with on the ice-cap.' Thus, the glaciers are being melted by a natural phenomenon and not replenished by snowfall during rainy seasons because of the increase in the earth's general temperature.

A weather station has been set up on the Northern Icefields to monitor the situation and record any further developments. A number of ice-core samples were taken in 2000 and studied to try and ascertain the history of the climate over the years. The results of these studies provided a unique perspective on the past and present global climate systems. The retreating glaciers are symptomatic of a larger, more significant problem that is causing dramatic changes to the earth's environment during our lifetime.

The findings on Kilimanjaro have massive implications. The potential ramifications of the loss of the ice fields on Kilimanjaro are immense; the local community will inevitably be affected since they rely on the ice as a source for drinking water, crop irrigation and hydroelectric power. Tourism will also suffer as the majority of people visiting the mountain do so in the hope of seeing the eternal snows that adorn the summit as Hemmingway saw them '... great, high, and unbelievably white in the sun'.

CLIMATE

'Asifuye mvuwa imemnyea.'
'He who praises rain has been rained on.'

Swahili proverb

It is very difficult to be precise about the climate on Kilimanjaro; as a result of its size, Kilimanjaro enjoys a number of climactic conditions and at any one time there are equatorial and arctic conditions present on the mountain. That said, the weather here follows remarkably regular patterns.

Although technically enjoying equatorial conditions, Kilimanjaro's climate is actually more tropical. On the warm, dry plains the temperature averages 30°C; as you ascend through the belt of tropical forest on the lower slopes, the temperature decreases, as does the level of rainfall, until you arrive at the permanent snows and freezing temperatures of the summit.

The weather on Kilimanjaro is the direct result of the seasons of the year. The conditions that you experience will also be directly affected by the side of the mountain that you are on and the altitude you are at.

Cloudforest on the mountain's lower sections is just one of the many environments created by Kilimanjaro's varied climate

Kilimanjaro lies just to the south of the equator. As such it is affected by the passage of the Intertropical Convergence Zone, a band of rain that moves across the region between northern Uganda and southern Malawi. The rains cross Africa twice a year and consequently there are two distinct rainy seasons.

The highest rainfall occurs between mid-March and early May. These are the long rains, *masika*, and are brought by the south-east trade winds from the Indian Ocean. During this season clouds pile up over the mountain and drop snow on the summit and rain on the slopes. Even if no rain falls, a belt of cloud encircles the mountain and visibility is drastically reduced. Marginally less rain falls between early November and late December. These short rains, *mvuli*, are carried overland by the north-east monsoon winds and are characterised by thunderstorms. However, rain and (higher up the mountain) snow can be encountered at any time of year, even during the driest periods of the year.

Rain occurs here because Kilimanjaro is a massive obstruction for the winds that bustle across the savannah. These winds hit the mountain and are deflected upwards. As the temperature and atmospheric pressure decrease with altitude, so the moisture condenses and becomes rain.

The heaviest and most sustained rainfall occurs in the forest zone on the south side of the mountain and can reach 2000mm/yr, giving these slopes the most favourable climate on the whole massif. Conversely, shorter and lighter rains fall on the northern and western slopes. The least rainfall lands on the summit itself.

The drier seasons between the two rains are associated with clear, dry weather. The middle of the year tends to be cold and dry while the end of the year is warmer, but similarly dry. These conditions can last for weeks at a time. January to February and September are the warmest, driest and clearest months on the mountain; peak trekking seasons correspond to these months, with the largest volume of climbers tackling Kilimanjaro from January to March and June to October

Regardless of the season, the best weather on Kilimanjaro is to be had during the morning. Cloud cover builds up during the day and convectional rainfall is more probable in the afternoon. The skies above the mountain

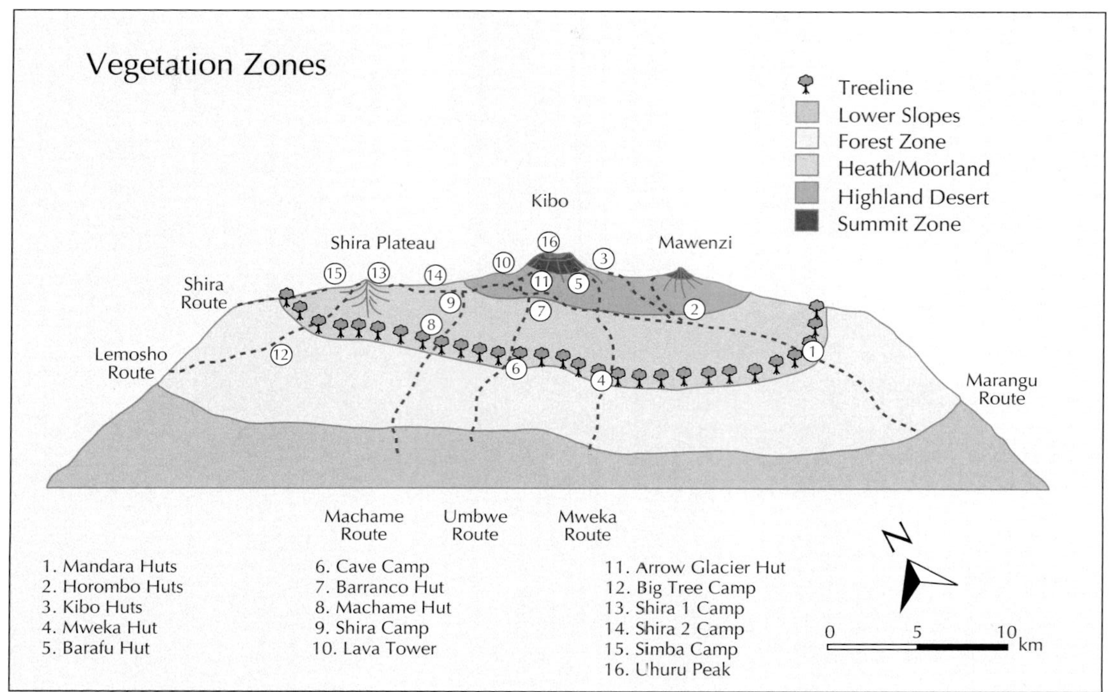

Vegetation Zones
Treeline
Lower Slopes
Forest Zone
Heath/Moorland
Highland Desert
Summit Zone
Kibo
Shira Plateau
Mawenzi
Shira Route
Lemosho Route
Marangu Route
Machame Route
Umbwe Route
Mweka Route
1. Mandara Huts
2. Horombo Huts
3. Kibo Huts
4. Mweka Hut
5. Barafu Hut
6. Cave Camp
7. Barranco Hut
8. Machame Hut
9. Shira Camp
10. Lava Tower
11. Arrow Glacier Hut
12. Big Tree Camp
13. Shira 1 Camp
14. Shira 2 Camp
15. Simba Camp
16. Uhuru Peak
N
0
5
10 km

will probably clear during the evening, ensuring that the summits are visible again come morning.

ANIMAL AND PLANT LIFE

In 1893–1894 the eminent botanist Georg Volkens spent a year on the Shira Plateau and northern slopes of Kilimanjaro, studying and identifying six separate vegetation zones. Beginning on the lower slopes, you pass through the forest zone and the heath/moorland zones before traversing the highland desert and entering the summit zone. These ecological bands occupy belts of approximately 1000m of altitude each and are distinguished from each other by the different association between altitude, rainfall, temperature, flora and fauna. A description of each zone and the plant, bird and animal life found in them is included at the end of the more general introduction to the region's wildlife.

Botanists have struggled over the years to apply a consistent nomenclature to the ecological zones and there has been frequent debate as to where they each begin and end. The uneven distribution of rainfall on the mountain means that the zones have formed an asymmetrical pattern. The northern side of Kilimanjaro receives far less rainfall than the southern half and consequently has a far narrower forest belt. Additionally, the trees found here are slightly different from elsewhere on the mountain.

As, in general, the temperature drops 1°C for every 200m of altitude gained and as rainfall also decreases with altitude, life is concentrated on the lower slopes. Plant life is most abundant in the areas of high rainfall and higher temperature, making the lower slopes and the forest zone far more habitable than the higher altitude zones. Since animal life is dependent on plant life being present, far fewer animals live at high altitude, congregating instead at lower elevations.

A huge number of plants thrive on Kilimanjaro, including a host of endemic species that are found nowhere else in the world. Many of the plants don't have common English names, and so their scientific name, derived from either Latin or Greek, is given here. The scientific name comprises two parts: the first part is the genus and the second is the name of that particular species. Many plants on the mountain have the species name 'kilimandscharica' or 'kilimanjari', which means that the plant was named after the mountain. A number of others have the species name 'usambarensis', which is a reference to the Usambara Mountains to the southeast of Kilimanjaro and is indicative that some of the flora has spread from this range of mountains to Kilimanjaro. There are also a number of commemoratively named plants on the mountain. Many of the explorers, climbers and botanists who played a part in the discovery or study of the mountain have plants named after them: Meyer, Purtscheller, Johnson, Thomson, Decken and New all have species named after them.

At one stage, Kilimanjaro was heavily populated by animals, as is evident in the early writings about the mountain and in the mid-20th-century animal count. In 1965 eyewitness reports of mammal sightings were correlated with contemporary fieldwork to create a checklist of 80 species found living in either the forest

Impatiens kilimanjari, unique to the slopes of Kilimanjaro, takes its name from the mountain

or heath/moorland zones. Nowadays, mammals are very rarely seen and you will have to be exceptionally lucky or incredibly patient to come across any of the shyer, larger game. Most of the animals simply slip away at the first sound of approaching foot traffic and vanish into the landscape. In some cases, the animals have quit the forest and retreated right off the mountain.

Early writings on Kilimanjaro that include descriptions of wildlife encountered and, in particular, big game sightings are usually confined to those reports that pre-date the second half of the 20th century. In 1964 a buffalo skeleton was found high on the east face of Mawenzi; elephant bones were also found as high as 4875m during the first half of the 19th century. Johannes Rebmann recorded seeing elephant on the day that he first sighted Kilimanjaro in 1848 and Hans Meyer wrote that he had seen elephants on the decent from his successful first summit in 1889. The frozen carcass of a leopard discovered on the summit in 1926 was the inspiration for Hemmingway's classic short story, while HW Tilman reported seeing 27 eland (small antelope) on the Saddle in 1933. Wilfred Thesiger was tracked during his push from Gillman's Point to Uhuru by a group of five wild dogs in 1962; his discovery of a host of paw prints in the ice led him to suggest that the dogs were frequent visitors to Kibo. In another incident, in 1979, a porter was savaged by wild dogs in the moorland zone and was only saved by the timely arrival of a large group of walkers. While you are unlikely to be as fortunate (or unfortunate, in some cases) as any of these individuals, you may still see monkeys, an array of birds and insects, and perhaps the tantalising evidence of something larger living in the forest.

Lower slopes

The first ecological zone on the mountain are the lower slopes, which stretch 800–1800m. This zone receives varying quantities of rainfall; on the southern side of the mountain 500mm/yr falls on the plains that mark the lowest extremity of the zone. In contrast, the forest boundary at the high end of the zone receives up to 1800mm/yr.

These slopes were originally earmarked by British and German colonisers as potential sites for settlements and farms because of what they described as the ideal 'European' conditions. There is now ample evidence of human use and activity on the lower slopes where local people graze livestock and grow subsistence crops including bananas, vegetables and coffee all around the mountain. This has had a negative impact on the natural vegetation and as a direct result, what was once bush and lowland forest is now largely grassland or farmland.

The lower slopes are nourished directly by rainfall and by rain falling in the forest zone; the water percolates down the mountain through underground channels to arrive on the lower slopes. The bountiful supply of water and the fertile, volcanic soils are the main reasons for the zone's successful plant and crop growth. The wealth of farmland in turn supports a number of densely populated settlements amid Kilimanjaro's foothills.

Flora

The lower slopes are decorated with a host of small colourful flowers that exist among the ferns and grasses that populate this region. The local grass, *Pennisetum clandestinum*, forms thick, short lawns and is identified by its peculiar filament-like white flower. A number of clovers are found here, in the vicinity of water; the attractive, pink/white flowers of *Trifolium semipilosum* and the darker, purple flowers of *T. usambarensis* are the most common examples. *Parochaetus communis* is a blue-flowered pea that is easily found in damp, shady spots. The most attractive flowers here are the African violet (*Streptocarpus glandulossinus*), and the long, violet coloured blooms of *Coleus kilimandscharica*. A number of other plants grow in scruffy looking, tall clumps. These include all of the *Vernonia* species whose huge shabby heads of small purplish flowers are very distinctive and the *Lippia* and *Lantana* species, which are most easily recognised by their lemony scented leaves and flowers. Tangled vines are evident in the trees: *Clematis hirsuta* has a host of pinkish flowers and the thorny *Pterolobium stellatum* displays a number of showy red seedpods that are frequently mistaken for flowers. The attractive blue *Ipomea* species, commonly called morning glory, is also found living on trees since it is a very fast growing, clambering plant. The seeds of the pink flowered *Erlangea tomentosa* adhere themselves to your clothes as you brush past and the recurved spines of the yellow-flowered *Mauritius thorn*, *Caesalpinea decapetala* or the three-leafed *Toddalia asiatica* inevitably catch and snag your clothes or skin as you climb.

Birds

A great many birds thrive on the lower slopes of Kilimanjaro, particularly where the cultivated ground ends and the forest reasserts itself, since the forest provides good, secure nesting sites and the cultivated land an abundant supply of food.

The ubiquitous common bulbul can be seen over much of East Africa at altitudes up to 3000m. It is an unpretentious, small brown bird that has white ear patches and a mottled breast. Generally found on the edge of forests in bushy areas, it has a melodious, high, up-and-down chortle. The white-browed robin-chat is also common in shaded woodland and at the fringes of the forest. This shy, colourful bird has a black face streaked by a long white superciliary stripe, an olive-grey rump and rich, tawny-orange underparts. Its repeated rich whistle can usually be heard at dawn and dusk. Also frequently seen is the gregarious speckled mousebird, a smallish, stout brown bird with a very long rigid tail, which makes it up to 30cm long. It has a brown crest, contrasting whitish cheeks and a thick bill. It whistles and chatters frequently, making a soft call except when alarmed, when the pitch becomes more insistent. The most attractive bird to inhabit this zone is the iridescent bronze sunbird. The male is generally black with gold, bronze and green reflections, and a long, curved bill; the female is a brownish olive colour and has a dusky facial mask. Found above 1200m, both sexes make an extended sputtering call that is interspersed with occasional louder notes.

Animals

The lower slopes host a few large game species, but these are much rarer than the smaller animals found here. Since you are most likely to start your climb towards the top of this zone and won't stay overnight within it, you probably won't see many of its inhabitants, a number of whom are nocturnal.

The tree-dwelling and vaguely cat-like, silvery grey galagos (bushbabies) may be seen in the dense vegetation up to 1800m. They have large leathery ears, enormous eyes and a bushy tail. Galagos are entirely nocturnal, emerging at night to forage for fruit, nectar, seeds, flowers, insects and larvae. Their baby-like cry can be repeated up to 100 times per hour, ensuring you are far more likely to hear than see them. Tree hyraxes also live almost exclusively amid the trees. These rabbit-sized herbivores are distant relatives of the elephant and are identified by their brownish coat and short coarse fur. Hyraxes are sociable and bond together in small colonies, and feed on leaves and shoots. For such small creatures they make a mighty din; the standard call begins with a series of groans and creeks and rises to a climax of eerie screams and shrieks – their alarm call is a high-pitched scream. Tree hyraxes are preyed upon by the common genet. This agile feline predator is attractively marked with dark spots on its creamy fur and has a banded tail. It hunts alone at night in trees or along the ground. In some places, genets have learnt to scavenge off human rubbish and may be seen haunting camp or hut sites.

Forest zone

The forest zone extends 1800–2800m. It is the richest zone on the mountain because it receives so much rainfall. The southern slopes enjoy as much as 2000mm/yr, while the drier northern and western slopes receive up to 1000mm/yr. Daytime temperatures reach 15–20°C, although the humidity makes it feel warmer. In contrast, the nights spent at either Mandara Huts (2720m) (along the Marangu Route) or Big Tree Camp (2790m) (on the Lemosho Route) can be very cold, especially if the sky is clear.

A wide band of lush montane forest encircles the whole of Kilimanjaro. The forest varies in width from a couple of kilometres to over 15km, according to its position on the mountain, the steepness of the slope and the extent to which human activity has impacted on its natural state. When 19th-century explorers first attempted to ascend Kilimanjaro, it took them two or three days simply to traverse this zone. Tree clearance has nibbled away at the forest and reduced it dramatically; the wetter southern slopes are still the densest and most verdant whereas the western and eastern slopes have been cleared in places for softwood plantations. Although these plantations are economically productive, they have adversely affected the wildlife by disrupting the migratory routes of elephant and buffalo. The extent of the disturbance has caused the numbers of these animals on Kilimanjaro to dwindle. Those that are left are increasingly cautious.

It has been calculated that 96% of the water on Kilimanjaro originates in the forest zone. The heavy rainfall is absorbed by the thick carpet of leaves and detritus on the forest floor. The water then enters the soil and percolates through the porous lava and a series of underground channels to emerge as springs lower down the mountain. The humus and porous lava act as natural water filters, cleansing the water of most impurities as it passes through the soil. The resultant springs are then channelled into both ancient and more modern Chagga irrigation systems.

Owing to the dampness and altitude of the forest, a wide band of cloud frequently forms around the upper third of this zone, which prevents the moisture within the forest from evaporating. This leads to high humidity and ensures that the forest remains damp. The moist cloudforest is an ideal climate for mosses and lichens, which thrive here and give the whole forest belt a timeless, primeval air.

Flora

The tropical forest is dense, lush and alive. Overrun by plants, it is a steamy, sensuous place to walk through and elicits strong responses in most walkers. As the mountaineer Rob Taylor wrote in his account of his assault on the Breach Wall: 'These plants are the powerful life force here, and they appear to grow before my eyes. I sense that if one stopped and remained still too long in this place, he would be entwined and overpowered, claimed as one of their own.'

Most obvious of the forest plants are the giant trees that dominate the zone. As you start the Marangu Route, the trail passes a giant spreading *Albizia schimperiana*, supporting a signboard. The leaves of this tree are reputed to have medicinal properties when burnt. By inhaling the smoke from the singed leaves you are supposed to be able to soothe headaches and reduce a fever. The commonest tree in the forest is the wild poplar, *Macaranga kilimandscharica*. It has smooth grey bark and large heart-shaped leaves that are dark on top and lighter below. The leaves are used by local people to make a hot infusion that prevents diarrhoea. You will also encounter the hefty *Tabernaemontana holstii,* which has rhododendron-like leaves and white flowers that can grow up to 3cm across. *Xymalos monospora,* with its shiny dark leaves and orange berries, and the gnarled *Agauria salicifolia,* which has rough reddish bark, small shiny oval leaves and pinkish flower spikes, are the two other most prevalent trees. The giant trees often play host to a multitude of mosses and grey green streams of bearded lichen (*Usnea sp.*). The most common of these is *U. barbata,* which is more commonly called old man's beard. At times the forest tree trunks support so many epiphytes that they more closely resemble vertical gardens. Moss-like plants from the *Lycopodium* and *Selaginella* species also blanket the forest floor. These plants send out runners to rampage across the slopes and clamber over or up everything in their path.

Usnea barbata, also known as old man's beard

Sycamore figs and palm trees are dotted throughout the forest, most usually in river gorges. Beneath the spreading canopy, the forest sustains a myriad of ferns. Botanists have identified over 130 varieties of fern in the forest zone. The most noticeable are the giant tree ferns that grow up to 6m tall. The stalks of the tree ferns are highly valued as poles for use in houses and verandas.

Very little light penetrates to the forest floor and, as a consequence, there is a dearth of wild flowers here. Those that do survive on the forest floor compensate by being especially striking. The most resplendent are the *Balsams* that make up the *Impatiens* species. These can be found in thick carpets around the buttressed roots of the great trees. The most exquisite is the endemic scarlet and yellow *I. kilimanjari.* This delicate, tropical busy Lizzy is shaped like an inwardly curled spur and is found nowhere else in the world. Its shocking pink relative, the violetesque *I. pseudoviola,* is also found in shady areas. Pink and mauve orchids, violets and the blue-flowered pea, *Parochaetus communis,* also grow here. Vines seen climbing over tree branches are most likely to be *Begonias;* the most common is the white flowered *B. meyeri-johannis,* which has a central clump of gold anthers amid delicate petals.

The Chagga collect the aerial roots from the fig trees and boil them in water. Once the mixture has cooled, it is drunk to combat skin diseases and stomach upsets. The *Dracaena* palm is also important to the Chagga, who use it to

Begonia meyeri-johannis

create a living fence around their homesteads. The palm sap has a medicinal value too.

As the forest is not uniform on each side of Kilimanjaro, the less dense, drier northern and western slopes harbour an entirely different collection of plant species. Of these, the tall, twisted cedar tree *Juniperus procera* is the most common. It grows to almost 40m tall and its fluted, shapely trunk is used commercially for the manufacture of furniture. Cedarwood oil is also used in soaps, while perfumes can be distilled from its sawdust. The African olive trees *Olea africana* and *O. kilimandscharica* grow to 10m and 30m respectively. The taller species is particularly important as a timber tree. Another common forest giant is *Podocarpus milanjianus*, whose smooth trunk and narrow curling leaves most closely resemble a yew tree. The pale yellow, straight-grained wood is even and uniform in texture, making it an excellent timber tree and earning it the nickname 'yellow wood'. The African holly, *Ilex mitis*, also grows here, as does the immense camphorwood, *Ocotea usambarensis*, which grows up to 40m tall. In contrast, the brittlewood *Nuxia congesta* is a bulky, crooked tree with a spreading crown. Frequently festooned with moss and lichen, it produces round clusters of white flowers after rainfall.

The forest zone on Kilimanjaro is unusual in one major respect: there is hardly any bamboo on the slopes, even though it is common on most other East African volcanic mountains, including Mount Meru, just to the west of Kilimanjaro. Bamboo is usually found in a belt 2100–2700m. Although very small clumps of bamboo exist on the northern and north-western slopes of the mountain, Kilimanjaro is essentially devoid of this species. The explanation for this dearth is that Kilimanjaro is higher and drier than other volcanic mountains and the transition from forest to heath/moorland happens much more abruptly. Instead of bamboo, Kilimanjaro supports vast quantities of giant heath trees, including the 3m tall *Philippia excelsa*, whose tiny white flowers nestle amid short, needle-like leaves. In addition to the giant heather, there are a great many bushes of *Hypericum*, which are easily distinguishable by their large, bright yellow flowers, and in sheltered, moist areas the handsome African rosewood *Hayenia abyssinica*, whose drooping clusters of dark red flowers and large leaves catch moisture from the mist. In the higher reaches of the forest there are also a number of attractive

Hypericum revolutum

shrubs that have brightly coloured berries. *Lasianthus kilimandscharica* has porcelain blue berries and white-mauve flowers, *Galiniera coffeoides* has red berries and *Pauridiantha holstii* has red berries and small white-yellow flowers.

At the very upper limit of the forest zone, the first endemic giant *senecio* appear. *S. johnstonii* has an open branched crown, cabbage-like leaves, small yellow flowers and grows up to 3m tall.

Birds

Due to the forest being so dense, you may not see a great deal of birdlife here. However, the calls and choruses that ring out are testament to a number of species.

The largest of the forest birds are the silvery-cheeked hornbill and Hartlaub's turaco. The hornbill is black and white and in flight its dark upper plumage contrasts vividly with its white lower back and rump. Only the male has the distinctive silvery grey feather tips on its cheeks and ear-coverts. They make a very audible whoosh while flying in the forest and their raucous, braying call is equally distinctive. While feeding, the hornbill makes softer grunting, quacking calls. The smaller turaco has a rounded bushy blue-black crest, white facial markings and a bright red ring around its eye. Its throat, breast and upper back are green, while its posterior parts are glossy violet-blue. When in flight, it displays a vibrant crimson underwing. It lives singly or in small groups and communicates using a gruff, harsh coughing sound.

The attractive bar tailed trogon is easily missed since it sits so still in the trees. The male has a scarlet chest, green back and black and white speckled wings. The throat and head are black. The female is similar, except her head and throat are brown and the chest plumage tends to be more orange. Both sexes have a very high, loud, crescendoing yelp. Mountain greenbuls, brown woodland warblers and olive thrushes are more lively but just as hard to spot owing to their drab green and brown plumage that camouflages them against the palette of forest colours.

Animals

The forest zone is home to most of Kilimanjaro's animals, both large and small. However, the vast majority are exceptionally shy, silent and very swift. The dense understorey keeps them hidden and the sound of your own passage will alert them to your presence far more quickly than you can detect them.

You are most likely to see monkeys, particularly black-and-white colobus monkeys. These incredibly acrobatic forest denizens have black fur, a flowing white cape and a long, white-tipped tail. They also have a highly distinctive, slightly sombre black face and white surrounding beard. They are gorgeous and graceful to watch. Colobus are sociable and tend to live in family groups numbering six to 10 individuals. They rarely venture out of the trees, obtaining water from hollows on the branches. They are strictly vegetarian and feed on leaves, fruits and seeds. At dawn and dusk the males can be heard uttering their guttural, purring territorial roar. Blue monkeys are also quite widespread. They are much less colourful than their name suggests, being mainly grey and black. They have a slender tail that helps them to move quietly through the trees while in search of fruit and leaves. Occasionally large troops of olive baboon are seen in the forest's lower reaches. These large, greenish monkeys have a shortish tail and bare, dog-like muzzle. They are omnivores who have been known to hunt and kill, as well as forage for fruit and grass. Their loud 'wahoo' alarm call sometimes rings out across the forest.

The forest is also home to a host of antelope. Of these, various species of duiker are the most common. Duiker is the Dutch for 'diver' and is a reference to its tendency to plunge headfirst into the undergrowth when startled. Abbot's duiker is a very rare, small dark red-brown antelope. It has the hunched back common to all duikers and a small pair of horns hidden in a patch of long reddish hair on its forehead. The red duiker is smaller, more brightly coloured and is often seen in pairs. It is chestnut-red and has a black blaze down its face. The bush duiker is the largest of the three and the most adaptable. It is fawn coloured and has the same distinctive black blaze on its face, which helps to break up its outline against the forest background. Generally found at higher levels of the forest, it sometimes ventures onto the heath/moorland.

The suni is smaller than any of the duikers and is nicknamed the 'dwarf antelope'. It is dark brown and hides in patchy forest, most usually on the western slopes of the mountain, where it feeds on the leaves of the brittlewood *N. congesta*. Bushbuck appear throughout the forest zone. Larger than the other antelopes, they are less secretive and more active during the day. The male tends to be darker brown than the female who is conspicuously red. Both sexes have large white throat patches and white stripes and spots along their flanks and face. The males can be distinguished by their medium-sized spiral horns. The compact, goat-like klipspringer used to be seen on the rockier stretches of the upper forest zone, but hasn't been sighted recently and is thought to now be locally extinct.

The antelopes share the forest with several other larger mammals. Nocturnal bush pigs range warily through the forest, feeding at night on shoots, roots and fungi. They have a large, distinct white stripe running from their face along a spinal crest the length of their back. The forest also houses eland, giraffe, buffalo and elephant, although the populations of these larger animals are unknown and probably transitory, passing through the forest on their way to other parts of the surrounding landscape. There have been no sightings of rhino on Kilimanjaro for many years and it's very unlikely that there are any resident in the forest.

As well as herbivores, the forest supports a number of carnivores, including mongooses, civets, genets, lions and leopards. Lions tend to simply pass through the forest on their way to the Shira Plateau, where they are recorded irregularly. The exact numbers of leopard living on the mountain are unknown and they are very rarely seen, preferring to hide in the forest and hunt rodents, antelopes and monkeys.

The forest also supports a huge range of insects. Safari ants and a range of attractive showy butterflies offer an alternative wildlife viewing experience. Large spectacular swallowtails can be seen in several forms; *Papilio rex* is black, cream and orange while *P. hornimanii* is black and turquoise. *P. sjostedti* is unique to the slopes of Kilimanjaro and Mount Meru.

Heath/moorland zone

The heath/moorland zone is in reality two intermingled ecological zones, which extend 2800–4000m and mark the transition from forest to low alpine desert. The edge of the forest receives more than 1300mm/yr of rainfall. This dwindles to 530mm/yr at the upper limits of the zone. The climate is usually cool and clear. Along the forest boundary there is frequently mist and low cloud, while above 3000m the sunshine becomes more intense and the plant life sparser. The temperatures drop as the slopes become more exposed and during the evenings frost regularly occurs. While the heath retains a number of plant species, the moorland is far more barren. In 1930 Eva Stuart Watt described the terrain in her book, *Africa's Dome of Mystery*: 'The whole landscape as far as the eye could reach was a medley of dull grey lava slabs, dotted with the red-leaf protea shrub and stunted heaths, which became smaller and smaller as we rose higher. Not a sound disturbed the silence of this uninhabited mountain mystery; not a sign of life broke the stillness save a little ashy-brown bird that hopped about the boulders, flipping its tail up and down. And to add to the impression created by the eerie scene, huge senecios lifted to a height of 20ft their black stems and greyish-yellow crowns and stood spreading out their arms in the deep moist gullies, like ghostly sentinels of the untrodden wilds.'

There are several huts and campsites within this zone. At the lower levels of the heath/moorland zone are the Machame Hut (3015m) and the Mweka Hut (3100m). In the higher reaches of the zone are the Horombo Huts (3720m), Shira campsites (3850m), Barranco Huts (3965m) and campsites at Kikelewa Caves (3600m) and Third Cave (3935m).

Flora: Heath

Heathers and shrubs dominate the heath. In the aftermath of the forest, the openness of the heath is a relief. The trees give way to large shrubs and giant heathers, the largest of which is *Erica arborea*, whose gnarled trunks grow to 10m tall in the upper forest, but only 3m on the moorland. The long slender trunks support tiny leaves and small white flowers clustered on the end of the branches. *E. rossi* is a smaller, bushier heather, distinguished by its flatter, cup-shaped white flowers. *Anthospermum usambarensis* is a cypress-like shrub that grows to around 3m tall and produces attractive clusters of green-white flowers. A similar sized shrub is *Stoebe kilimandscharica*, whose slender branchlets support tiny scale-like silvery leaves and minute dirty yellow flowers. *Kotschya recurrifolia* is a small shrub whose frequently forked branches support gold coloured flowers. *Myrica meyeri-johannis* is a diminutive shrub, adorned with catkin-like flowers. Mingled with all of the shrubs are quantities of spiny gorse, *Adenocarpus manii*, that reach a height of 2m.

The heath is resplendent with attractive, brightly coloured, highly visible flowers. The most characteristic are everlastings. These simple, hardy flowers, which occur in a variety of colours, grow in clumps: *Helichrysum meyeri-johannis* has simple pink daisy-like flowers with red tips; *H. argyranthum* has greenish white flowers, while *H. kilimanjari* produces yellow brown flowers and lemon-scented leaves. *H. cymosum* is taller than its relatives and produces tight clumps of yellow blooms. In the mid-20th century, the porters used to make garlands from these flowers for climbers who successfully made it to the summit. This practice has since stopped.

The heath is also home to various species of *Protea*. More common further south, it is the floral emblem of South Africa. The most widespread species found on the mountain is *P. kilimandscharica*, which is more usually known as the 'sugar bush'. It stands almost 4m tall and has a large number of big, creamy flower heads, similar in appearance to a white globe artichoke, which consist of a mass of upright white filaments arising from a shallow, bowl-shaped rosette.

Amid the grasses and shrubs are a plethora of vibrant flowers. The most distinctive is the red-hot poker, *Kniphofia thomsonii*, whose candle-like spike of red, orange and yellow flowers waves in the breeze. The most beautiful flower on the heath is the delicate red or salmon pink *Gladiolus watsonioides*, whose flower hangs gracefully from a curved stem. The gently arching, pink-flowered *Dierama pendulum* and the white-flowered *Anemone thomsonii* are often hidden by clumps of grass, as is the small pink-flowered orchid *Disa stairsii*. The heath's phosphorous-rich volcanic soils support two types of clover, the blue-flowered *T. cryptopodium* and the pink and white-flowered *T. burchellianum*. *Lobelia holstii* sometimes grow on the upper edges of the heath, although *lobelia* in general are more common higher up on the moorland.

Flora: Moorland

The higher section of this zone, the moorland, is characterised by hardier plants. Clusters of giant *lobelia* and *senecios* are the archetypal symbols of African mountain vegetation and are found here in numbers, most often in valley bottoms and beside streams. There are two types of giant *Dendrosenecio*: *D. cottonii* and *D. kilimanjari*, each especially adapted to the rigours of living at altitude. They both have tall stems that act as reservoirs and collect water. The stems fork into two and then each branch forks again higher up; these support the large cabbage-like rosette of leaves that sits atop the stem. They are almost grotesque in appearance, and look misshapen and ungainly. The plants flower approximately once every 25 years; after this the parent branch forks again and grows for another 25 years before repeating the cycle. Therefore, by counting the number of forks that one branch makes and multiplying this by 25, you will be able to roughly determine the age of the plant. The delicate central growing shoot is protected from the sub-zero temperatures on the moorland by a dense leaf bud that insulates it. The plant retains these large leaves when they die, using them to form a shaggy skirt of dry material, which insulates and protects the trunk.

D. cottonii is the most widespread giant *senecio*. It grows high on the moorland and can reach almost 5m tall. It has the classic *senecio* shape and produces a metre-long spike of dull mustard coloured flowers and has very thick, cottony leaves. *D. kilimanjari* is endemic to the mountain. Less common, it grows at slightly lower altitudes to a similar size, but has much brighter, lemon yellow flowers.

Dendrosenecio kilimanjari

The moorland also supports two smaller, scrubby *senecios*. *S. meyeri-johannis* and *S. purtschelleri* are similar to their relatives in shape, but are a fraction of the size.

The other visually striking plants on the moorland are the endemic *lobelias*. The name *lobelia* derives from the 17th-century botanist Mathias de L'obel. They are essentially giant overgrown herbs that have adapted to survive in this harsh environment. *Lobelia deckenii* stands almost 3m tall. It has a hollow stem and a pronounced flower spike that supports regular spiralling leaf-like bracts that hide small blue flowers. These flowers are frequently sought out by sunbirds hunting for insects and nectar. The *lobelia* has a rosette of leaves at the base of the stem that fold over the central core of the plant at night to insulate and protect it from the cold. These rosettes exude a slimy, water-like secretion that freezes in the cold; the water below this layer of ice never freezes and consequently the sensitive leaf bud is protected from sub-zero temperatures.

Giant lobelia

There have been suggestions that you could drink the fluid found trapped in the *lobelia's* reservoirs: do not be tempted to do so since *lobelias* contain lobeline which is highly toxic. The author and historian Audrey Salkeld reported that the mountaineers Ian Howell and Phil Snyder tried it when short of water and found it 'viscous, tasteless, and home to colonies of little worms'.

Lobelia deckenii

The moorland also gives rise to the wiry shrub *Euryops dacrydioides*, which grows in clumps on rocky ridges. It has scale-like leaves and bright yellow flowers. As you climb higher, you will encounter especially adapted everlastings. These are even hardier than their lower altitude relatives and have evolved smaller leaves covered in dense, fine hairs that reduce moisture loss and safeguard the plant from the extremes of temperature. The most common everlastings are the yellow and brown flowered *Helichrysum cymosum*, the gaudy yellow flowered *Helichrysum splendidum* and the large white-flowered *Helichrysum newii*. This final species is named after the missionary Charles New, who observed it while climbing

Kilimanjaro in 1871 and described it as having 'frosty-looking leaves and exceedingly pretty flowers'.

A number of species of grass, including blue-stem grass, unicorn grass and crested hair grass, grow in tussocks, intermingled with clumps of the minty herbs, *Satureia biflora* and *S. kilimanscharica*.

The moorland supports a number of bogs. These unique environments are incredibly fragile and delicate. Do not walk on theses habitats as this will damage and drastically alter them. Bog sedge, *Carex monostachya,* is the dominant plant here and is often accompanied by groups of giant *Dendrosenecio*. Delicate flowers, including blue flowered gentians, *Swcrtia crassiuscula*, bright yellow buttercups, *Ranunculus oreophytus*, and pink-purple thistles, *Carduus keniensis*, hug the ground and take advantage of the bountiful water supply.

Birds

The higher you climb on Kilimanjaro the fewer birds you encounter. At the lower reaches of the heath/moorland a number of smaller birds frequent the heathers and tussock grasses, while a number of larger raptors hunt small rodents and other prey.

The alpine chat is a widespread, companionable bird. Above 3400m it is the most common bird on Kilimanjaro. It is mostly brown and has a short, white-sided tail. It can frequently be seen standing bolt upright on rocks and boulders, where it surveys the lie of the land and utters its loud piping call. The streaky seedeater is another common moorland bird. Although generally brown, it has boldly streaked underparts and broad, pale streaks along the side of its face. It flits from boulder to bush in search of seeds and feeds on the ground. It has a high-pitched, long drawn cry.

The alpine swift is a large, highflying swift. It has dark brown upper feathers, white underparts and a dark brown breast band across its pale chest. Its tail is deeply forked. The swift nests in colonies, high on crags. It has a strident rising and falling scream-like call. The only sunbird on the moorlands is the dazzling scarlet-tufted malachite sunbird. The long-tailed males are mainly metallic green and have bright scarlet pectoral tufts. The rump and upper tail feathers have blue-black reflections. The female has brown feathers on her upper body and is paler below. The feathers have orange-red pectoral tufts. It feeds on nectar from the flowers of the giant *lobelia* and has a rather mellow sounding song. The small montane yellow-crowned canary has a bright yellow head, yellow-olive rump and yellow wings. Its tail is discernibly forked. It makes a prolonged, bright jumble of trills that rise attractively.

Ground birds such as Shelley's frankolin and the cape quail are also found on the moorland. The shy, secretive frankolin resembles a western grouse and has a tawny head and a white-flecked neck. Its cream underparts are blotched and banded with brown streaks. It has streaked chestnut plumage on the rest of its body. When startled it rises from the ground with a great clatter, omitting a shrill squeal. The quail is pale brown and slightly squatter than the frankolin. It has a distinctive call that sounds like a series of short whistles.

The commonest bird of prey on the moorland is the augur buzzard. It is very broad winged and has a short stubby tail. The feathers on its back are black and its underparts white. The buzzard soars on raised wings and is able to hover motionless. It relies on stereoscopic vision to judge the changing distance accurately as it dives on its prey. The augur buzzard has a loud clamorous cry. The smaller mountain buzzard is similar in colour and markings to the augur buzzard. It tends to hunt in pairs and is quite vocal, making a loud mewing cry. The African crowned eagle is another impressive bird of prey. This large bird proudly sits bolt upright. It is blackish brown above and has heavily mottled tawny cream underparts. It has broad rounded wings and flies remarkably silently. It feeds on large birds and mammals to the size of small duiker, but prefers colobus monkeys. It has a melodious, far-ranging cry. The largest bird of prey is the exceptionally rare lammergeier. This striking vulture has long pointed dark wings, a wedge shaped tail and a distinctive white head and black mask. Its underparts are pale and its neck is frequently rust coloured. It soars over the slopes with its wings held slightly below the horizontal and has a whistling call. The white-naped raven is a large scavenger that occasionally hunts in its own right. It has jet black feathers and a broad white collar. It has broad wings, a short tail and a very large tipped black bill. It has a series of short, guttural, harsh cries. It has learnt to scavenge from campsites and lunch stops along the various routes. It is bold and audacious and will confidently come close enough to pilfer food.

Animals

The most widespread animal on the heath/moorland is the four-striped grass mouse. This small banded grey rodent has colonised the area around the Horombo Huts and its numbers have risen steadily to almost plague proportions. Scavenging on scraps and benefiting from the wastefulness of people, these mice have prospered. Slightly less visible but still present are the climbing mouse and the harsh-furred mouse. Most extraordinary of the rodents found in this zone is the naked mole-rat, a hairless burrower that lives in large underground colonies and attacks plant roots from below. Small mounds of earth along the paths indicate the presence of a colony and if you approach slowly and carefully you may see the workers digging near the surface, throwing up puffs of soil like miniature volcanoes.

The various species of mouse are important prey for small cats, such as the African civet, which hunt on the heath. This truculent loner is an aggressive nocturnal predator of small animals. It has white fur that is variously speckled, blotched, striped and banded with black.

East Africa's largest and slowest antelope, the eland, is a regular visitor to the heath. It is nomadic and journeys over the heath while traversing migration routes. It is about the size of an ox and has humped shoulders and a pronounced dewlap at the base of its neck. Both male and female elands have tightly twisted, spiral horns. The bush duiker also ventures onto the heath to feed and can be seen at the zones lower reaches.

Larger species, including buffalo and elephant, are also very occasionally encountered on the heath, usually as they negotiate the mountain on their way to new territories. Their tracks and spoor are often the only indication of their passage. A Chagga legend maintains that there is an elephant graveyard high on the mountain. Elderly or dying animals climb Kilimanjaro in order to cast themselves into a pit high on the slopes, thereby thwarting the poachers and hunters who are after their ivory. The location of this legendary pit isn't recorded but may be the ash pit on the summit.

Of the larger predators, the much maligned African hunting dogs (wild dogs) and lions have very occasionally been known to frequent the Shira plateau, climbing out of the forest to hunt the open spaces. Hunting dogs work in packs and use their remarkable stamina to run down prey. They are some of the most efficient predators on the savannah. Their fur is ochre, tan, black and white. They are slenderly built and have long legs, a prominent muzzle and powerful jaws. The famous, tawny coat and black and golden mane of the lion is a classic African symbol. They are the largest and most powerful big cat in Africa.

Reptiles don't usually frequent places as cold as the heath/moorland zone, but on Kilimanjaro you may see brown or grey lizards basking on the exposed rocks, using the sun's direct light and the absorbed heat of the rocks to warm themselves.

There are also a few butterfly species here, including the greenish white *Catopsila florella* and the bluish *Harpendyseus aequatorialis*.

Highland desert zone

This is a desolate, lunar-like landscape that stretches from 4000–5000m. It is much drier than lower sections of the mountain and receives as little as 250mm/yr. Professor Hedberg, an expert on Afro-alpine plant adaptation, described this alpine zone as enduring 'summer every day, and winter every night'. The exposed landscape suffers from intense radiation and very high evaporation. Huge daily fluctuations in temperature, from 40°C in direct sunlight to well below freezing at night, ensure that only the hardiest plants can survive. Sudden cloud cover and an increase in wind speed can result in temperatures plummeting 20°C in almost as many minutes. Water is particularly scarce and the soil struggles to retain any moisture. To combat this, many of the plants have evolved to sieve water from the cloud and mist so that it drips down the leaves to be absorbed by the roots. Plants must also combat the process of solifluction. When ground water freezes, the soil water expands and disrupts the soil, potentially uprooting the plants. Consequently, only the most enduring plants can exist here and the hut and campsites at this altitude, Kibo Huts (4710m), Barafu Hut (4660m), Lava Tower (4655m) and Arrow Glacier (4850m), are all set in bleak, inhospitable environs.

Flora

Botanists have calculated that only 55 species of plant survive above 4000m on Kilimanjaro, in contrast to the many hundreds that exist at lower altitudes. The most common of these are the pale green and rust red lichens, which are able to avoid the soil entirely and choose to encrust the lava that is predominant here.

Rather than spread over rocks in the usual fashion, mosses at this altitude curl around soil nodules and form rootless spheres, known as grimmia, which are able to freely roll around the landscape. The moss feeds on the soil that it encloses and soaks up any available moisture that it encounters, like a sponge.

Flowering plants can't subsist in these conditions as readily because they rely on roots to stabilise and nourish them. Leaves and flowers are prone to damage by frost and the extremes of temperature. Those plants that do exist here are nearly all small *senecios*, including *S. telekii*, *S. meyeri-johannis* and *S. purtschelleri*, or woody-stemmed, tough everlastings. Even these have had to adapt in order to survive. *H. newii*, *H. cymosum*, *H. splendidum* and *H. citrispinum* all exist in the highland desert as well as lower on the mountain. The higher altitude variations are smaller and hug the contours of the ground. They have developed leathery leaves, a thick skin and small stomata to aid water retention and prevent them drying out. Fine silver hairs reflect solar radiation and trap air next to the leaves in a bid to reduce heat and water loss.

Small grass tussocks rely on clusters of dead matter to insulate their shoots and retain sufficient moisture for them to survive, but endure up to 4700m. The most common grass is *Pentaschistii minor*, whose narrow, wiry leaves reduce water loss. Where grasses manage to bind the soil together, other plants huddle and take advantage of the stabilised surface. These are almost universally ground hugging, cushion plants. Their leaf rosettes provide a degree of insulation and the shiny leaves reflect the harsh sunlight. The most unlikely plant in this zone is the small, delicate *Arabis alpina*. More commonly found in the Alps or Lapland, it is a surprisingly fragile plant to exist at this altitude.

Birds

In general, the air is too thin and the wind too strong for all but the strongest birds to fly here. White-naped ravens and larger birds of prey occasionally forage at altitude during the day but return to lower elevations to nest.

Animals

No large animals live in the highland desert zone, only ever passing through it on their way elsewhere. Eland are fairly regular visitors to these slopes and their tracks are common on the Saddle. The mountaineer HW Tilman encountered 27 eland there in 1933 and observed: 'Their normal habitat is the open plains at heights of 5,000 feet to 6,000 feet, but so far as one could tell the eland up on the "saddle" at 16,000 feet were in no way different except for apparently shaggier hair. This particular herd seemed to be subsisting very happily on a diet of little more than shale, and were very shy.'

Elusive predators including serval, African hunting dogs and leopards also occasionally pass through this zone. The only other inhabitants of the zone are small, sedentary, wingless insects. The insects hide in tussocks and under the clumps of grass for protection. Little spiders living in the zone feed on small ground-dwelling insects that have been caught on gusts of wind and carried here. These are probably the highest resident animals on Kilimanjaro.

Summit zone

The summit zone comprises land above 5000m. It is very barren and hostile and is characterised by arctic conditions. It receives as little as 100mm/yr of rain and supports virtually no life. What rainfall there is, is immediately absorbed by the porous rock and lost. There is virtually no surface water present here, the vast majority of it being locked up as snow or ice.

The temperatures are burning hot by day and well below freezing at night. There is little atmosphere present to protect anything from the force of the sun's radiation and there is 50% less oxygen than at sea level.

Yet remarkably there is still life present in this extreme environment. The occasional lichen clings to exposed lava and grows at an excruciatingly slow rate, as little as 1mm/yr. Thus the red and grey lichens around the crater rim are very old. The highest recorded flowering plant on the mountain is an everlasting. A very compact version of *H. newii* was found growing inside the Kibo crater at 5670m. Fumaroles emit warm sulphurous steam inside the crater and create unique microclimates that, incredibly, provide just enough ingredients for life, enabling the everlasting to survive.

Summit wildlife sightings have been confined to the discovery of the frozen leopard carcass in 1926 at Leopard Point and the report by Wilfred Thesiger of five African hunting dogs that accompanied him and two companions to the top in 1962. Thesiger marvelled: 'It was an amazing thing to have found wild dogs at 19,000 feet, about 10,000 feet higher than they normally ever go. They looked like wolves in the snow as they followed us, or sat and watched us. I have often wondered if there is any record of mammals having been found at a higher altitude.'

Lava rubble leading to the Southern Icefields

ACCLIMATISATION TREK

Mount Meru ash cone (photo: David Evison/Shutterstock.com)

In order to aid acclimatisation and their chances of success on Kilimanjaro, many people undertake an earlier acclimatisation trek that sees them climb to a reasonable altitude before descending once more. The climb closest to and most accessible from Kilimanjaro is the ascent of Mount Meru, north of Arusha. Mount Meru is located in the Arusha National Park, which was once described by the British biologist, Sir Julian Huxley, as 'a gem amongst parks'.

At 4566m high, Mount Meru is more than 1000m lower than Kilimanjaro and, assuming you discount Mawenzi, is the second highest mountain in Tanzania and the fifth highest on the African continent. As such, it must not be underestimated. Overshadowed by the larger mountain to the east, Mount Meru is nonetheless a very impressive freestanding volcano in its own right. It makes a superb four-day trek that is very rewarding and picturesque, while also serving as an excellent introduction as to what to expect on Kilimanjaro. The trek involves walking through forest and grassland on the lower slopes, before completing a dramatic and exhilarating ridge-walk to the summit that provides stunning views of the Ash Cone lying several hundred metres below in the crater.

The local Waarusha people maintain that the volcano is sacred. Although they conducted animal sacrifices on its slopes, it is unlikely that they ever climbed to the top. First sighted by Europeans in 1862, the mountain was probably first climbed in either 1901, by Carl Uhlig, or 1904, by Fritz Jaeger, well over a decade after Kilimanjaro's summit had been claimed. Without the prestige of its neighbour, it has since received far less foot traffic than Kilimanjaro.

Mount Meru is a perfectly conical shape. It was formed by volcanic activity associated with the creation of the Rift Valley a quarter of a million years ago. It has an internal crater surrounded by precipitous cliffs, some of which are more than 1500m high. More recent eruptions, some within the last 100 years, have resulted in the formation of a resurgent ash cone.

One of the great advantages of tackling a climb here is the superior abundance of wildlife; over 400 species of birds and animals make their home on these slopes. The forests are also home to larger game than is seen on Kilimanjaro and you may spot giraffe, bushbuck, warthog, colobus monkeys and even elephants and buffalos in the course of your climb through the forest and moorland. As the mountain receives less visitors than Kilimanjaro, the animals are yet to be scared away by the frequent and heavy presence of people.

For a four-day trek, expect to pay upwards of US$350 in fees. In order to climb Mount Meru, you must pay a Conservation Fee, previously called the Arusha National Park entrance fee. This is US$45 per day. There are also hut fees (US$30 per day), a rescue fee (US$20 per trek) and, as all groups are obliged to take a national park guide, guide fees (US$15 per day) to pay. The national park guide who has to accompany you is a national park ranger, who is there to make sure that you remain safe on the mountain, rather than show you the way. These guides carry guns in case of unexpected contact with wild animals, but they will avoid having to use them.

While you can trek on Meru independently, albeit with the compulsory national park guide, the saving is negligible once you've factored in your own food, transfers and the fact you'll probably still want a porter or two to help ease the burden of climbing with all your kit. So, although you don't need to take porters on the trip, you may wish to. Most outfitters that organise climbs on Kilimanjaro will also be able to set up an ascent of Mount Meru and, if using an agency to arrange your trek, expect to have to factor in the cost of a guide, cook and porter team. Agency rates for climbing Mount Meru start around US$700 per person for four days. Tips for the guide and any porters that you hire are not included in this price and your budget ought to allow for this. A guideline would be for each climber to pay around US$50 per day on the mountain, to be split by the whole porter team.

There are opportunities to camp on the Momela Route – there are pitches adjacent to each of the huts along the trail. The huts can not be booked and instead operate on a first come, first served basis, so it may be as well to carry a tent in case you arrive late and find that the huts are already full. Whether you choose to camp or find yourself doing so out of necessity, you will have to pay the hut fees.

ROUTE X

Mount Meru Momela Route

Start/Finish	Momela Gate
Distance	38km; or 35km
Grade	Moderate/hard
Time for the round trip	4 days
Altitude gain	3066m
Note	Some groups combine the third (summit) day and the fourth (descent) day. This is entirely possible, but does mean that the summit day is very lengthy, since you must descend right off the mountain in the same day.

The Momela Route is the only available route to the summit of Mount Meru. It begins on the eastern side of the mountain and climbs to the summit via the northern shoulder of a horseshoe-shaped crater. The climb takes four days. Since this is most often done as an acclimatisation trek, there is no point in rushing and wasting the opportunity on hand.

Day 1 Momela Gate to Miriakamba Huts

The first day is a 4–5hr trek over almost 14km that ascends just over 900m. The trek begins at **Momela Gate** (1600m), from where it crosses the Ngare Nanyuki River and climbs through the increasingly dense and verdant forest. There are good opportunities for spotting wildlife on these early stages so keep your eyes peeled for baboons, dik dik and other antelope. The path crosses a number of streams and passes several excellent viewpoints that show the wide open plains and Momela Lakes. There are also several well signposted Kilimanjaro viewpoints that gaze across to the enormous massif nearby too. Ascend under a sacred **Fig Tree Arch** created by a giant strangler fig that bridges the path and past the **Itikoni Clearing**. Beyond here, there's the potential to step off the path and explore the **Maio Falls** before re-joining the track and continuing towards the crater. The path emerges onto more moorland-like terrain, which it crosses, affording you unrestricted views. At the far side of this scenic plateau the path descends slightly to the **Miriakamba Huts** (2504m).

There are two smart bunkhouses at **Miriakamba Huts** (with bunks and mattresses) that can accommodate 48 people, along with a dining hut. Long-drop toilets and a good water source are nearby.

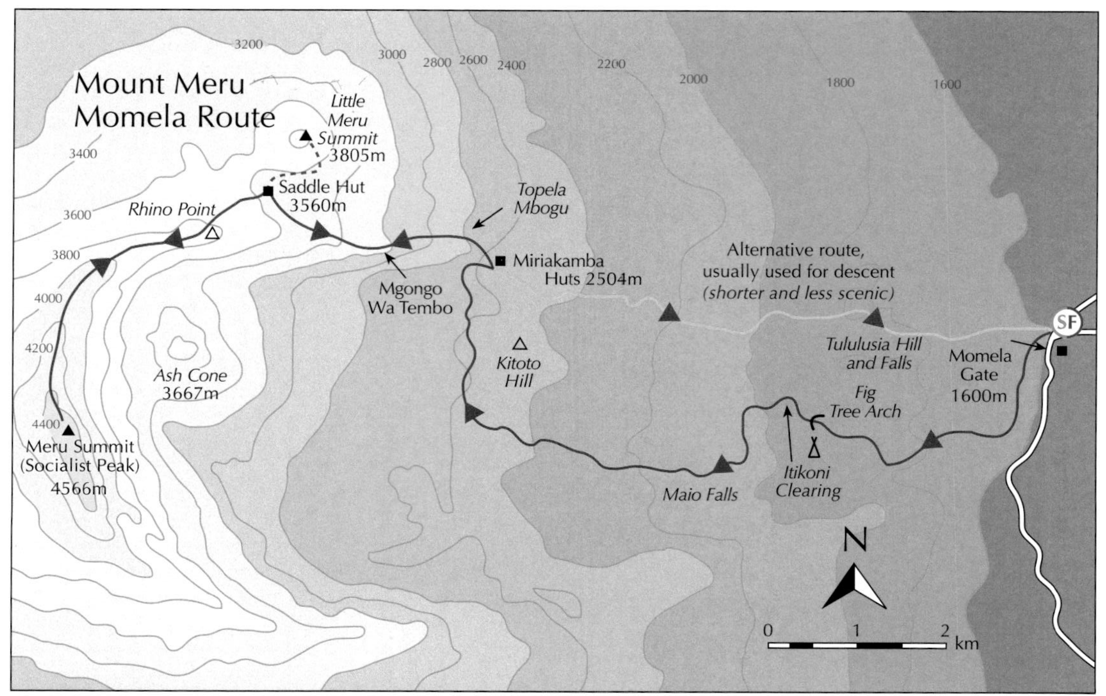

Mount Meru
Momela Route
Little Meru Summit 3805m
Saddle Hut 3560m
Rhino Point
Topela Mbogu
Miriakamba Huts 2504m
Mgongo Wa Tembo
Alternative route, usually used for descent (shorter and less scenic)
SF
Kitoto Hill
Ash Cone 3667m
Tululusia Hill and Falls
Momela Gate 1600m
Fig Tree Arch
Meru Summit (Socialist Peak) 4566m
Maio Falls
Itikoni Clearing
N
0
1
2 km
3200
3000
2800
2600
2400
2200
2000
1800
1600
3400
3600
3800
4000
4200
4400

Mount Meru at sunset seen from Shira Plateau on Kilimanjaro

Day 2 Miriakamba Huts to Saddle Huts

The second day covers 6km over 3hrs, climbing steeply to gain 1056m. The path winds through the pleasant forest, passing prosaically named **Topela Mbogo** (Buffalo Swamp) and **Mgongo wa Tembo** (Elephant Ridge), where you may still encounter wildlife and will certainly have good views of Kilimanjaro. From the ridge there are exceptional views into the crater. The path leaves the forest and continues up through the heath. It clambers onto a wide col between the slopes of Mount Meru and the secondary peak, Little Meru. The **Saddle Huts** (3560m) are set here.

> **Saddle Huts** comprise two decent bunkhouses, and long-drop toilets. Water is retrieved from a stream about 10mins away. Due to the short nature of the day, it is possible to take a detour to the top of Little Meru (3805m). The ascent takes a further hour and affords you superb views of the summit and of Kilimanjaro.

Day 3 Saddle Huts to the summit and return to Miriakamba Huts

This is a 5½km climb, ascending just over 1000m to the peak followed by an 11½km descent to Miriakamba Huts for the evening. This will take 9–11hrs. By leaving Saddle Huts at 2.00am, or just after, you ought to be on the summit of Mount Meru in time to see the sunrise behind the great bulk of Kilimanjaro.

The ascent to the top, along a narrow ridge rather than up a giant scree slope, is ideal preparation for an assault on Kilimanjaro's higher reaches but is not for the faint hearted.

The drops on one side are sheer and the exposed nature of the path can prove too much for more timid trekkers.

Aim first for **Rhino Point** (3875m), by heading across a plateau behind the hut before climbing steeply. The point is marked by a cairn and takes around 1hr to reach. The path then drops slightly before rising more steeply to start to edge around the rim of the crater. Walk around the rocky crater rim for a further 4–5hrs climbing steeply and precariously in places to reach the summit (4566m), once known as Socialist Peak, from where the views are outstanding. There are vistas over Arusha to the west, towards Kilimanjaro and Mawenzi to the east and Mount Meru's own ash cone lying just below you.

The descent (altitude loss: 2062m) is along the same path, although it looks entirely different with the sun upon it. It takes 3–5hrs to return to Saddle Huts depending on the conditions, and a further 1½–2hrs to descend to Miriakamba Huts.

Day 4 Miriakamba Huts to Momela Gate

It takes 2–3hrs to descend the 10km from Miriakamba Huts to the Momela Gate the following day, along the same route that you used to climb the mountain.

Alternative descent

Alternatively, there is a shorter, slightly more direct route that takes 2hrs to descend around 7km through a scenic stretch of forest, across an open plain and back to the gate. If you've time, there's also a detour to take in the impressive **Tululusia Falls**, which lie just a little way off the path.

CLIMBING KILIMANJARO

Karanga Camp, Machame Route (photo: Steve Lagreca/Shutterstock.com)

There are a number of ways to approach and climb Kilimanjaro. Six forest and heath/moorland routes begin on the lower slopes and ascend to 3500–4000m. These routes then usually merge with the Southern Circuit Path before linking to one of three final summit ascent routes. From the summit there are two separate descent routes that are affiliated to each of the earlier climbs. The easiest way to make sense of this jumble is to study the Kilimanjaro region map.

Typically, when you sign up with an outfitter to tackle Kilimanjaro, you sign up for a particular combination of routes; the most common might see you undertake the Machame-Mweka Route, which would climb the mountain along the Machame Route and then return to its foot along the Mweka Route. The second most popular trek uses the Marangu Route as both an ascent and descent route. If you sign up for one of the other paths, you will agree to tackle a particular combination of ascent and descent routes in advance of your departure.

Each of the six initial ascent routes – the Marangu (Route A), Machame (Route B), Umbwe (Route C), Lemosho (Route D), Shira (Route E) and Rongai (Route F) routes – are all detailed in the Ascent routes section (please see the Routes on Kilimanjaro map and the Route comparison table at the beginning of the book). There are also full descriptions of the three final ascent routes – Normal/Marangu Route (Route I), Barafu Route (Route J) and Western Breach Route (Route K) – to the crater rim in the Summit ascent routes section. There is a description of the Southern Circuit Path (Route G) and Northern Circuit Path (Route H) that circle Kibo at around 4000m in the Circuit paths section. After a full description of the summit, there follows descriptions of the two descent routes – the Marangu (Route L) and Mweka (Route M) routes – in the Descent routes section.

ASCENT ROUTES

ROUTE A

Marangu Route

Start	Marangu Gate
Finish	Kibo Huts
Distance	29km
Grade	Moderate/hard
Time	3 days
Altitude gain	2810m
Total time on the mountain	5 days
Summit route	Normal/Marangu Route; no option of Western Breach
Descent route	Marangu Route

The Marangu Route is the oldest and one of the quickest methods of ascending Kilimanjaro, typically taking 5 days in total to climb, ascend the summit via the Normal/Marangu Route and descend again, retracing your steps via the Marangu Route. It's also one of the seemingly easier and more popular routes on the mountain, at one time drawing over 80% of trekkers on Kilimanjaro. As a consequence of its mass appeal and accessibility, it came to be known as the 'Coca-Cola route'. It is also somewhat unfairly referred to as the 'tourist route'. This is to underestimate the ascent, which is in reality still a challenging undertaking. Much of the misconception about its simplicity stems from the fact this is the only route on the mountain where you sleep in huts rather than under canvas. Nonetheless, you must still gain a similar altitude to some of the longer routes, just in less time, which goes some way to explaining why there is a surprisingly poor success rate on this ascent.

Numbers on the Marangu Route have fallen with the improvement and promotion of alternative routes on the mountain. However, because it is also used as a means of descending the mountain, you are unlikely to ever feel truly alone or isolated in the huts or campsites along the track.

The Marangu Route ascends up the south-east side of Kilimanjaro through fine forest and moorland scenery. Although this is far from a genuine wilderness experience, the route is still very beautiful and the forest sections in particular are attractive. The route passes to the south of Mawenzi before it crosses the desolate Saddle heading towards Kibo Huts. The summit ascent is then conducted via the Normal/Marangu

Route on an arduous scree slope that culminates in the arrival at Gillman's Point on the crater rim. Uhuru Peak can then be reached from here.

The descent route for this particular trail is traditionally back along the Marangu Route. Steps are retraced from the summit to Horombo Huts, before you eventually walk off the mountain via the Marangu Gate.

Most people complete the route in only five days and as a consequence it has a surprisingly low success rate for getting trekkers to the top. Many people fail to acclimatise properly on the way up the mountain and as a result succumb to the debilitating effects of altitude on the final haul to the crater rim, or simply peak at Gillman's Point. In order to increase your chances of reaching Uhuru Peak, you should try to factor in an extra day for acclimatisation purposes. Ideally this should be taken at Horombo Huts, from where you can enjoy a number of fascinating side trips to explore various features of the mountain.

To the trailhead

The Marangu Route begins from the Kilimanjaro National Park Headquarters at the Marangu Gate. This is best accessed from the small town of Marangu, on the southeast side of Kilimanjaro, some 40km drive from Moshi. Most trekking companies will ensure that you are transported to the trailhead from where you are staying. On the drive to the Marangu Gate take the time to observe your changing surroundings.

From Moshi, follow the sealed Arusha–Taveta road towards Dar es Salam for just over 20km. At the small, bustling town of Himo, the road turns left and heads north for 13km to arrive at the sprawling, unkempt Marangu. The fact that the road is paved all of the way to the town is a reflection of the economic impact that Kilimanjaro has had on the region in general and on Marangu in particular. In the centre of town, at the main junction, turn left again and follow the track uphill for 6km to the park gate. The journey from Moshi to the trailhead takes 45 minutes to an hour and represents a gain in altitude of almost 1000m.

At the park gate, all the formalities for entering the national park can be completed. This can be a laborious process and you should expect to spend up to an hour registering and paying the requisite park fees. Your guide ought to take responsibility for ensuring that you are registered correctly and that your park fees are paid in full. In addition to the registration office there is a visitor centre, toilet block, picnic area and souvenir shop. If you find that you're missing a piece of kit, you can hire various bits (including gaiters and trekking poles) from the Kilimanjaro Guides Cooperative, who have a small hut at the gate. This is also the headquarters of KINAPA, the Kilimanjaro National Park.

Huts and accommodation

The Marangu Route is the only route on the mountain to have sleeping huts provided at every night stop. A-frame buildings house communal dormitories, where basic bunks and sponge mattresses are supplied – note that although you can leave the thermarest or roll mat behind, you'll still need to bring a sleeping bag. The huts have solar powered lights and cold running water. Basic toilet facilities are also present at each hut. Groups dine together in a large communal hut, resulting in a jovial, lively atmosphere and a great deal of interaction. It is often possible to purchase soft drinks, bottled water and even beer at the huts, although the prices increase as you climb higher up the mountain. Make sure that you carry small Tanzanian notes to pay for things bought along the route.

During the peak season, huts can sometimes be over full as a result of large groups altering their itineraries. As a result, the facilities can become overstretched. Each hut has a number of tent pitches in the immediate vicinity and it is possible to camp at each site. Those camping can take advantage of the toilet and water facilities provided but are forbidden from using the hut dining or communal areas.

The first night stop is at Mandara Huts. The lowest hut on the Marangu Route was originally constructed before World War I. It was christened Bismarck Hut, after the Iron Chancellor of Prussia in recognition of his significant role in the construction of the German Empire. The original stone hut has since been replaced by a series of comfortable wooden A-frame huts, built by a group of Norwegians as part of an aid programme. The largest hut comprises a communal dining area and an upstairs bunkroom. Smaller huts sleep up to eight people each. In total some 80 walkers can be accommodated here. There are flush toilets behind the main cabin. Water is retrieved from springs above the hut and is piped to the toilet block.

The second and fourth nights are spent at Horombo Huts. This was originally named Peters Hut, after Karl Peters, the German explorer and arch-imperialist. Similar to Mandara Huts, this vast complex comprises a number of wooden A-frame huts and

Horombo Huts and Kibo in the background

resembles a small village. Horombo is designed to support up to 160 people, making it the busiest overnight stop on the entire mountain. Groups both ascending and descending the mountain use the site. There are flush toilets to the south-east of the main hut, down the slope a short distance. Water is piped from a stream to the north of the huts. It is forbidden to access the valley that contains the stream in a bid to ensure that the water supply remains clean and uncontaminated.

Kibo Huts, the third hut visited, is set at the foot of the final push to the summit. The original hut was built in 1932 and contained four bunks and a small stove. This has been replaced by a larger stone blockhouse that contains a small dining area and a number of dorm rooms that lead off a main corridor which sleeps around 60. A series of long-drop toilets are set to the south-west, behind the hut. There is no water available at Kibo Huts and all supplies must be carried here from the last water point on the ascent.

STAGE 1

Marangu Gate to Mandara Huts

Start	Marangu Gate (1905m)
Finish	Mandara Huts (2720m)
Distance	8km
Time	3–4hrs
Altitude gain	820m

This is a deceptively gentle introduction to the climb that may lull you into a false sense of security despite the fact that you are ascending almost all the time. The trail is clear and well maintained, and so you should be able to maintain a steady, gentle pace through the lower forest sections, ensuring that you arrive at Mandara Huts after three to five hours. If there have been quantities of rainfall, the going may be wet and slippery underfoot and the approach to the night's accommodation may take longer. You ought to aim to begin the route in the morning since the forest zone is prone to showers in the afternoons. Birds also tend to be more active first thing in the morning. This way you can enjoy a leisurely stroll through the forest and still have the afternoon spare to explore your surroundings.

The ascent begins by following the broad, well-maintained track that leads north behind the booking office into the forest. Just beyond the gate, on the left-hand side of the track, is an archway that marks the start of the trekker's path to Mandara Huts.

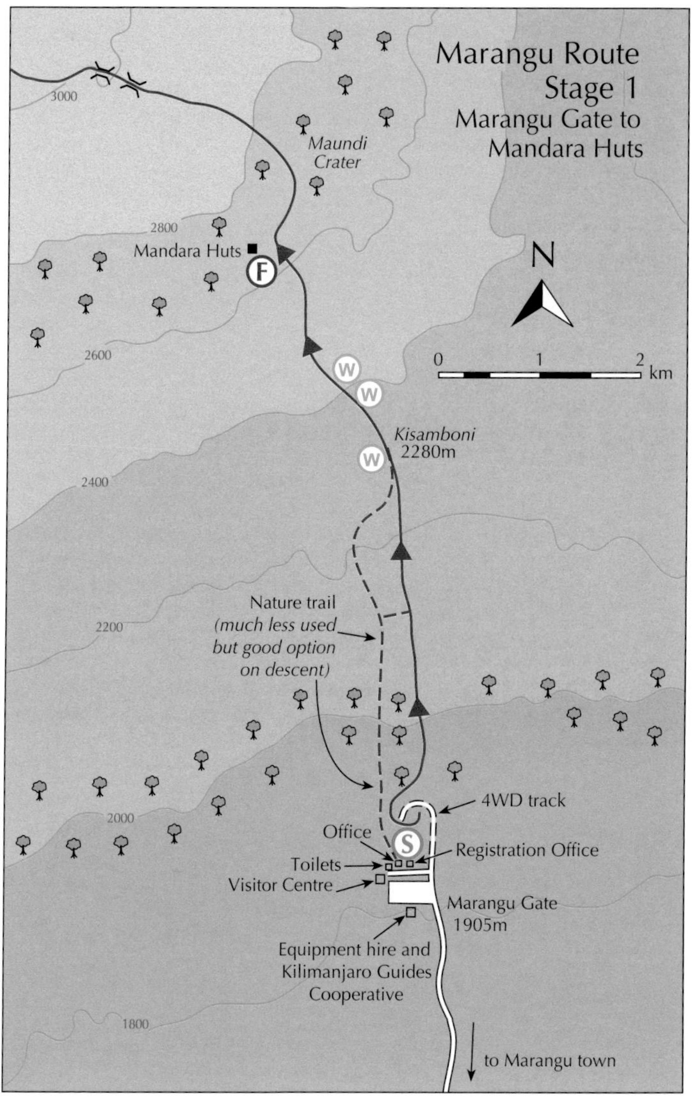
Marangu Route
Stage 1
Marangu Gate to
Mandara Huts
N
0
1
2
km
3000
2800
2600
2400
2200
2000
1800
Maundi
Crater
Mandara Huts
F
W
W
W
Kisamboni
2280m
Nature trail
(much less used
but good option
on descent)
4WD track
Office
S
Registration Office
Toilets
Visitor Centre
Marangu Gate
1905m
Equipment hire and
Kilimanjaro Guides
Cooperative
to Marangu town

MARANGU GATE

Your guide ought to take responsibility for ensuring that you are registered correctly and that your park fees are paid in full. The process is protracted and slow and can take up to an hour to complete. In the interim, relax, stroll around the gate area and visit the small shop located here. Admire the vast spreading *Albizia schimperiana* tree that supports the signboard at the trailhead and prepare yourself for the first stage of the ascent.

Near to the Marangu Gate is a short detour that visits a beautiful river gorge. Take the trail that leads to the left of the booking office and follow it west into a valley. Here there is a small seasonal waterfall, some tree ferns and a number of splendid trees whose huge oval leaves shade and shelter the smaller plants beneath.

Note also that there is a more westerly 'nature trail' that leads north from the car park and registration office that joins the main track about 2.5km further up. This path is much less frequently used and consequently much more overgrown, but makes for an interesting variation when you're descending the mountain, rather than simply retracing your steps. See Route L for details.

A broad **4WD track** leads straight ahead. This used to be the main route up the mountain, but in response to overcrowding and erosion, the path has been re-routed slightly. The original 4WD track is still used by porters to help accelerate their ascent and to ease the footfall on the forest path.

The forest path, for trekkers only, is a narrow clearly defined trail that provides intimacy and interest as you pass through this beautiful, chaotic aspect of the mountain. The path climbs steeply but gently, passing beneath huge *Macarangu kilimandscharica* trees and on into denser, more verdant forest that limits the amount of light that penetrates to the forest floor. The path is well graded and has drainage channels cut alongside it.

The trail sides are brimming with **plants and wildlife**. Overgrown and the cascading vegetation hides quantities of scarlet and yellow *Impatiens kilimanjari*, violet *I. pseudoviola* and the sweet-scented white *Begonia meyeri-johannis*. Away from the main gate you may see, or more likely hear, blue monkeys or black-and-white colobus monkeys moving through the tree tops as they search out and feed on fruits and leaves. Keep an ear out for the loud thrum of wings as Hartlaub's turaco flaps clumsily through the forest.

The trail heads towards and then runs alongside a small stream. After an hour, the path passes a small pool to the right that is backed by a waterfall. If there has been recent rain this can be a very attractive spot. There are also good views out over the

Typical montane cloudforest on the early stage of the Marangu Route

plains to the west of Kilimanjaro here.

Crossing the stream on a small bridge, the path comes to a junction where you continue straight on. The smaller path crosses a wooden bridge to Kisamboni, a picnic table and lunch area that lie adjacent to the 4WD track used by the porters. At this point you are approximately halfway between Marangu Gate and Mandara Huts.

The trail continues its consistent climb, passing another side path and bridge as well as a couple of small waterfalls. As the path becomes a little rockier it bridges another small stream and steepens slightly. This marks the final ascent to Mandara Huts.

The dense **Podocarp forest** becomes increasingly damp and bearded lichens, old-man's beard and other mosses become increasingly apparent, hanging from the trees like tattered lace, as you move into the alpine heath and moorland. *I. kilimanjari* continue to be visible amid the tree roots and buttresses.

Half an hour after crossing the bridge, the forest gives way and you emerge into the clearing that houses **Mandara Huts** (2720m).

This **collection of huts** is named after the legendary local chieftain who terrorised so many of the early western explorers as they sought to access and ascend Kilimanjaro in the late 19th century. The huts themselves are modern wooden A-frame buildings that have cold running water and flush toilet facilities. They can sleep up to 60 walkers. Surrounded by dense forest, they are frequently shrouded in mist during the afternoon and often have a peculiarly spectral air.

Excursion to Maundi Crater

If you arrive early and have the energy left to explore your surroundings, it is possible to stow your packs and clamber up nearby Maundi Crater. Or if your guide allows,

Mandara Huts sign at the Marangu Route first overnight stop

consider a detour so early at the start of the second day's trekking as the route to Horombo Huts passes quite close by.

From Mandara Huts the path heads north through the last vestiges of forest and emerges onto the heath and moorland after 500 metres. Beyond a small bridge is a junction, signposted to Maundi Crater. This small parasitic cone on the south-east flank of Kilimanjaro is an interesting geological feature, rich in wild flora and home to both colobus and blue monkeys.

The path climbs 500 metres to the top of the small grass and shrub-cloaked amphitheatre and affords you spectacular views on a clear day, both of the main peaks of Kibo and Mawenzi to the north and of lakes Chala and Jipe to the south-east, as well as the distant Pare Mountains. The trip there and back, to the top of crater, takes 1hr in total. See Marangu Route Stage 2 map for an outline of the route.

STAGE 2

Mandara Huts to Horombo Huts

Start	Mandara Huts (2720m)
Finish	Horombo Huts (3720m)
Distance	12km
Time	5–6hrs
Altitude gain	995m

This is an attractive day's walking that enables you to clear the confines of the forest and secure your first inspirational views of Kibo and Mawenzi. The steady climb through the more exposed, bleaker heath and moorland, past the unusual groundsel and *lobelias* found here, is relatively gentle although you ascend almost 1000m. The path is clear and even, ensuring that five to six hours of gentle walking should see you arrive at the village-like Horombo Huts complex.

From Mandara Huts the trail leads north through the remaining stretches of the forest zone.

In this section you will notice that the **vegetation** begins to change with Podocarps giving way to giant heath trees (*Philippia excelsa*) and bushes of *Hypericum* and *Erica*. Keep an eye and an ear out for monkeys active in the morning.

After 500 metres the trail emerges from the forest, crosses a wooden bridge and forks. A side path leads right to Maundi Crater while the main trail curves north-north-west and heads towards the Saddle. If you didn't explore it the previous evening, it is possible to detour to Maundi Crater and then cut across the scrub to rejoin the main path 500 metres further up the trail. It skirts the base of Maundi Crater and progresses towards the higher reaches of Kilimanjaro. Crossing a further two bridges over frequently dry waterways, the path winds gently between a series of thickets where the trees are festooned with lichen, before crossing several small bridges and ascending into the open moorland. The orangey-red path, visible between the tussocks of grass and heather, stretches into the distance enticingly.

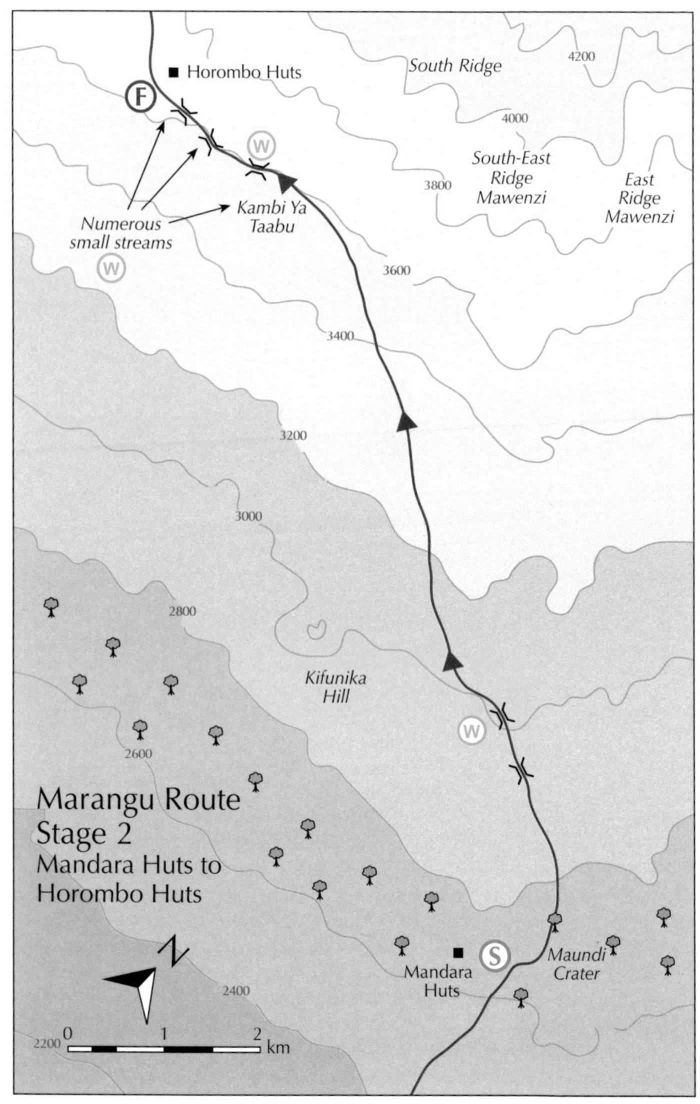
Horombo Huts
South Ridge
4200
4000
South-East
Ridge
Mawenzi
East
Ridge
Mawenzi
3800
Numerous
small streams
Kambi Ya
Taabu
3600
3400
3200
3000
2800
Kifunika
Hill
2600
Marangu Route
Stage 2
Mandara Huts to
Horombo Huts
Maundi
Crater
Mandara
Huts
2400
2200
0
1
2
km

Senecio kilimanjari close to Horombo (photo: Vadim Petrakov/Shutterstock.com)

From here you will get your first proper **views** of Kilimanjaro's two main peaks, with rugged Mawenzi in the foreground and snow-capped Kibo in the distance. Already they are looming large, but in fact the main summit is still two days' walk away from this point.

The trail undulates on its way to the Horombo escarpment, rising and falling as it negotiates a series of moorland ravines, which frequently have small streams running along the bottom. *Lobelias* can be seen growing in the damper, shadier parts of these ravines. As you drop into and then climb out of each hollow, the peaks of the mountain fall from view only to reappear fractionally closer as you clamber back up the other side.

The path climbs steeply onto a ridge and arrives at **Kambi Ya Taabu** 3½hrs after leaving Mandara Huts and so is frequently used as a lunch stop. The picnic table and rickety shelter here mark the three-quarter point to Horombo Huts.

The section of track immediately beyond this point is exceptionally pleasant, especially if the weather is clear and warm. The gradient decreases and the path eases across the flank of Kilimanjaro through a very pretty stretch of grasses, heathers and wild flowers. The small, colourful flowers and the spikes of 'red hot pokers' stand out against the palette of greens, browns and yellows that constitute the moorland vegetation.

A series of massive **wild fires** badly damaged a large section of the mountainside here. The evidence of these fires is still visible, with blackened shrubs, charred branches and ashy plants apparent along the path. However, there has been considerable regeneration in the interim period and new growth is flourishing and erasing the scar on the landscape.

HOROMBO HUTS

The Horombo Huts complex is a lively, noisy overnight stop, as a great many groups collect here. Both those going up the mountain on the Marangu Route and those on their way down from either the Marangu or Rongai routes use the huts. In addition, those opting to spend an additional day ascending on the Marangu Route for acclimatisation purposes are likely to do so here, further adding to the press of bodies.

As well as hut accommodation, there are extensive camping sites. Mawenzi's craggy spires rise from behind a ridge to the north of the complex, while above the huts a clear stream runs through the flora-filled valley, allowing giant *senecio* and *lobelia* to flourish. You must not enter this valley for any reason since you risk contaminating the complex's water supply.

As well as supporting a large number of walkers and their porters, the Horombo area is densely populated by four-striped mice. These opportunists have taken to scavenging for scraps and leftovers in and around the huts and during particularly mild seasons their numbers can reach plague proportions.

Directly below Horombo Huts are some interesting lava flows. The surface of these flows cooled more rapidly than their molten interiors, creating a tube-like crust. This crust sealed in the volcanic gasses and insulated the molten lava from the cool air, allowing it to continue to flow downhill, leaving behind a hollow tunnel. The hot interior lava re-fused some of the tube lava, which consequently re-crystallised as a glassy rock. Fragments of this can be seen all around the hut site.

The trail crosses a couple of small streams on little wooden bridges and climbs again to a point where you can see clearly up a *senecio*-filled valley. This valley lies to the north of the Horombo Huts and houses the stream that supplies the complex with water. Continuing to undulate, the path turns west to skirt a knoll and exposes the vast vista of plains and forest to the south of Kilimanjaro.

Having walked 1½hrs from Kambi Ya Taabu, the path rises sharply and enters a rocky valley at the foot of Mawenzi's southern lava ridges. The **Horombo Huts** (3720m) are situated here.

Optional acclimatisation day to Zebra Rock

If you choose to spend an extra day acclimatising on the Marangu Route, you are most likely to spend it based at Horombo Huts. On the extra day try to persuade your guide to climb above the huts with you to explore the lower section of the Saddle. See the Marangu Route Stage 3 map for an outline of the route. Follow the path as it leaves Horombo Huts and walk north-west until you reach a junction. Take the right-hand fork, which heads north towards Mawenzi and the Mawenzi huts.

The distinctly patterned Zebra Rock

After walking 1.5km from Horombo Huts, on the edge of the moorland zone, is a low, overhung cliff. Water seeping down the rock face from above has left pale encrustations deposited on the dark lava. The light and dark vertical bands on the cliff have led to this feature being known prosaically as **Zebra Rock**. From here it is also possible to explore the area around the lower slopes of Mawenzi, admiring its dramatic fluted visage and many shattered ridges. The trek to **Mawenzi Hut** takes about 2hrs while the return to Horombo can be completed in a little over 1hr, making it a good half-day outing and opportunity to further acclimatise.

STAGE 3

Horombo Huts to Kibo Huts

Start	Horombo Huts (3720m)
Finish	Kibo Huts (4710m)
Distance	9km
Time	5–6hrs
Altitude gain	990m

By this stage the enormity of Kilimanjaro will begin to sink in. The five to six-hour ascent from Horombo Huts to Kibo Huts is a lengthy trudge across the very exposed, starkly beautiful Saddle that allows you to contemplate the great mound of Kibo rising ahead of you. As you plod across the barren highland desert you will be rewarded with great views of Kibo and Mawenzi, at least until the clouds boil in and obscure the summits.

The trail leaves Horombo Huts and heads north-west then north, climbing steeply through an area of changing vegetation. As you gain height, the variety and quantity of plants diminish becoming smaller, hardier species: heathers and everlastings replace the *senecio* as you wind between large boulder outcrops.

There are two routes to the Saddle: the Southern Path and the Northern Path that merge again at Jiwe Lainkoyo.

The start of the less regularly used **Northern Path** branches right from the main path at the first junction you reach. This stony and badly eroded track veers north, past Zebra Rock, before curving north-west at East Lava Hill and bending left to pass by West Lava Hill and a pair of tarns. The path continues north, curving north-west past the junction with the Northern Circuit Path and crosses the Saddle to the north of Middle Red Hill before converging once more with the main Marangu Route at Jiwe Lainkoyo.

The Southern Path, the most commonly ascended of the two, continues north-west from the junction with the Northern Path briefly, before forking again. The left-hand fork here joins the Southern Circuit Path, which contours across the side of the mountain below the Saddle before curving around the southern side of Kibo to link up with the southern and western forest/moorland approach routes and the other summit access routes.

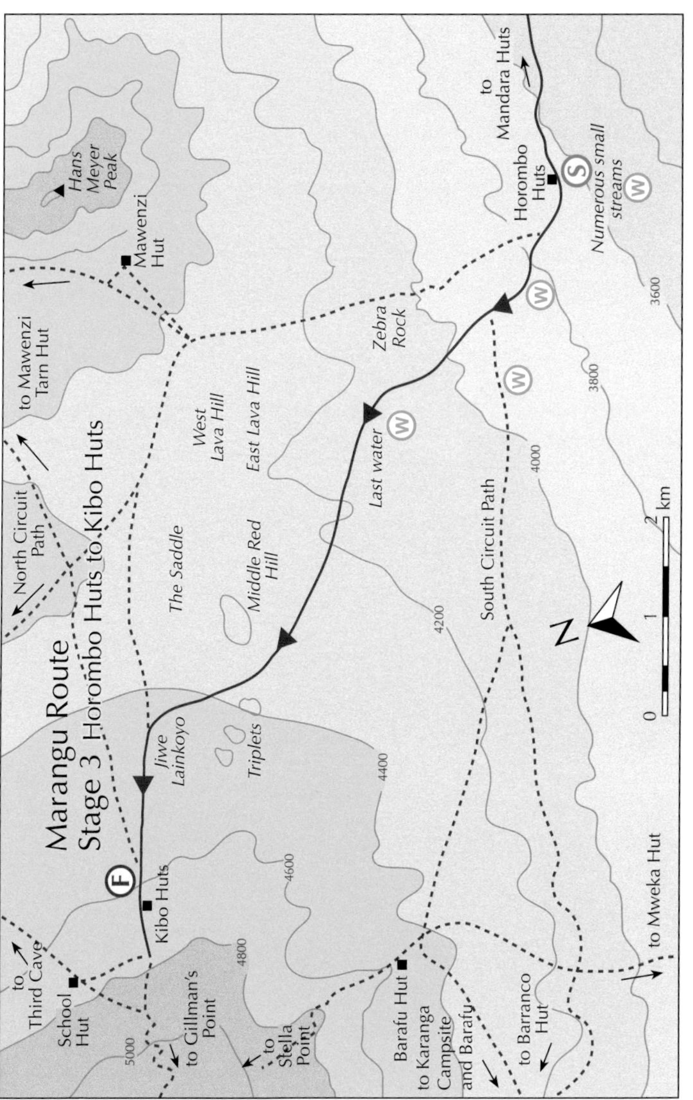
Marangu Route
Stage 3 Horombo Huts to Kibo Huts
Hans Meyer Peak
Mawenzi Hut
to Mawenzi Tarn Hut
North Circuit Path
West Lava Hill
East Lava Hill
The Saddle
Middle Red Hill
Zebra Rock
Last water
to Mandara Huts
Horombo Huts
S
Numerous small streams
W
3600
3800
4000
4200
4400
4600
4800
5000
South Circuit Path
Jiwe Lainkoyo
Triplets
F
Kibo Huts
to Third Cave
School Hut
to Gillman's Point
to Stella Point
Barafu Hut
to Karanga Campsite and Barafu
to Barranco Hut
to Mweka Hut
N
0
1
2 km

Take the right-hand fork instead and head north then north-west, gradually gaining height. After an hour's walking the path crosses the Maua River, where you can collect water. The path continues on this setting, rising and falling as it traverses the rumpled flank of the mountain, until it reaches the official, signposted last water point on this route. There are picnic tables adjacent to the stream.

This is the **highest running water** on the Marangu Route, although in reality it is a small, muddy stream that is generally inferior in quality to the Maua River. The explorer and mountaineer Hans Meyer named this point Schneequelle, meaning 'snow stream', since the stream he encountered here on his first ascent of Kilimanjaro emerged from a snow drift at that time.

About an hour beyond the last water signpost is another sign indicating that you are arriving on the Saddle.

Hans Meyer recorded that when breaching the **Saddle** in the 19th century he encountered six-foot drifts of snow on the southern slopes. This is likely to be an alien situation for most modern walkers since the Saddle is resolutely bare for much of the year now. Occasional blizzards do blanket the barren landscape in snow, but even without a white dusting, the expanse of sterile desertesque landscape is harshly beautiful.

The path continues to meander through this desolate place over orangey-red lava gravel, between small boulders and lava bombs and amid tough tufty grasses and

Lava bombs littering the barren Saddle

everlastings. The path passes to the south of **Middle Red Hill**, a large parasitic cone that provides some shelter from the gusting wind that bustles across the Saddle, and then bends to the north of the **Triplets**, some of Kibo's many parasitic cones.

Just north of the Triplets the two approach routes from Horombo Huts, the Southern and Northern paths, merge at **Jiwe Lainkoyo**, whose name translates as 'the painted rock'. This is reputed to be an old campsite once popular with local hunters. A third path that heads across the northern side of the Saddle from Mawenzi Tarn Hut converges with the two from the south here as well.

The broad path then heads west directly towards Kibo. Although the Kibo Huts are visible in the distance, sat on the lowest slopes of the summit cone, it is still a soul destroying and rather tiring hour trudge further on through an increasingly bleak landscape. Ascending past a large rocky outcrop the path arrives at the wind blasted, basic stone blockhouses that comprise **Kibo Huts**.

The **Kibo Huts**, sunk into the foothills of the summit they are named after, are a fairly hostile place to wait and prepare for the early morning ascent to Gillman's Point and Uhuru Peak. There are fine views to be enjoyed, however, of Mawenzi's austere, arresting west face, visible across the curving slope of the Saddle.

Continuing on from Kibo Huts to Gillman's Point and Uhuru Peak

From Kibo Huts the Normal/Marangu Route heads up Kibo's eastern scree slopes to Gillman's Point on the crater rim amid the eastern ice terraces (see Summit ascent routes, Route I). From here it is then possible to access the actual summit of the mountain. In total it's a gruelling 5hr plus climb over a little more than 6km of steep, unstable scree and rock, gaining around 1180m to finally stand on Uhuru Peak.

ROUTE B

Machame Route

Start	Machame Gate
Finish	Barafu Hut
Distance	35km
Grade	Hard
Time	4 days
Altitude gain	2850m
Total time on the mountain	6–7 days
Summit route	Barafu Route; option of Western Breach
Descent route	Mweka Route

The Machame Route is the westernmost route to scale the southern slopes of Kilimanjaro. Some people consider it to be the finest forest/moorland ascent route on the mountain. Hans Meyer wrote 'Without doubt Kibo is most imposing as seen from the west. Here it rises in solemn majesty, and the eye is not distracted by the sister peak of Mawenzi, of which nothing is to be seen but a single jutting pinnacle. The effect is

Lobelia growing below Kibo, viewed from Machame Route, Barranco Hutto Karanga Camp (photo: Steve Lagreca/Shutterstock.com)

enhanced by the magnificent flowing sweep of the outline, the dazzling extent of the icecap, the vast stretch of the forest, the massive breadth of the base, and the jagged crest of the Shira Spur as it branches away towards the west.'

The path itself begins climbing slowly through thick, leafy forest on the west flank of Kilimanjaro before emerging on the moorland. It then takes in the dramatic Shira Plateau, providing a glimpse of an unusual side of the mountain, before joining the Southern Circuit Path and contouring around the southern face of Kibo. The final summit bid can be made either via the perilous Western Breach, from Lava Tower and Arrow Glacier Hut, or, more usually, via the Barafu Route, which is reached by circumnavigating the peak beneath the spectacular Southern Icefields. Descent from the summit is then conducted on the Mweka Route, which drops quickly and steeply off the southern side of Kilimanjaro by way of the Mweka Hut to finish at the Mweka Gate. Whether you team the climb with either a thrilling ascent of the Western Breach or more commonly with the climb via the Barafu Route to the crater rim and then the traditional Mweka descent route, this is one of the loveliest, most complete outings on the mountain.

The route is slightly more challenging than some of the other forest/moorland routes but, like the other routes described here, it does not require any technical ability. Although the terrain is in parts tougher to negotiate than on other routes, the variety of vegetation, scenery and the stunning views of the Shira Plateau, the Western Breach and Kibo make this a highly attractive option.

The Machame and Mweka routes used to be simply rough tracks used by the park rangers or groups of mountaineers looking to access the technical climbing routes on this side of Kibo. Although improvements were made to the Machame trail in the 1970s, it wasn't until the 1990s that it began to gain in popularity as people recognised its myriad charms and began to appreciate that it offers you a better chance to acclimatise while ascending. Subsequently, it became known as the 'whiskey route', since it was harder, more expensive and much more intoxicating than the 'Coca-Cola route' (Marangu Route). A lot of work has been done in recent years to improve the track conditions further and promote this route as an alternative to the Marangu Route, largely to reduce the pressure of numbers on the traditional main tourist path. The result has been a significant upgrade in the track quality, which in turn has ensured that there has been a marked increase in foot traffic on this side of the mountain. The route has now surpassed the Marangu Route in terms of popularity and is the busiest on Kilimanjaro. As the total number of users has multiplied, so the campsites have swelled under the wave of new interest, meaning this route is no longer the wilderness experience it once was.

The success rate for reaching Uhuru has traditionally always been higher on the Machame Route than on the Marangu Route. No doubt this has been at least partly due to the fact that it provides a longer ascent and that consequently you are allowed to acclimatise better ahead of the final summit bid. It is also likely that the greater success was in part due to only more experienced groups choosing to ascend Kilimanjaro via this route. With the popularisation of the Machame Route, the percentage of people that successfully summit may fall as less capable groups opt to try this ascent route rather than the traditional Marangu Route. Maximise your own chances by building in extra acclimatisation days: if using the Barafu Route to the crater rim, stay an extra night in the Karanga Valley on the way to Barafu Hut. There is no obvious place on the Western Breach final ascent route to pause so, instead, stay an extra day at Barranco Hut.

Start of the Machame Route (photo: Polina Meleca/Shutterstock.com)

To the trailhead

The Machame Route begins from Machame Gate, adjacent to Machame village on the south-western side of the mountain. All of the registration formalities can be completed at the national park office found in one of the buildings here. Park fees are also paid at this point. Your outfitter will ensure that you are ferried to the gate by bus.

Machame village is 25km from the town of Moshi. To reach the village, follow the tarmac road from Moshi first west and then north for 45mins. Machame village itself is a straggling affair set amid fertile farmland. The final 3km approach to Machame Gate is through a series of banana and coffee plantations and via a small stretch of natural forest; it takes 15mins. The road that scales the final ridge to bring you to the gate is only a dirt track, but it is clear and well maintained. The gate itself is at 1810m.

There are toilet facilities at the gate. Local men are often stationed by the start in a bid to sell walkers water, gaiters or trekking poles, some fashioned from tree branches.

Huts and accommodation

Everyone on the Machame Route is obliged to camp. Although there are a series of old corrugated metal uniport cabins along the trail in varying states of disrepair, walkers are not intended to use them. Adjacent to each of these huts is an area cleared for camping. There are long-drop toilet facilities at each of the campsites, as well as, with the exception of the Barafu Hut, good water sources. Barafu is dry and all water supplies must be carried to this point.

The basic Machame Hut is a tatty uniport. There is a park ranger stationed here who will require you to register once you arrive at the campsite. The Shira Hut is a similar basic structure that is in such a state that most groups actually choose to camp south of the hut by the Shira Cave or, even further south, at the Shira Camp. The Barranco Hut, erected in 1966, is idyllically located but it is nonetheless a little shabby. There are two small uniports at Barafu that also date from the 1960s. Set amid a desolate lava landscape, they are as inhospitable as they look.

STAGE 1

Machame Gate to Machame Hut

Start	Machame Gate (1810m)
Finish	Machame Hut (3015m)
Distance	11km
Time	5–6hrs
Altitude gain	1205m

This is a fairly lengthy introduction to climbing Kilimanjaro, which passes through some of the finest forest scenery to encircle the mountain. Ascending steadily on a straightforward path, you are transported through lush montane cloudforest to arrive at the Machame Hut on the edge of the heath/moorland zone.

The ascent begins by following a broad 4WD dirt track as it loops around the warden's hut and begins to climb north and then north-east into the forest. The 4WD track rapidly dwindles and within 3km is reduced to a single track. At the end of the 4WD track is a **signpost**. Reached 45mins after leaving the gate, it states that the Machame Route is only to be used as an ascent route.

The path from this stage used to be a rough and unkempt way to access Kilimanjaro that involved scrambling over tree roots and up slippery, uneven sections of mountainside. However, a great deal of work has been carried out on this lower section of the route and the path is now well graded and even. Roots have been covered or cleared and drainage ditches dug alongside the track to ensure that it doesn't degenerate into a river channel during the heavy rains. In some places the new track crosses the remains of the older path and you can see just how different the two are. The transformation should make you appreciate just how much hard work has gone into creating the current highway, which has seen the track upgraded all of the way from the gate to Machame Hut.

The path meanders through close, intensely green **forest** where lianas and mosses cover camphor, cedar, juniper and olive trees. The endemic *Impatiens kilimanjari* is also prevalent here, as are *I. pseudoviola* and *Viola eminii*. This stretch of the forest is particularly attractive. Birdlife here is abundant and vocal, although you will need to have quick eyes or boundless reserves of patience to actually see the turacos, hornbills and other avifauna that are creating the diverting sounds.

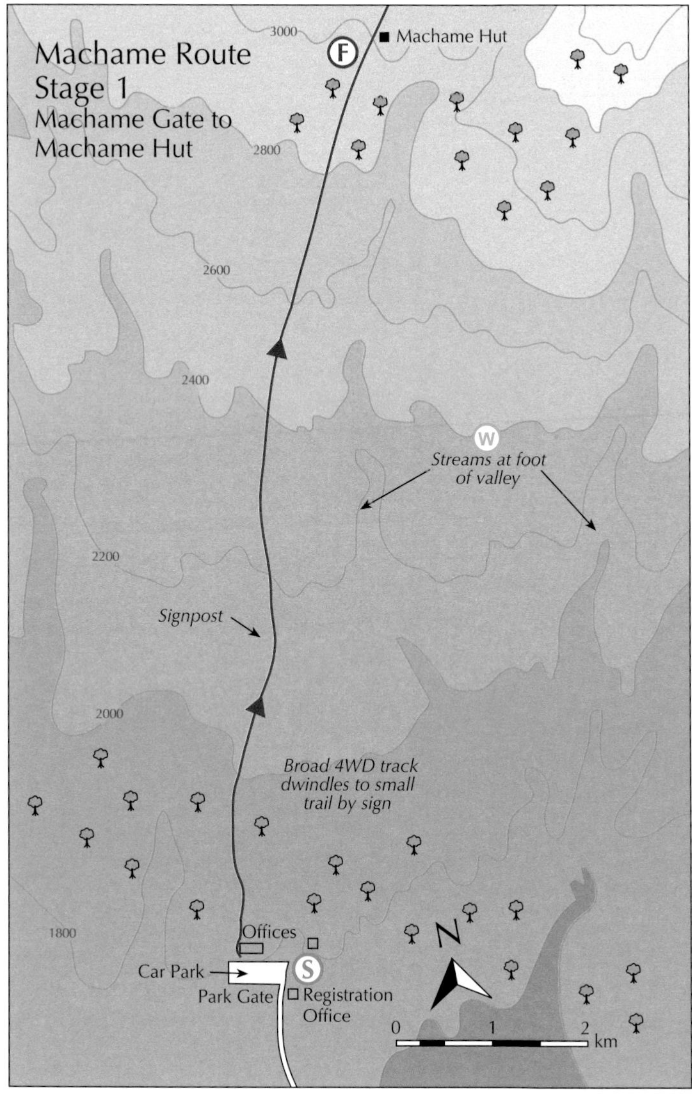
Machame Route
Stage 1
Machame Gate to
Machame Hut
3000
Machame Hut
2800
2600
2400
Streams at foot
of valley
2200
Signpost
2000
Broad 4WD track
dwindles to small
trail by sign
1800
Offices
Car Park
Park Gate
Registration
Office
N
0
1
2
km

Porters ascending through the forest towards Machame Hut

The track rises along an increasingly vertiginous ridge, although the drops to either side are largely obscured by the thick vegetation. What breaks there are in the undergrowth reveal stunning views across forest-blanketed ridges. There is a lot of interest here and walking slowly and carefully will allow you to absorb what's around you.

After 2½hrs the trail passes through a large clearing in the forest that is often used as a lunch stop. There is a long-drop toilet here. After this point the gradient increases somewhat as the ridge steepens slightly. To the north you can frequently hear the sound of water, rising from the stream, which runs parallel to the track, at the foot of the ravine. It is also possible to spot a miniature waterfall to the right of the track where another small stream passes close by the foot of the ridge. The path continues to ascend through the forest on a clearly discernible path for a further 2½hrs.

This section transitions from **forest to scrub**; the larger trees loaded with moss and old man's beard merge with and then give way to giant heathers and

Trees festooned with old man's beard at Machame Hut

scrub. Scarlet *Gladiolus watsonioides* and red and yellow red-hot pokers lie among the grasses. A signpost adjacent to the track warns of potential fire hazards and the risk of dropping lit cigarettes in this often tinderbox-dry area.

After 15mins of this transformation beginning, the path breaks cover and arrives at **Machame Hut** (3015m).

MACHAME HUT

There are a handful of tent pitches along the approach to the battered uniport, but the majority of the better pitches are on the higher ground above the hut. There should be a park warden resident in a registration hut here who will require you to sign a register upon arrival. He can also sell you water or even beer at this point. There are long-drop toilet facilities in the vicinity of each tent pitch and water can be retrieved from a small stream found 30m from the campsite to the north-west of the site, down a steep slope.

Unfortunately, the campsite is frequently cloaked in mist and low cloud during the afternoon, so views of the mountain will be obscured. Early mornings are often clear, however, and you will be able to see the dome of Kibo rising above a ridge to the east. Looking the other way, out across the plains to the south-west, you will be able to pick out Mount Meru amid the morning haze.

STAGE 2

Machame Hut to Shira Camp

Start	Machame Hut (3015m)
Finish	Shira Camp (3840m)
Distance	5.5km
Time	5–6hrs
Altitude gain	825m

Following an energetic start to the day and an aggressive ascent of a steep volcanic fin that juts out of the mountainside, the terrain levels and the path eases onto the Shira Plateau, an atmospheric, ancient part of Kilimanjaro with excellent views onward to Kibo and away to Mount Meru.

As the early morning sun climbs above Kibo to the east of Machame Hut, follow the path that heads north-east towards a rocky ridge. The ridge, made from a petrified lava flow, protrudes from the mountain and is clearly visible from the Machame Hut. As you traipse up through the scrub, keep an eye open for glimpses of Kibo to your right, looming larger as you climb above the surrounding foothills. There are several clearings on the ascent, the first reached half an hour after leaving the hut site; from here you can gaze back over Machame Hut and the closely packed canopy of trees that stretch westwards towards Mount Meru.

The path loops from one side of the ridge to the other, crossing the crest of the ridge several times. As the path climbs, the vegetation around it alters and you find yourself leaving the skeletal trees to walk amid hardy tussock grasses and *senecio*. There are several large boulders on the ridge top that offer a superb view east to Kibo, although mid-morning cloud frequently mounts up and obscures the summit.

The path arrives at the foot of an 8m-high semi-circular rock cliff 2hrs after leaving Machame Hut. The ascent used to be relatively straightforward, amounting to nothing more than a scramble, but it has been further simplified with the creation of some cut steps in the rock face.

Having surmounted this obstacle, take a **break** for lunch and admire the views. Beyond here you can see the renovated path returns to its rougher original format and drops into a relatively sheltered, scenic valley dotted with *senecio* and everlastings.

The valley below is another point where some groups pause to have lunch. Large white-necked ravens often scavenge and can be seen soaring above the area or hopping awkwardly from boulder to boulder in search of scraps. The route ahead is visible from here and it is possible to make out the path as it skirts the head of the valley beneath the lip of the Shira Plateau, before rising north to access the plateau.

The path eases horizontally across a steep slope above the head of the valley. It crosses several small, smooth streambeds before clambering past a series of large boulders and rocky outcrops onto the flatter, easier ground of the Shira Plateau. The path then meanders over the plateau on an almost level gradient, winding around rocky patches of shale and clumps of everlastings. *Lobelias* also appear here for the first time.

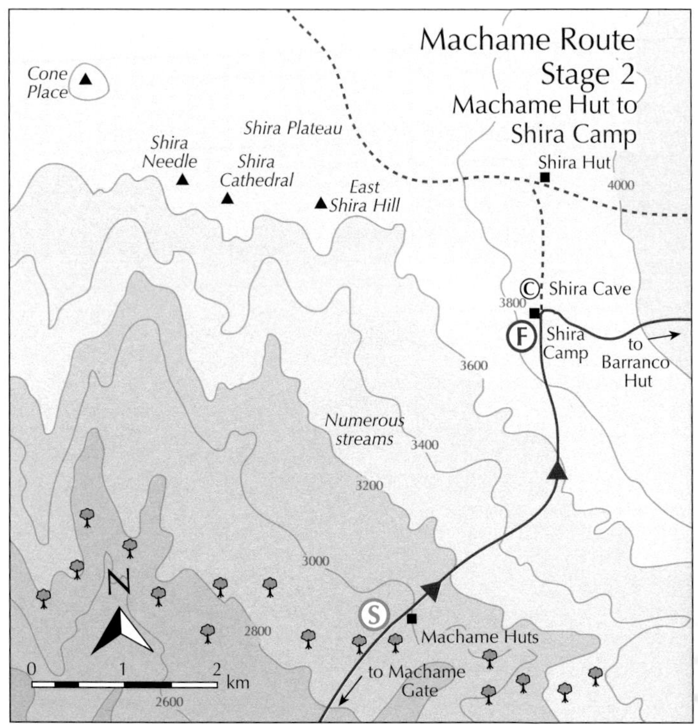

Shira Camp on the Shira Plateau

Shiny black chunks of obsidian, formed by the very rapid solidification of lava, litter the Shira Plateau and act as potent reminders that this area is in fact the remains of the oldest of the three volcanic cones that comprise the Kilimanjaro massif. Indeed, the final descent to the campsite, across the caldera, is on a giant solidified lava flow, clearly visible amid the dust and gravel beneath your feet.

Continuing north, the path arrives at a rough cleared patch of ground an hour after the lunch stop. This is the overnight campsite for most groups. The **Shira Camp** (3840m) is just south of the **Shira Cave** and about 30mins south of the Shira Hut, which sits on the Shira Route to Kibo. At the campsite there are long-drop toilets, and a clean stream can be found some 10mins to the south-east of the site.

THE PLATEAU

The plateau is exposed and barren, but has a number of fascinating features. From the campsite you'll be able to see the striking, jagged Shira Ridge edge to the west, about 1–1½hrs' walk away. The three high points on the sheer ridge, looking west to east, are the Shira Needle, Shira Cathedral and East Shira Hill. The Shira Needle has a small, precarious summit that can be reached by scrambling awkwardly up a serious rock face. The Shira Cathedral is a dramatic rock buttress set amid a series of pinnacles and spires, with sheer drops of several hundred metres apparent on the southern face. The small rounded, grassy peak behind this ridge is the Shira Cone (3840m), which is also known as Cone Place. The highest point on the plateau is its far western extremity, where Johnsell Point (3962m) and Klute Peak are visible behind the Shira Cone. If you pan left from the end of the ridge, you'll get great views of Mount Meru to the south-west, particularly at sunset when the sun drops below the horizon adjacent to Meru's perfect cone.

STAGE 3

Shira Camp to Barranco Hut

Start	Shira Camp (3840m)
Finish	Barranco Hut (3985m)
Distance	10.5km
Time	5–6hrs
Altitude gain	145m

This is a superb day's walking that showcases some of Kilimanjaro's finest features as you move around the mountain's flank. The path climbs across the Shira Plateau to a high point by Lava Tower, an ascent of around 800m, before dropping around 650m into the Barranco Valley to arrive at Barranco Hut, a mere 145m higher than the day's start point. This climb-high, sleep-low approach to scaling Kilimanjaro maximises your ability to acclimatise and improves your chance of successfully reaching the summit. The views of the Shira Plateau, Lava Tower and the western face of Kibo are sumptuous, and the final campsite affords you with some of Kilimanjaro's classic viewpoints.

From the Shira Camp, the path heads east aiming directly towards Kibo. As it negotiates the rocky plateau, the path intersects one that leads from Shira Cave. The path climbs gently east along a fin of petrified lava, undulating across the creases of the **Shira Plateau**.

After 2½hrs, the track is joined from the left by a small trail that leads from Shira Hut and is part of the Shira and Lemosho routes. Ignore the junction and continue on what is now technically part of the **Southern Circuit Path**. The path veers south-east, drops into a broad, rock-strewn valley and then regains the lost height, rising evenly and gently towards Kibo. To the left of Kibo, in the foreground, is a line of hills; this is the Oehler Ridge. The path leads in a southerly direction and passes through an area of interesting rock formations.

There is a very real sense of being in the **wilderness** here. Large boulders are perched precariously on eroded plinths of smaller stones bound together by mud, providing surreal looking sculptures. The rocks are variously patterned with grey and orange lichens and provide scant protection for small clumps of everlastings. The walk in towards Kibo is startlingly austere. Ahead the impressive ice-frosted cliffs of Kibo are visible, as are the first views of the Western Breach.

If the weather is clear the views are astounding. Swirling cloud teases and tantalises you with glimpses of the summit. The high-speed winds that race across the summit create unusual cloud formations and can cause a cloud cap to form that sits snugly atop the summit.

After half an hour the path splits, with forks passing either side of a distinctive black wedge-shaped outcrop of rock. To the left of this landmark is the orange-black volcanic plug known as the **Lava Tower** (4635m). Those tackling the Western Breach ascent to the crater rim will camp in the lee of the Lava Tower overnight before climbing to Arrow Glacier Hut for their summit bid. See Route K.

Regardless of which ascent to Uhuru Peak you plan to undertake, most groups will follow the left-hand fork, which climbs slightly up to the Lava Tower to make the

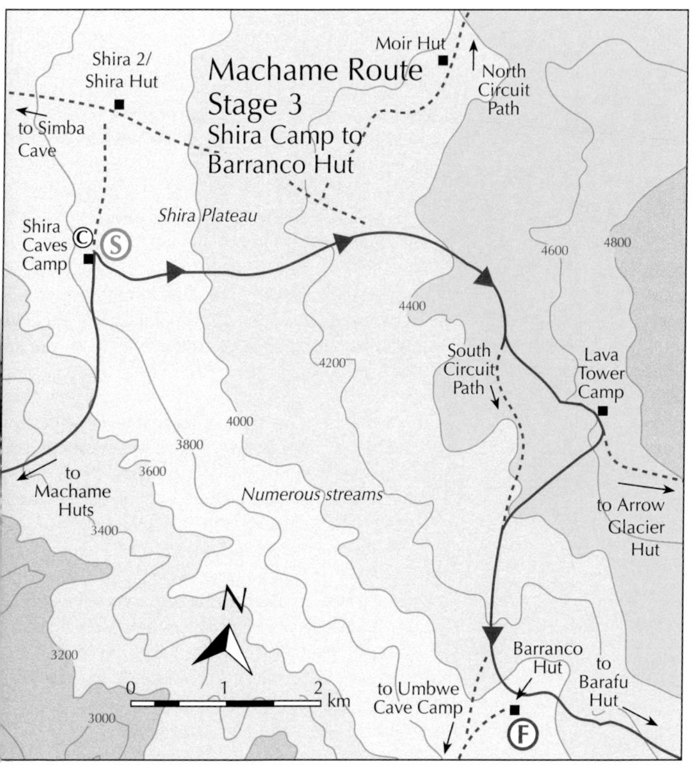

Path on the Machame Route (photo: Lexan/Shutterstock.com)

most of being at this elevated altitude before descending to camp at Barranco Hut. The right-hand fork passes to the south of the Lava Tower, and is re-joined by the path descending from the Lava Tower after 1km. Your porters will almost certainly take this route, since it is a shorter, more direct route to the Barranco Valley. This is undertaken to benefit from acclimatising at a higher altitude before dropping lower to sleep; you also get the best possible views of the Western Breach. It is possible to climb the 60m tower itself although the scramble up the northern side of the Lava Tower is not clearly indicated at any point. Ask your guide to show you the way and take extreme caution while climbing the steep rock face. There are exemplary 360° panoramic views from the top of the tower (4635m). The sheer immensity of the landscape seen from here is staggering. The climb up and down takes half an hour from the foot of the tower.

Take the path from the far side of the Lava Tower that drops into a rocky valley, fords a small stream of meltwater and climbs a slope in order to crest a ridge before re-joining the path that leads to the Barranco Valley.

After the paths have rejoined to the south of the Lava Tower, the path drops down a loose scree slope in a series of zigzags. At the foot of the slope it crosses several branches of Bastions Stream. The path them scrambles back up a rock-strewn ridge and passes a well-signposted junction to the left that leads directly to Arrow Glacier and the foot of the Western Breach.

The path continues south for an hour, descending a stony ridge, before dropping steeply into the Great Barranco Valley past quantities of *senecio* and *lobelia*.

The **Great Barranco Valley** is the result of an enormous landslip that occurred over 100,000 years ago. The slip broke away part of Kibo's crater rim, creating the less steep gradient of the Western Breach, and scored a deep gash in the mountainside. The views of this enormous gash, which is over 300m deep here, are superb and offer virtually unparalleled sights of the Western Breach and Southern Icefields. To the right of the Western Breach, the vast, vertical, Breach Wall and other sheer cliffs rise imperiously from the head of the valley to create an almost impenetrable rampart. On the far side of the valley, the 300m Barranco Wall stands, appearing to block the following day's progress around the southern face of Kibo.

Perched on the edge of the final descent to the floor of the Great Barranco Valley is the dramatically sited **Barranco Hut** (3985m).

Barranco Hut is an old uniport that is battered and grubby, but fortunately there are very attractive sites to pitch a tent all around the area. There are long-drop toilets to hand and several streams from which to draw water.

STAGE 4

Barranco Hut to Barafu Hut

Start	Baranco Hut (3985m)
Finish	Barafu Hut (4660m)
Distance	8km
Time	7–8hrs
Altitude gain	675m

This is a potentially long and difficult day because of the distance and altitude. The early stages are focused on traversing the attractive Great Barranco Valley and overcoming the stiff challenge posed by the ascent of the Barranco Wall. Having overcome this obstacle, the gradient relents as the path contours around the southern face of Kibo, under the massed ranks of the Southern Icefields, before making an arduous, tiring approach to Barafu Hut. Some people choose to split the section, camping overnight in the Karanga Valley to aid acclimatisation.

It is well worth waking early to catch the sunrise at Barranco Hut, since it can be spectacular to watch the light strike the dramatic slopes and catch the eternal snows.

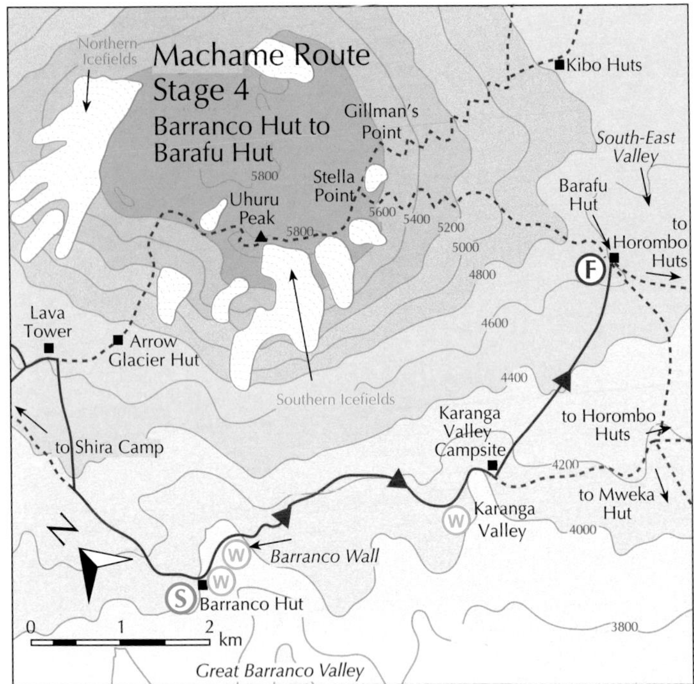

From the Barranco Hut the path descends into the **Great Barranco Valley**, passing tall *senecio* and winding around tussock grasses as it goes. The path drops to the valley floor and crosses boggy ground and a stream. Be sure to mind your footing here since the ground is marshy and many of the rocks used as stepping-stones are unstable and may simply sink into the soft ground under your weight. On the far side of the stream, at the foot of the Barranco Wall, is a giant boulder with a small cave beneath it. Most groups pause here to regroup before tackling the Wall.

Although the **Barranco Wall** is imposing and looks to be very steep, it isn't actually very difficult to climb. The rock face is close to vertical in places, but a series of cairns and splashes of red paint highlight a diagonal line that zigzags up the face to avoid the sheerest sections. The rock is relatively exposed and can be very slippery after rainfall, requiring you to use your hands in order to scramble safely in some places. While tackling the Wall, spare a thought for the porters as they attempt to scale up it, many carrying your kit on their heads or strapped to their own bags. The 300m climb to the top of the Wall takes 1–1½hrs.

A view from the top of the Western Breach across Kilimanjaro's crater to Mawenzi, while Uhuru Peak looms top right

Upon successfully **cresting the Wall**, there is a great sense of achievement to be had and the views of the bulk of Kibo from this vantage point are outstanding. The Heim Glacier, part of the Southern Icefields, is also clearly visible from here. A series of small cairns marks the indistinct path that leads to the snout of the glacier and the start of some of the technical climbing routes to the summit.

The path above the Wall crosses a high alpine plateau in a south-easterly direction, dipping and climbing to cross small gullies housing streams, while the Heim, Kersten and Decken glaciers reveal themselves high above your left-hand side. The path drops into the Karanga Valley 1½hrs after scaling the Barranco Wall.

The **Karanga Valley** is windswept but hosts a variety of flora, including numerous *lobelia*, in stark contrast to the rather barren surrounds that you have recently traversed. The Karanga River at the bottom of this valley is the last water point before the summit for those climbing the Barafu Route to the crater rim. Your guide should ensure that there is enough water gathered to last until you retreat from the peak to Mweka Hut. Make sure that all the water collected from here is properly sterilised since there are a number of toilets adjacent to the stream and there is a slight possibility of contracting giardia from untreated water.

On the eastern side of the Karanga Valley the path climbs a series of switchbacks to escape the valley; this ascent takes 15mins. At the top is the rather exposed and bleak **Karanga Valley Campsite**, used by trekkers taking this section slowly. There are toilets here too.

The path from the Karanga Valley Campsite continues north-east, climbing across the mountain for almost 2hrs on a relentless trajectory through the barren scree and rock-littered landscape here. The Southern Icefields are visible to the left. Scramble up a small cliff face and begin the final approach to the Barafu Hut, which is the last campsite before the assault on the summit.

The path curves to the north and rises more steeply for a further 30mins until it arrives at **Barafu Hut** (4660m), on the western lip of the South East Valley.

BARAFU HUT

Barafu is the Swahili for 'ice', and the exposed, hostile campsite here merits its moniker. A pair of old uniports are in reality little more than rusted shells and the tent pitches are scattered amid outcrops of rough lava. Long-drop toilets are set on the edge of the ridge. There is no water available at Barafu or indeed anywhere in the immediate vicinity.

Be careful when moving around the campsite after dark as the cliffs adjacent to the campsite are precipitous and the terrain underfoot is very uneven and unstable in places. There have been a number of serious and indeed fatal accidents here as a consequence of people losing their bearings in the dark.

By virtue of its elevated and exposed position, the views from Barafu are very good. Having approached from the western side of Kilimanjaro, this will be your first chance to examine the jagged outline of Mawenzi, now visible across the broad expanse of the Saddle. There are also expansive views of Kilimanjaro's broad southern flank, which reveal just how huge the mountain actually is.

Continuing on from the Machame Route

The Barafu Route to the summit begins to the north of the campsite and climbs to Stella Point on the crater rim and then Uhuru Peak. This involves almost 5km of arduous ascent gaining around 1230m in height in around 6–8hrs. See Summit ascent routes, Route J, for further details.

ROUTE C

Umbwe Route

Start	Umbwe Gate
Finish	Barranco Hut
Distance	14km
Grade	Hard
Time	2 days
Altitude gain	2335m
Total time on the mountain	5–6 days
Summit route	Barafu Route; option of Western Breach
Descent route	Mweka Route

The Umbwe Route is an exceptionally direct, beautiful method of scaling Kilimanjaro's western flank. Lying between and parallel to the Machame and Mweka routes, the Umbwe Route is a very steep, wild, exhilarating climb. As a consequence, it is rarely used and should only be considered by more experienced, acclimatised walkers. The mountaineer Iain Allen wrote 'An ascent of Kibo by the Umbwe Route is one of the finest non-technical mountaineering expeditions in East Africa'. For this reason, it's held to be Kilimanjaro's best-kept secret.

The standard version of the route, opened in 1963, provides the shortest ascent route to Kilimanjaro's Western Breach and summit ascent routes. The trail relentlessly scales the steep, thickly forested slopes beneath the Great Barranco Valley before climbing to Barranco Hut. Walkers then have the option of detouring around Kibo via the Southern Circuit Path to approach the summit from Barafu Hut, which is the most common approach, or of accessing the summit via the Western Breach, which is perhaps the signature combination. If you climb the Western Breach it's the shortest route from start gate to summit on the mountain, covering less than 25 miles. Regardless of your eventual summit path, you will be required to descend via the Mweka Route.

The climb generally only takes five days to complete. It is without doubt arduous but still non-technical, requiring strength and stamina plus an iron will rather than ropes and crampons to reach your goal. The climb itself showcases some of Kilimanjaro's finest features and the views from Barranco Hut are outstanding. The sense of isolation and wildness on this route are the main lures for walkers, with it being the closest thing Kilimanjaro offers to a full-on wilderness outing, at least until you join the rest of the trekkers at Barranco Camp, which is one of the busiest on the mountain.

The downside to using the Umbwe Route is that the rapid ascent to altitude doesn't allow much time for proper acclimatisation. In fact, if you arrive in Moshi and ascend without factoring in any time for additional acclimatisation, you can gain as much as 4000m in just three days, which is way too fast to be healthy and could seriously compromise your chances of reaching the summit. However, there is scope to build in additional, vital acclimatisation days on the ascent; if planning to attempt the Western Breach there is the option to spend an extra night at Barranco Hut or higher at Lava Tower; otherwise, on the Barafu Route you may wish to consider spending an extra day at the Barranco Hut or stopping overnight in the attractive Karanga Valley.

To the trailhead

The Umbwe Route begins at the Umbwe Gate. The gate is set amid Kilimanjaro's western foothills at 1650m. Your outfitter will organise transport to the Marangu Gate – where you must register and pay the requisite park fees – and then on to the Umbwe Gate.

To reach the Umbwe Gate, follow the Moshi–Arusha Road west from Moshi for 15km. At the junction with the Lyamungo Road, turn right and head north. When the road arrives at a T-junction, turn right and head towards the village of Mango. Before reaching the village take the left-hand turn signposted to Umbwe village. This track climbs to the Umbwe village, mission and school. The Umbwe Gate is located several kilometres beyond the village up a dusty 4WD track. The drive to the gate from Moshi takes 1½hrs. At the gate itself there is very little, aside from an office and some toilets.

Huts and accommodation

There are no sleeping huts on this little-used ascent route, although at higher elevations there are the traditional metal uniports at each campsite. Everyone ascending the Umbwe Route is required to camp.

The first campsite, Cave Campsite, is adjacent to a shallow cave that is in reality little more than an enlarged overhang. The second campsite, at the Barranco Hut, is set next to the old, corrugated uniport. At both of these sites there are long-drop toilets. There are also obvious water sources in the vicinity of each site.

Above this point you will climb to either the Lava Tower or Arrow Glacier campsites to reach the Western Breach, or cross to the Barafu Hut to begin the Barafu Route to the crater rim. There are no huts below the Western Breach – the uniport that once stood at Arrow Glacier was destroyed by a rock fall and hasn't been replaced. There are, however, two old uniports at Barafu. Built in 1968 these are now essentially only aged and dirty shells. There are long-drop toilets at each of these points. It is important to note that there are no water sources at Lava Tower, Arrow Glacier or Barafu Hut. All supplies must be carried to these points.

STAGE 1

Umbwe Gate to Cave Camp

Start	Umbwe Gate (1650m)
Finish	Cave Camp (2940m)
Distance	9.5km
Time	4–6hrs
Altitude gain	1290m

The first day on the Umbwe Route comprises a relatively short sharp ascent up Kilimanjaro's western flank. Starting on a dusty 4WD track the path transforms into an adventurous climb along a ridge through thick lush forest, clambering over tree roots to arrive at Cave Camp on the upper limits of the forest zone.

Having registered at the Marangu Gate, your outfitter will convey you around the skirts of Kilimanjaro to the Umbwe Gate. From the gate a 4WD trail quickly enters thick forest and begins to ascend north-east along an increasingly narrow ridge.

The **vegetation** is so tightly packed that it appears to surround and bear down on the trail and obscures much of the sunlight and certainly prevents you from enjoying any views of the summit ahead. In the gloom it is still possible to detect swathes of *Impatiens kilimanjari* and *Impatiens pseudoviola* nestled among the buttressed tree roots. Bright balsam flowers add vibrant splashes of colour to the myriad of greens surrounding the path.

The trail today is far more accessible than it used to be. The mountaineers **Rob Taylor and Henry Barber** used the Umbwe Route to access the foot of the Breach Wall on their ill-fated attempt to be the first to scale it in 1978. Taylor recorded the ascent: 'Side by side we begin together, groping our way up the trail, a six-inch gap between two bushes, a slight crimp in waist-high weeds, a dimpled depression in the black peaty mud. It is not so much a path we follow as our intuition.'

Having followed the 4WD trail for almost 2hrs through the forest, it gives way to a proper footpath. The path continues on the same trajectory, scrambling up a ridge between two valleys. The path snakes along, with the Umbwe River flowing to the right at the foot of a forested ravine and the Lonzo River to the left of the arête. Tree roots and ruts make the going uneven, but do ensure that there are handholds available to haul yourself up the steeper sections of path. The way is generally clear and obvious, but red

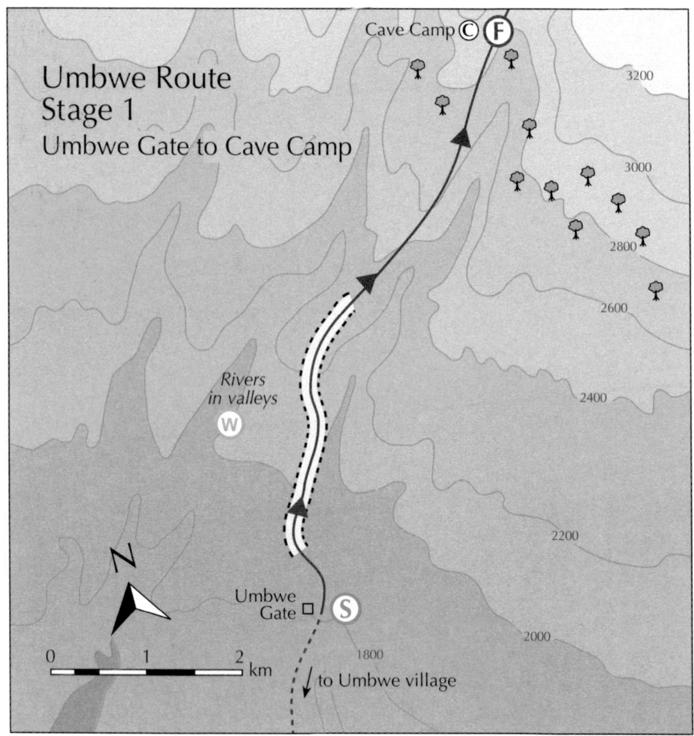

splashes of paint on trail-side trees act as a reassurance that you are indeed heading in the right direction as you make your way up one of the steepest sections of path on the mountain, through some stunningly beautiful forest.

After 4–5hrs the path starts to climb through grasses and heathers and reaches a cave, just within the uppermost reaches of the forest zone. The cave is ostensibly a large overhung wall made of slotted blocks that appear to be stacked perfectly and give the impression of a charred half igloo. This is **Cave Camp** (2940m). This is an attractive, flat area adjacent to the cave with a number of tent pitches. Water is readily available, most easily from a small pool 15 metres back along the approach trail.

STAGE 2

Cave Camp to Barranco Hut

Start	Cave Camp (2940m)
Finish	Barranco Hut (3985m)
Distance	5km
Time	4–5hrs
Altitude gain	1045m

The relentless climb towards Kibo continues and, as it does so, the path steepens further and narrows before breaking out of the forest, weaving through the rampant heath and edging along the rim of the Great Barranco Valley before arriving at the Barranco Hut, which is shared with trekkers on the Machame and Lemosho routes.

From Cave Camp, the trail climbs north-east once more, initially through thick heather forest and heathland, full of lichens. It is ascending a knife-like arête and if you peer either side of you, through the vegetation, you'll be able to see the slopes plummet away. After 30mins the path breaks clear of the forest and passes onto the heath/moorland zone. Heathers and tussock grasses are abundant here. Shortly after leaving the forest the path arrives at the foot of a 10m-high cliff, colloquially known as **Jiwe Kamba**. Once there was a rope fixed here to aid ascent but these days you'll be faced with a series of rocky steps, branches and roots to help you scramble up this minor obstacle. At the top of the cliff you will be able to see the western face of Kibo and the Southern Icefields for the first time. The initial view is immense and quite intimidating. Afternoon mist and cloud may obscure the summit.

The trail continues to climb and 1½hrs after leaving Cave Camp it reaches the first of two rocky outcrops. There are good water sources in their vicinity which can be reached by dropping down to a spring on the western side of the path. By now the track has begun to edge above the Great Barranco Valley on a series of interconnecting ridges. Alongside the path there are vertiginous drops of up to 400m to the Umbwe River at the foot of the valley.

The **Great Barranco Valley** is the result of an enormous landslip that occurred over 100,000 years ago. The slip broke away part of Kibo's crater rim, creating the less steep gradient of the Western Breach, and scored a deep gash in the mountainside.

Above the second rocky outcrop the incline decreases slightly and the trail becomes easier and broader. Eventually you descend slightly from the ridge,

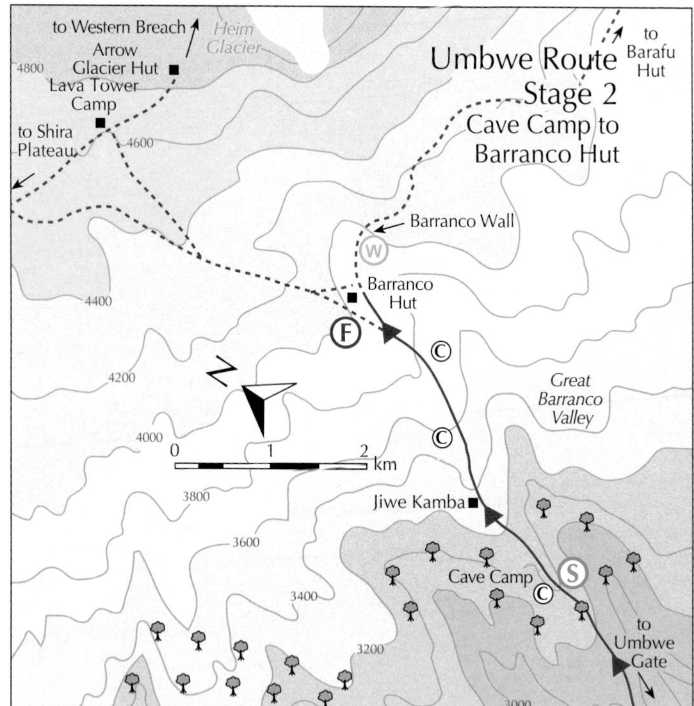

BARRANCO HUT

At the Barranco Hut campsite there are numerous tent pitches and a couple of long-drop toilets located near the hut, which is surrounded by groundsel and *lobelia*. Water can be fetched from a stream 5mins further up the valley. The shabby green uniport is delightfully sited and is frequently adjudged to be the most dramatic campsite on the mountainside.

The views back down the Great Barranco Valley, over the forest or across to the looming Barranco Wall are especially impressive. The views ahead, beyond the scree and moraines, of Kilimanjaro's snow-capped summit and Kibo's southern face are similarly dramatic. The rugged gash of the Western Breach disturbs the uniformity of the crater rim and the vast Heim Glacier hugs the curving dome closely. Kibo's bleak, savage beauty is encapsulated in this image.

Kibo (photo: Peter Zaharov/Shutterstock.com)

potentially the only real descent on the entire route, and arrive at **Barranco Hut** (3985m). Here there is a fork: the left-hand fork veers north-west towards Lava Tower, Arrow Glacier and the Western Breach. The right-hand fork heads east to Karanga and Barafu. Which one you take will have been predetermined by your choice of summit ascent path.

Continuing from the Umbwe Route

From here the trail now joins the Southern Circuit Path, from where you are faced with two options. You can either head north-west for 3.5km towards the Lava Tower and approach the tricky Western Breach from Arrow Glacier, or turn east and cross the conspicuously rumpled slopes of Kibo's southern face for 8.5km to arrive at Barafu Hut (see Stage 4, Machame Route, Barranco Hut to Barafu Hut) in order to make a final ascent to Uhuru via the Barafu Route. See Route J (Barafu Route) and Route K (Western Breach) for the details of these summit ascent routes.

Optional acclimatisation day

Whichever option you plump for, you would do well to consider building an additional day into your itinerary to supplement your acclimatisation. This can either be taken on route to your final night's camp or here at Barranco Hut. The advantages of taking an extra day at Barranco Hut are multiple: the hut is particularly attractive and magnificently located in an area of outstanding beauty that merits further exploration. From here you are ideally situated to explore the stunning Great Barranco Valley, scale the imposing Barranco Wall, revel in the heady views and even make an approach to the classic technical climbing route over the Heim Glacier.

To reach the Heim Glacier from the top of the Barranco Wall follow a faint trail marked by occasional cairns that leads in an easterly direction along a rocky rib directly towards the moraines and scree that litter the snout of the Heim Glacier. The scramble to the foot of the glacier takes over 2hrs from the top of the Barranco Wall. Allow at least 6hrs for the return trip from the Barranco Hut.

Kibo from the Umbwe Route (photo: Pavel Samsonov/Shutterstock.com)

ROUTE D

Lemosho Route

Start	Lemosho Glades
Finish	Shira 2 Camp
Distance	23km
Grade	Moderate/hard
Time	3 days; plus 2 days to reach Barafu Hut
Altitude gain	1500m
Total time on the mountain	7–8 days
Summit route	Barafu Route; option of Western Breach
Descent route	Mweka Route

The Lemosho Route is a longer ascent of Kilimanjaro that begins below the Shira Ridge, rises through the forest sections gradually and then crosses the Shira Plateau before joining the Southern Circuit Path and connecting with a summit ascent via the Western Breach or Barafu Route. As such it is an excellent, rounded outing with additional opportunities for acclimatisation, improving your chances of reaching Uhuru Peak.

Historically the route has been used significantly less than the more popular paths and is positively quiet in parts. The path approaches Kibo through unspoilt forest on the western flank of the mountain. Its remote, untampered nature means that much of the forest remains intact and the thick understorey shelters buffalo and other large game, although you are still unlikely to actually see any of the animals that live here. Once on the Shira Plateau, the path merges with the Shira Route and tracks towards Kibo, in turn intersecting with the Machame Route. The summit bid can be made via the Western Breach or the Barafu Route, while the descent is traditionally along the Mweka Route. Bear in mind, however, that some agencies describe this as the Shira Route. There are also a large number of faint and alternative tracks across the plateau in particular, so your guide or group may take a variation of what is outlined here. There's also a chance that you could join the Northern Circuit Path instead of the Southern Circuit Path and head round the north side of Kilimanjaro to ascend via School Hut and Gillman's Point...make sure you check with your operator which version of the route you're signing up to tackle when you arrange your trip.

The length of time spent on the Lemosho Route can vary considerably. It is possible to complete the entire climb in as little as five days or stretch it to last as many as eight or nine days. A reasonable compromise that allows you to ascend slowly and carefully while making the most of your surrounds is the seven-day trip outlined here. This incorporates two short days of walking but does ensure that you acclimatise well and enjoy a very comprehensive walk to the foot of Kibo. An extra day can be built in by staying in the Karanga Valley on the Barafu Route.

To the trailhead

The trailhead is at Lemosho Glades, however, prior to starting the walk you must first register and pay all park fees at the Londorossi Gate. The journey from the town of Moshi to the Lemosho Glades, via Londorossi, is an interminable one. The 80km of poorly maintained roads take 2–3hrs to negotiate. Your outfitter will arrange all transport to the trailhead.

To reach Londorossi, take the Moshi-Arusha Road west for 25km. At the village of Boma Ya Ng'ombe the road forks, the right-hand fork curving north around Kilimanjaro to the village of Sanya Juu, 22km away. Sanya Juu is the final place from which to stock up on provisions and foodstuffs. From here the road circumnavigates Kilimanjaro for a further 30km, until it reaches Londorossi. The gate is just beyond the small, ramshackle town.

Following registration and payment of park fees here, follow a 4WD track back south for 11km, until you reach a left-hand fork that is signposted to Lemosho Glades. At the junction you may be required to pay a toll fare to the Forest Authority before being able to progress to the trailhead. The journey from Londorossi Gate to the Lemosho Glades takes 45mins to an hour.

Huts and accommodation

As with all of the less heavily used routes on Kilimanjaro, there are no huts at all on the early stages of the ascent and no other option other than to camp in tents on the entire route.

At each of the designated campsites there are long-drop toilets and good water sources. Once the trail merges with the Southern Circuit Path, each campsite is set adjacent to an old metal uniport. These corrugated metal structures are little more than shells, like the Barranco, Barafu and Mweka Huts. Mostly built in the late 1960s, they were originally used as basic shelters for early climbers on the mountain. They have long since fallen into a state of disrepair and are much too small to accommodate the heavy traffic that now uses the relevant trails.

STAGE 1

Lemosho Glades to Big Tree Camp

Start	Lemosho Glades (2390m)
Finish	Big Tree Camp/Mti Mkubwa (2790m)
Distance	5km
Time	2hrs
Altitude gain	400m

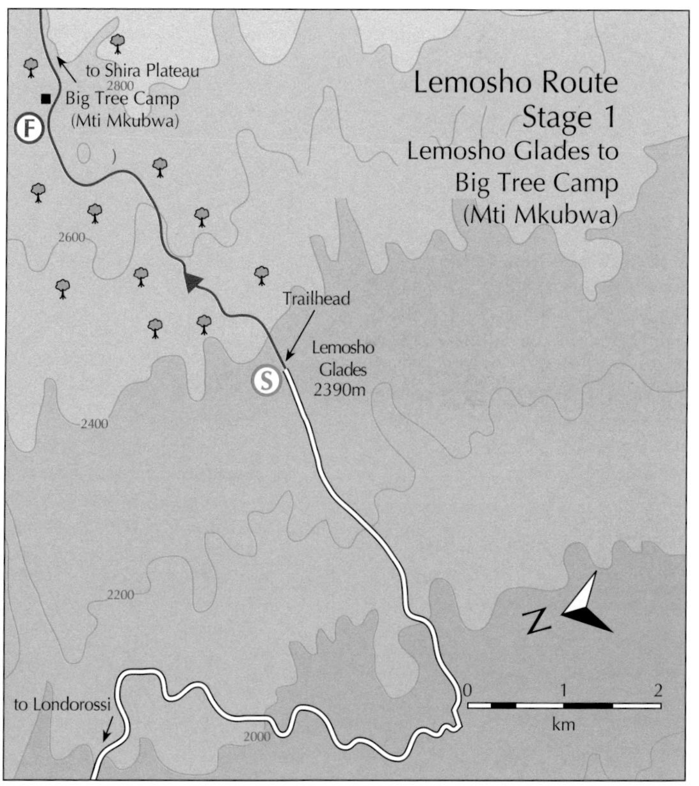

After registering and paying park fees at Londorossi, you then head on to the Lemosho Glades trailhead by vehicle. You will eventually begin climbing the mountain on foot. By this stage of the day, however, there is only time for a brief foray onto the forested lower western slopes of Kilimanjaro.

From the trailhead deep in the forest the path begins to ascend through a swathe of thick cloudforest. It leads in a generally eastern direction as it weaves through the trees to the north of the Lemosho River.

The forest is stunning and full of **wildlife**. Birds and insects are particularly prevalent here. An armed park ranger used to accompany groups on this section due to a slightly higher likelihood of encountering big game but this practice has been abandoned. Buffalo and even elephant do live in the forest around the Lemosho Glades although you are unlikely to encounter them, simply coming across tracks and piles of dung. Instead, keep an eye out for colobus and blue monkeys.

After 2hrs the path ascends a ridge and enters a small clearing in the upper reaches of the forest zone. This is **Big Tree Camp** (Mti Mkubwa) (2790m).

The official name for **Big Tree Camp** is Forest Camp (as marked on some maps) but none of the outfitters or guides refers to it as such, preferring to use the nickname that is derived from the giant trees found in its vicinity. Water is available from a stream about 1.5km south of the campsite.

STAGE 2

Big Tree Camp to Shira 1 Camp

Start	Big Tree Camp/Mti Mkubwa (2790m)
Finish	Shira 1 Camp (3505m)
Distance	8km
Time	4–5hrs
Altitude gain	715m

This is a longer day that sees you trek through and then finally leave the confines of the forest and gain the edge of the Shira Plateau, from where there are exceptional views of Kibo, far to the east.

The path leaves Big Tree Camp/Mti Mkubwa and continues to undulate mainly eastwards, ascending gently as the forest thins and the vegetation surrounding the path alters. Climb on to a ridge and then follow it upwards. As the taller trees give way and the thick understorey thins, you emerge on the heath/moorland zone, amid giant heathers. The plateau is a relaxing, rewarding place to explore and there are a host of trails and indistinct tracks that criss-cross its surface.

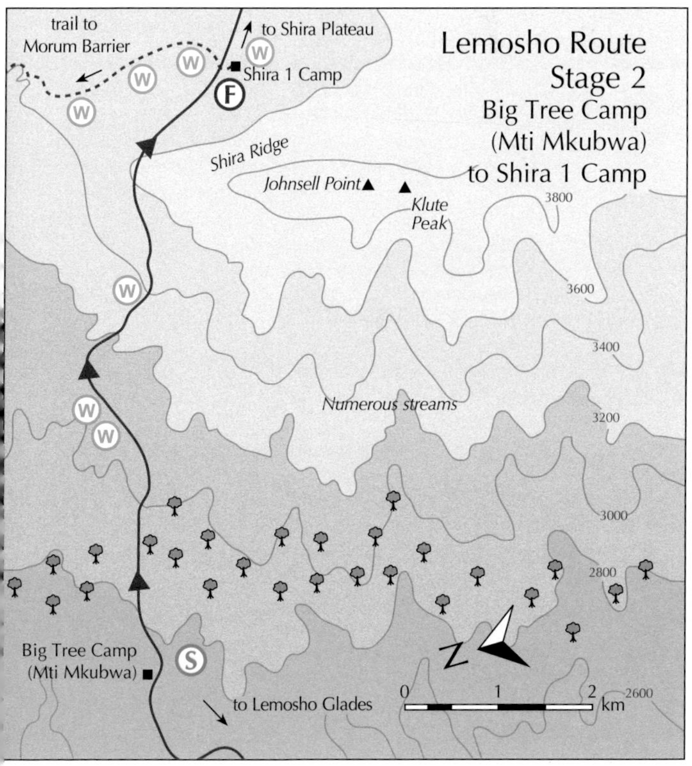

Kibo from a campsite on the Shira Plateau (photo: Oprea George/Shutterstock.com)

The gradient increases as the path progresses, only levelling or dipping slightly to cross one of the many small streams here. Most of the streams are dry throughout the year, unless there has been some recent rainfall. The path crests the rim of the Shira Plateau at around 3540m.

From here there are sweeping **views** of the entire rolling, crumpled plateau as it stretches south-east. To the right of the trail is the Shira Ridge and on it the highest points of the Shira Plateau, Johnsell Point (3962m) and Klute Peak. Ahead of you is your end goal, Kibo.

Having gained the **Shira Ridge**, the main path drops slightly as it negotiates heathers, everlastings and small boulder outcrops on its way to the **Shira 1 Camp** (3505m).

There is a tangible sense of **isolation and remoteness** here on the edge of the plateau. Few people come this way and at this stage at least you can appreciate the enormity of the undertaking faced by early explorers as they hurled themselves against Kilimanjaro's ramparts. There are a number of tent pitches and long-drop toilets spread around. Water can be fetched from a nearby stream.

STAGE 3

Shira 1 Camp to Shira 2 Camp/Shira Hut

Start	Shira 1 Camp (3505m)
Finish	Shira 2 Camp/Shira Hut (3890m)
Distance	10km
Time	3–4hrs
Altitude gain	385m

This is a short, gentle day that goes via the Shira Cathedral and the southern rim of the plateau. There is an alternative route from the Shira 1 Camp to the Shira 2 Camp that transports you across the heart of the plateau but most people take the slightly longer, tougher trek as it gives you superb panoramic views from the top of the Cathedral and also aids your acclimatisation as it results in only a slight altitude gain.

Keep an eye out for the sunrise, which can be dramatic from the start point of this stage. As the sun rises behind the bulk of Kibo and climbs above the peak, it suddenly shifts and shoots brilliant beams of light from the snow-capped heights of the mountain.

From the edge of the Shira Ridge, the path bends slightly to follow a south-easterly course across the plateau. As you set off you are walking straight into the sun and directly towards the mass of Kibo. Usually clear first thing in the morning, Kibo will rapidly become lost to mounding cloud that arises and shrouds the summit.

The path undulates across the surface of the plateau, hugging the lay of the land and following its every detail as it drops into small gullies containing tributary streams of the Engare Nairobi River. Beyond the streams lie two large boulders. After the second one the path splits, take the right fork ascending in a southerly direction to the rounded dome of the **Shira Cathedral**. The left fork undulates on an alternative, shorter path south-east crossing the heart of the plateau. From the Cathedral the trail tracks east and descends past **East Shira Hill**, undulating through an attractive high alpine meadow of heather and everlastings.

The walk across this section of the oldest part of Kilimanjaro is gentle and can even be completed at a reasonable pace. As you yomp towards Kibo, the path passes the **4WD emergency track** that the Shira Route uses to access the Shira Plateau beyond the Morum Barrier. Together, the paths forge a route south-east for 4km towards **Shira 2 Camp/Shira Hut** (3890m), which is equipped with the standard long-drop toilets and is close to a good water supply.

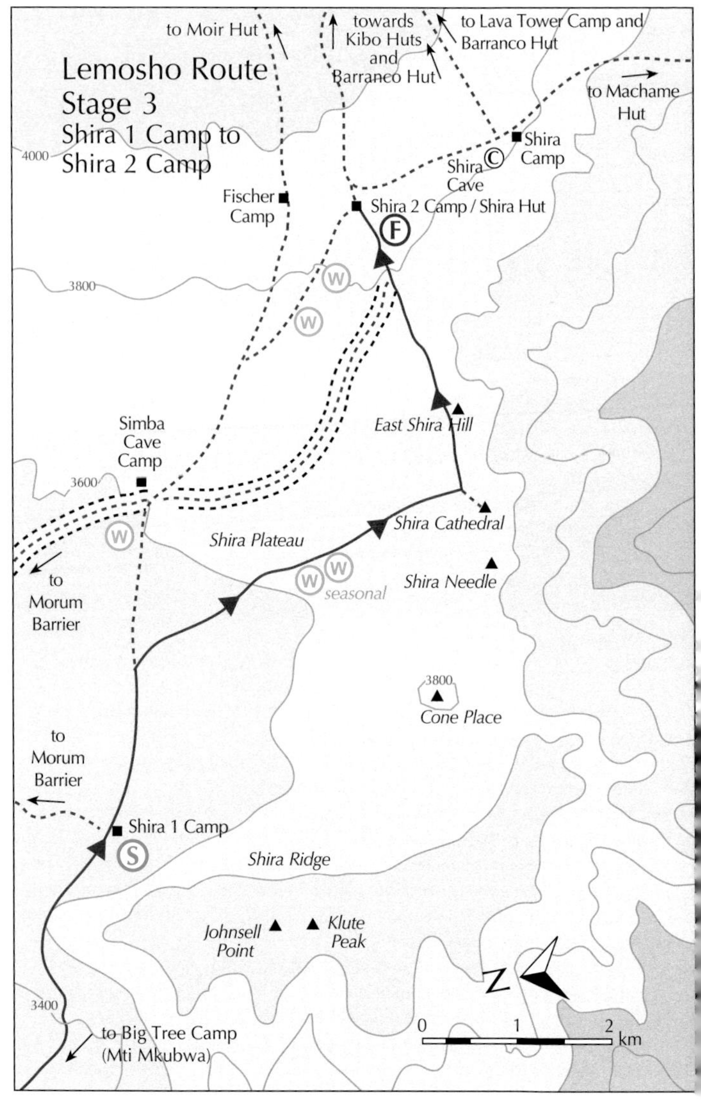

to Moir Hut
towards Kibo Huts and Barranco Hut
to Lava Tower Camp and Barranco Hut
Lemosho Route
Stage 3
Shira 1 Camp to Shira 2 Camp
to Machame Hut
Shira Camp
Shira Cave
4000
Fischer Camp
Shira 2 Camp / Shira Hut
3800
Simba Cave Camp
East Shira Hill
3600
Shira Cathedral
Shira Plateau
Shira Needle
seasonal
to Morum Barrier
3800
Cone Place
to Morum Barrier
Shira 1 Camp
Shira Ridge
Johnsell Point
Klute Peak
N
3400
to Big Tree Camp (Mti Mkubwa)
0
1
2
km

Strange highland desert sculptures – boulders perched on plinth of mud and pebbles

Because the walk into Shira 2 Camp/Shira Hut only takes a couple of hours in total, you should have an entire afternoon free to devote to the exploration and enjoyment of the **Shira Plateau**. Short forays will allow you to discover the strange and unusual flora of the heath/moorland zone, while longer, more energetic excursions will enable you to explore the further reaches of this impressive, ancient caldera.

Continuing on from the Lemosho Route

From Shira 2 Camp/Shira Hut the Lemosho typically progresses eastwards for 5km before merging with the Machame Route, on the way to Lava Tower Camp, and Southern Circuit Path in turn. This opens up the summit approach routes of the Barafu Route (Route J) and the Western Breach Route (Route K), depending on your level of fitness and experience. See the Summit ascent routes section for the route descriptions.

Alternatively, on the more direct trail from Shira 1 Camp to Shira 2 Camp/Shira Hut, skipping the detour to Shira Cathedral, and shortly after passing Simba Cave Camp at the junction with the 4WD track up from Morum Barrier, you can break eastwards across the Shira Plateau, past an old camp, Fischer Camp, and join the Northern Circuit at Moir Hut. This is the Alternative Lemosho Route or TK Lemosho Route, an unofficial path on the mountain that combines the Lemosho, Northern Circuit and Rongai Route to reach the summit, contouring around the rarely visited northern side of Kibo before climbing to the crater rim via School Hut and Gillman's Point. This combination, detailed under the Northern Circuit Path (Route H), makes a great wilderness outing on the mountain, escapes the majority of crowds and gives you a better chance of acclimatising by virtue of it being a longer route.

ROUTE E

Shira Route

Start	Londorossi Gate
Finish	Shira 2 Hut
Distance	13.5km
Grade	Moderate/hard
Time	2 days
Altitude gain	490m from Morum Barrier, plus a further 1400m on the drive from the Londorossi Gate
Total time on the mountain	6–7 days
Summit route	Barafu Route; option of Western Breach
Descent route	Mweka Route

Sometimes referred to on maps and by outfitters as the Londorossi Route, this is an infrequently used ascent route that scales Kilimanjaro from the north and approaches Kibo via the Shira Plateau, climbing the mountain from almost the exact opposite direction as the Marangu Route. It is sometimes known as the Shira Plateau Route. The path begins above the forest zone and snakes across the Shira Plateau for two days, connecting with the Lemosho Route along the way. It then intersects with the Machame Route and joins the Southern Circuit Path. From here there are then two options for approaching the summit. While some groups opt to tackle the Western Breach, most tackle the final climb along the Barafu Route. Descent from the summit is via the Mweka Route.

The 80km approach to the Londorossi Gate (the trailhead) is a gruelling, lengthy drive on rapidly deteriorating roads. However, there are great views to be had of the mountains that dot the Great Rift Valley; Mount Meru and Longido are particularly prominent as you drive north around Kilimanjaro. The early stage of this trek is essentially a driving route, and isn't much fun for trekkers. Because of this, the Shira Route is rarely offered and rarely tackled.

For those so inclined, the trek begins with a drive along a 4WD track from the gate (2000m) to the Morum Barrier (3400m) from where the walking starts. Cleared in 1968 by the Kilimanjaro District Forestry Department in order to improve access to this side of Kilimanjaro, the track is also occasionally used for emergency or rescue vehicles. The major drawback is that, by driving this high on the mountain, you will only see the forest sections through a car window as you bounce up a dusty, rutted track.

More pertinently, by beginning the walk high on the heath/moorland zone, you impede your ability to acclimatise properly. The very rapid gain in altitude as a result of the distance driven can lead to the equally rapid onset of altitude sickness. Even though the next two days are relatively short, you will not have given yourself the most solid start to your ascent.

The Shira Plateau itself possesses great beauty and is host to a number of fascinating geological features. The Shira Cone rises 200m above the plateau, but is shaded by the dramatic Shira Ridge to the west, which is up to 400m higher than the plateau. The prominent Shira Needle, Shira Cathedral and East Shira Hill mark the southern edge of the plateau. Exploring this area makes a great outing on Kilimanjaro. However, you are better combining it with an ascent through the forest via the Lemosho Route to get a more rounded appreciation and improve your chances of successfully tackling the summit.

To the trailhead

The Shira Route begins at the Londorossi Gate on the northern side of Kilimanjaro. The Gate is 2½–3hrs from the town of Moshi. Park fees can be paid and registration formalities completed at the gate itself. Most walkers will be shuttled to the gate by their outfitter or agency.

To reach Londorossi, follow the Moshi-Arusha Road west from Moshi. After 25km the road passes through the village of Boma Ya Ng'ombe. There is a signposted junction right here that curves north around the flank of the mountain to West Kilimanjaro. The small town of Sanya Juu is passed 22km after the junction; this is the last point at which it is possible to pick up additional supplies or foodstuffs. From here it is a further 40km to Londorossi. This small, ramshackle town is almost exclusively constructed from wood. It has a frontier feel to it and provides no proper facilities for the casual visitor. Signposts indicate the Londorossi Gate, where there is a park warden's hut.

From the gate, a rough 4WD track continues through the forest. This 11km stretch of pitted, rutted track leads all the way to the Morum Barrier; at 3400m this is the highest point on the mountain readily accessible by vehicle. In dry conditions the track can be fairly easily used although progress is slow and awkward. The track climbs through the forest zone for about half its length, emerging onto the heath/moorland at around 2700m. From here the path bounces across the high alpine landscape to reach Morum Barrier Gate, from where most groups start to walk.

Huts and accommodation

There are no huts on the lower sections of the Shira Route and all overnight stops are taken at campsites. Most groups don't even detour to the damaged uniport at Shira Hut anymore, opting to camp further north at the Shira 2 Camp.

At each campsite there are clearly visible tent pitches and long-drop toilets. Water is readily available from streams in the immediate vicinity of each overnight spot.

After the Shira Route merges with the Machame Route and joins the Southern Circuit Path, you will either (if climbing the Western Breach) camp at Lava Tower and then at Arrow Glacier Hut, or (if ascending by the Barafu Route) camp adjacent to the uniports at the Barranco and Barafu Hut.

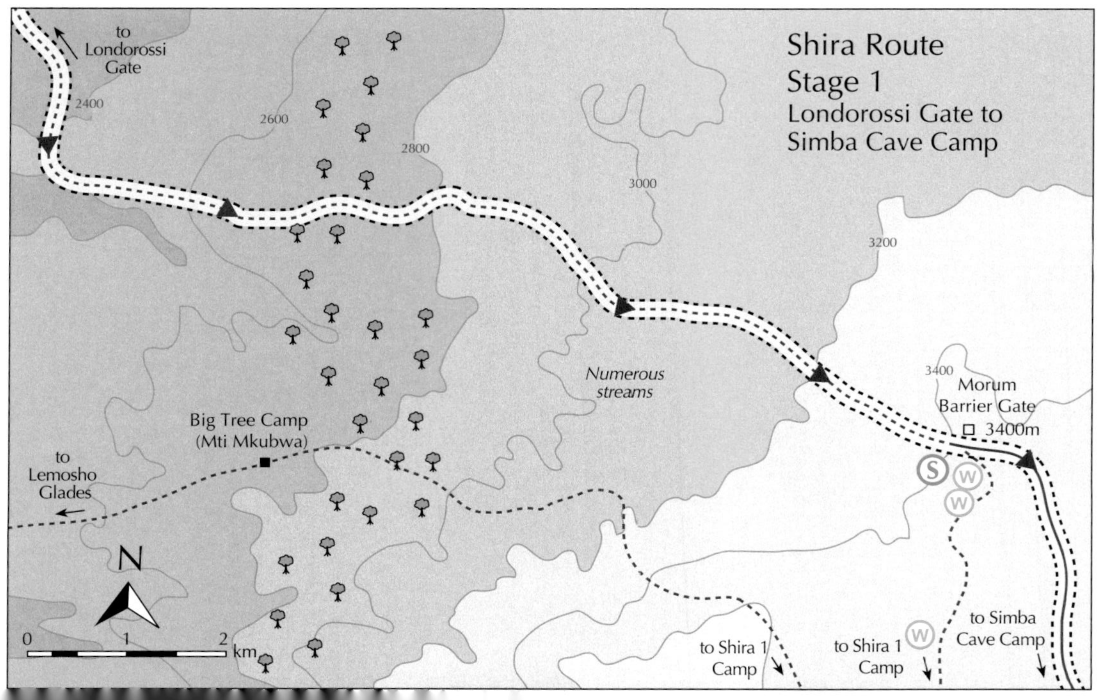

Shira Route
Stage 1
Londorossi Gate to
Simba Cave Camp
to Londorossi Gate
2400
2600
2800
3000
3200
3400
Numerous streams
Big Tree Camp (Mti Mkubwa)
to Lemosho Glades
Morum Barrier Gate
3400m
to Shira 1 Camp
to Shira 1 Camp
to Simba Cave Camp
N
0
1
2
km

STAGE 1

Morum Barrier to Simba Cave Camp

Start	Morum Barrier (3400m)
Finish	Simba Cave Camp (3640m)
Distance	6.5km; 17.5km including the drive from Londorossi Gate
Time	1½hrs; 3½hrs including the drive from Londorossi Gate
Altitude gain	240m, plus a further 1400m on the drive from the Londorossi Gate

This is a lengthy day, although it is dominated by the drive from the village of Moshi to Londorossi Gate, where all of the requisite formalities for entering the national park are completed. From here you will then be driven for a further 11km to the Morum Barrier Gate. Only at this stage will you actually begin walking, and then only briefly, since the day will most likely already be drawing to a close.

If you set off late from Moshi or make especially slow progress to the Morum Barrier, it is possible to camp here overnight. Most people make for the Simba Cave Camp around 90 minutes away, although some operators prefer the Shira 1 Camp, a little over an hour away. Others head to Moir Hut with the aim of joining the Northern Circuit Path and exploring the northern side of Kibo.

From Morum Barrier Gate, for Simba Cave Camp, the **4WD track** continues across the centre of the Shira Plateau towards Kibo. The track curves right and heads almost due south through open heath/moorland, fording several small streams and tributaries of the Engare Nairobi River. After walking for 4km (it should take 1½hrs) the path arrives at **Simba Cave Camp** (3640m). Here there are tent pitches and long-drop toilets; water is available from the nearby streams.

The views and sense of open space on the **Shira Plateau** are remarkable and quite unlike any other aspect of Kilimanjaro. Take the time to savour them, picking out features such as the Shira Cone, Cathedral and East Shira Hill stood across the heath and moorland, before you join the busier stretches of track in the forthcoming days. Look out too for deer tracks – klipspringer or dik dik most likely but possibly those of buffalo as well – as they make their way across the plateau in search of grazing.

STAGE 2

Simba Cave Camp to Shira 2 Camp

Start	Simba Cave Camp (3640m)
Finish	Shira 2 Camp (3890m)
Distance	7km
Time	2hrs
Altitude gain	255m

This is a second short day that sees you ease further onto the Shira Plateau. Following the dramatic gain in altitude the previous day, the gentle nature of the short ascent to the next campsite should be welcome. The short day also means that you are left with plenty of spare time to explore the surrounding ridges and conspicuously rumpled surface of the plateau.

From the Simba Cave Camp the **4WD track** continues in a roughly southwards direction. Most agencies take one of the trails ascending gently south-east instead. These paths are clearly visible and well signposted as they climb gently past boulders and clumps of tussock grasses and everlastings. The walk is deceptively simple. Although the gradient is gentle and the terrain not unduly tough, your body is unlikely to have adjusted to the altitude gained the previous day and consequently progress is likely to be slower than you might anticipate.

After 45mins you reach a fork marked with a rudimentary signpost, with the left-hand trail tracking east towards Moir Hut and the Northern Circuit Path (see below). Instead, take the right-hand fork and follow it south-east for another hour. Towards the end of this time, the Lemosho Route joins the path from the right. Together the Shira and Lemosho Route continue south-eastwards until, a mere 2hrs after leaving Simba Cave Camp, you arrive at **Shira 2 Camp/Shira Hut** (3890m), where there are long-drop toilet facilities and a readily accessible water supply.

Having arrived by late morning, you will have time to **explore the area**, weather permitting, during the free afternoon. Simply being able to stroll on the rolling plateau is a relaxing experience. For the more energetic, there are good side trips that can be undertaken in the vicinity. One attractive option is to explore the area to the west of the Shira 2 Camp that boasts the Shira Needle, Shira Cathedral and East Shira Hill.

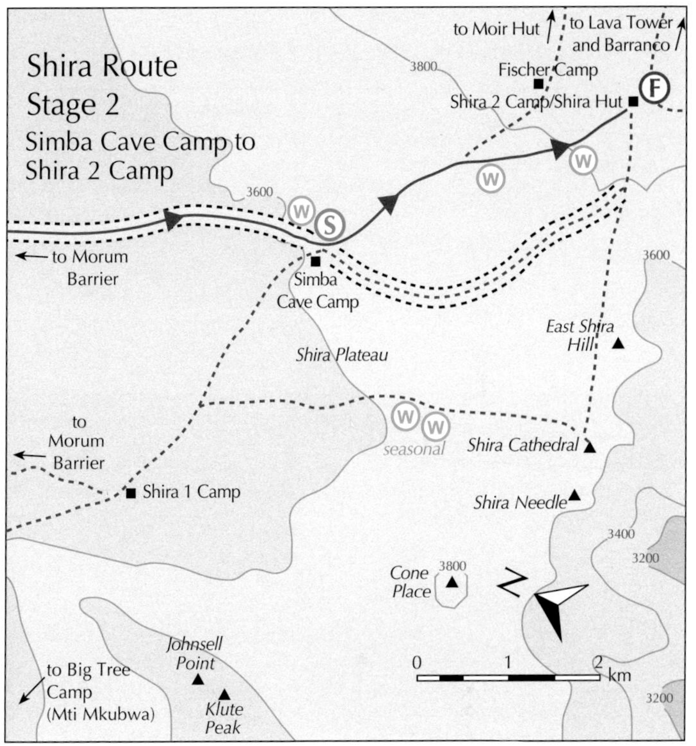

Northern Circuit

Beyond Simba Cave Camp, on the way to Shira 2 Camp, there is a path that breaks left across the desert of the Shira Plateau. Having passed an abandoned campsite, Fischer Camp, it joins the Northern Circuit at Moir Hut. This little used option is part of what some operators refer to as the Alternative Lemosho or TK Lemosho Route, which combines the Lemosho, Northern Circuit and Rongai Route to interesting effect, creating a largely untramped section of track that allows you to enjoy a genuine wilderness experience on Kilimanjaro before reconnecting with an official route to the summit. See Route H in the section Circuit paths.

CONTINUING ON FROM THE SHIRA ROUTE

The following day's route from Shira 2 Camp/Shira Hut is determined by which final ascent route you will tackle. Initially, you will follow the path from the campsite and ascend over 5km to join the Southern Circuit Path. As on the Machame Route, you will then be able to access the Western Breach via Lava Tower and the Arrow Glacier (Route K), or the Barafu Route via the Barranco and Barafu Hut (Route J).

Kilimanjaro at sunrise with Kibo (right) and Mawenzi (left) (photo: Antonia Jorge Nunes/Shutterstock.com)

ROUTE F

Rongai Route

Start	Rongai Gate
Finish	Kibo Huts; or School Hut
Distance	33km; or 27.5km
Grade	Moderate/hard
Time	4 days
Altitude gain	2710m; or 2750m
Total time on the mountain	5–7 days
Summit route	Normal/Marangu Route; no option of Western Breach
Descent route	Marangu Route
Note	Time on the mountain is 6 days; or 5 days

Once upon a time this was an unusual and less-heavily used method for ascending Kilimanjaro but these days it is a popular, genuine substitute to the treks on the south side of the mountain. Originally it was set up in the 1960s to act as an alternative to the Marangu Route, which was at that time the only real walking route on the mountain. The local chief, Salakana, set up facilities on his tribal land and charged walkers to use the huts and facilities there. The money raised was then ploughed back into the local community, which thus benefited directly from the presence of tourists.

A number of small routes sprang up, all of which began on the northern flank of Kilimanjaro and tended to converge at the Second Cave before progressing either towards Mawenzi or heading directly towards Kibo, depending on the speed of the chosen ascent. The polarised nature of relations between Kenya and Tanzania and the proximity of the start points for the Rongai, Loitokitok, Outward Bound and Naromoru Routes to the border between the two countries meant that they fell into disuse for many years. However, in response to overcrowding on the other routes and because people are again recognising that its relative quietness, unspoilt nature and spectacular views make this a very pleasant way to climb Kilimanjaro, the Rongai Route has returned to being popular.

What is now known as the Rongai Route is actually something of a misnomer, since the path followed runs parallel to, but slightly east of, the original Rongai Route on a path akin to the one-time Loitokitok Route that started from the village of Loitokitok in Kenya. The perceptive walker may also spy a couple of way signs on the early stages of the route that are labelled 'Nalemoru Route', further adding to the confusion.

Regardless of what you call it, this ascent of Kilimanjaro is quite extraordinary. Taking advantage of the drier northern slopes, you are able to approach the Saddle

The distant view of Kibo, here seen across the heath/moorland, is the ultimate goal for trekkers on Kili

relatively easily. The views north over the arid, flat Maasai lands in southern Kenya reveal the sheer scale of your endeavour and make the ascent seem very grand indeed. By opting to complete the walk in six days rather than in five (for the five-day route see Stages 2A and 3A), you are able to detour to Mawenzi Tarn Hut, situated just below Mawenzi's North Corrie. This is a truly stunning campsite that allows you to admire the jagged peaks and to explore the foothills of Kilimanjaro's second summit more effectively than on any other route.

The only drawbacks to ascending this route are the lengthy drive around Kilimanjaro to the start point and the disappointing early stages of the first day's walk. Much of the lowland forest has been cleared for farmland and as a consequence you only climb through a small section of genuine forest before reaching the heath/moorland zone. This is in some way recompensed by the fact that you traditionally descend via the Marangu Route, which has some attractive forest scenery on its lower sections. The gruelling final ascent to the crater rim is conducted from either School Hut or Kibo Huts and is via the Normal/Marangu Route.

Nonetheless, the scenic variety, emptiness and technically easy nature of the walk more than compensate for the drawbacks, making this an excellent method of ascending and enjoying Kilimanjaro.

To the trailhead

Plans to set up a national park gate at Naromoru have led to the creation of the Rongai Gate. Even so, it is still necessary to register and pay the requisite park fees at the Marangu Gate first. Your outfitter will ensure that you are shuttled to the gate and then transported on from here, around the eastern side of Kilimanjaro to the actual trailhead

The trailhead is 50km from the Marangu Gate. What was once a dusty, difficult track that became interminably muddy after rain is now a much more modern, tarmac road that passes through a series of Chagga towns and villages, allowing you a glimpse of local life. After driving for 1½hrs you arrive at the town of Tarekea, 40km from Marangu, on the north-eastern side of Kilimanjaro. Here the road forks. The right-hand fork crosses the border and heads into Kenya, while the left-hand fork curves north-west around the mountain, following the border on the Tanzanian side. Beyond Tarekea is the village of Loitokitok. A small junction heading up a track leads to a motley collection of huts adjacent to the Snow Cap Cottages. This inauspicious huddle, including a wooden office and small shelter, is the park gate and start point for the trek. Once your guides and porters have divided up all of the equipment and food, you'll need to register your name and party in one of the rickety huts.

Huts and accommodation

Although there are a couple of uniports along the Rongai Route, you will need a tent for each of the overnight stops on the ascent. Camping is the only option on the early stages of the climb, but there is the possibility of staying in the hut at Kibo and again at Horombo on the descent, although you are almost certain to camp throughout your time on the mountain.

There is a corrugated iron uniport at the First Camp and at Mawenzi Tarn Hut. Though there are structures at Mawenzi Tarn, which date from the early 1970s, and School Hut neither are suitable for walkers to stay in and they aren't used for this purpose. School Hut used to be known as the Outward Bound Hut, but the park authorities are now referring to it by this new moniker.

The larger stone blockhouse at Kibo Huts accommodates a number of people, but is primarily designed for those ascending the Marangu Route. The same is true for the A-frame complex at Horombo. In either case, camping may well provide you with a more peaceful, better night's sleep than you would get in a communal bunkroom.

STAGE 1

Rongai Gate to First Camp

Start	Rongai Gate (2000m)
Finish	First Camp (2635m)
Distance	7km
Time	2–3hrs
Altitude gain	635m

The first day on the Rongai Route is a fairly ropey and unspectacular start to the ascent of the largest mountain in Africa. After a couple of hours' drive from Marangu Gate, the climb begins by ambling gently through an area of heavily deforested land that is now being used for cultivation. Fortunately, it improves rapidly and before too long passes into a small copse of natural forest. Beyond this it emerges amid some scrub and heather close to First Camp, from where you have the first exceptional views of Mawenzi's serrated outline and Kibo's snow-capped dome.

Head south-west along the dusty 4WD track ahead of you. The trail circles a pine forest and then sets off across a series of small, cultivated plots of land. This whole area used to be lightly forested, but the pressures of human encroachment have resulted in the destruction of most of the natural forest in this area.

Continue along this fairly shabby track as it winds between plots of maize and potato and past pitiful shacks, gradually gaining height. You will most likely run into groups of raggedy boys and girls shouting 'Jambo, Chocolate!' around here. The path passes two signposts marked 'Naremoru', which refer to a previous incarnation of the route, and after 1hr bends right and dips to cross the Nare Moru River before entering a stand of forest.

The forest, which is quite small, shelters a variety of **birds and animal** life. As you enter the forest you may see a resident troop of black-and-white colobus monkeys in the treetops, making huge leaps of faith and moving agilely from branch to branch in search of fruit and seeds.

Once inside the forest, the track curves left and climbs past a third 'Nalemoru' sign. There is a makeshift picnic table and long-drop toilet here. The gradient then increases and the going underfoot becomes more uneven. Jumbled roots and fallen

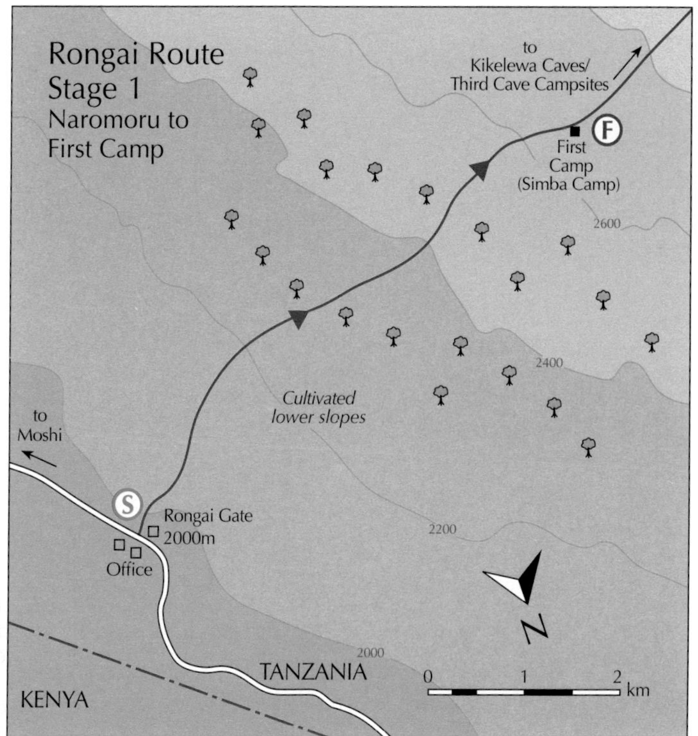

branches lie on the path in untidy heaps. Small, brightly coloured flowers lurk amid the overwhelming palette of greens.

All too quickly the trees thin and the undergrowth recedes as you enter an area of giant heathers and scrub. The forest briefly reasserts itself but quickly gives way once more to the rampant heath. The path continues to gain height gently, undulating through the pleasant scenery. Having dropped to cross a frequently dry riverbed, the path climbs once more to reveal views north-east. Kilimanjaro's foothills taper into the dusty, wheat-coloured Kenya plains. The path picks its way across a second stream on polished blue-grey rocks and re-enters the scrub.

There is often evidence of larger **wildlife** here, even though you'll be lucky to actually see any. Although you may come across an elephant skull beside the

View of Mawenzi above tents at First Camp

path and quantities of spoor, you are more likely to have to content yourself with spotting birds and insects.

Quite suddenly, a little over an hour after leaving the forest, the path comes to a number of cleared patches of scrub. This is the site of **First Camp** (2635m), also referred to as Simba or sometimes Sekimba Camp.

The grassy pitches at **First Camp** afford reasonable camping opportunities and the tall scrub hides a number of the pitches, making the site feel smaller than it really is. Upon arrival you will have to register your group with the warden stationed in the uniport here. There are several long-drop toilets in the area, but little else. Water is available from the stream you crossed about 50 metres back along the track. Kibo and Mawenzi are both visible, weather allowing, and make for a stirring and inviting view.

STAGE 2

First Camp to Kikelewa Camp

Start	First Camp (2635m)
Finish	Kikelewa Camp (3680m)
Distance	12km
Time	5–6hrs
Altitude gain	1045m

This is a fairly long day that sees those completing the climb in six days separate from those who will only take five days to summit and drop off the mountain again. All walkers start together and follow the same trail to Second Cave. At this point the paths diverge, those taking five days heading to Third Cave (see directions in Stages 2A and 3A) while those taking six days turn towards Kikelewa Camp.

First thing in the morning there are glorious **views** of Mawenzi to the south and Kibo to the west. The peaks are visible through and above the scrub for the first part of the day, until early cloud drifts over the Saddle and smothers the summits.

Leaving First Camp, the trail continues on a south-westerly heading, rising steadily onto the heath/moorland zone, aiming for Kibo's northern flank. The trail coils between tussock grasses, sweet-smelling herbs and small garish flowers that stand out against the ubiquitous yellows and browns of this part of the mountain. Trees are stunted, skeletal or non-existent at this altitude. The track passes a rocky outcrop and begins to rise a little more sharply, climbing onto a small plateau.

Looking back there are good **views** of where the fingers of forest reach down Kilimanjaro and flatten to form the yellow, broad Kenya plains. It is also possible to see the shine of Lake Chala on the border, to the east. To the left of the trail you can also see a shallow canyon, carved by mountain runoff that flashes down from the higher slopes after heavy rain. For much of the year it is dry though.

From here the path ascends alongside the riverbed via a rocky outcrop and another level stretch of terrain. As it gains the lip of this second level patch of ground, the trail passes a faint junction to the right. This used to be the point at which the original Rongai Route joined the main track up the mountain. Some 2hrs after leaving

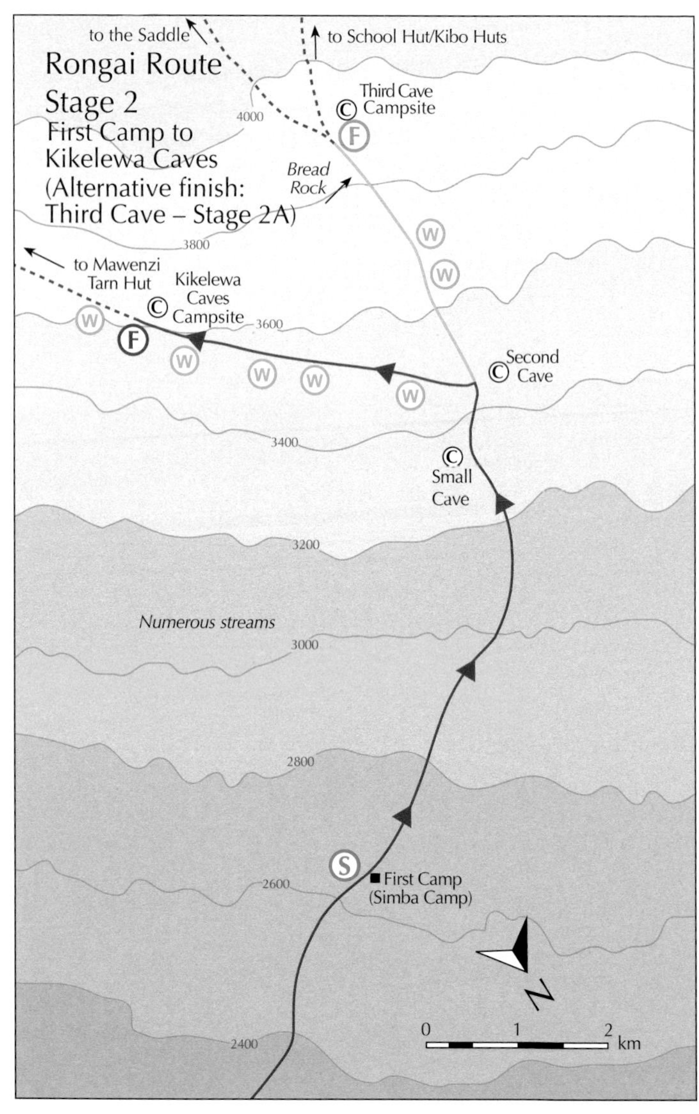
to the Saddle
to School Hut/Kibo Huts
Rongai Route
Stage 2
First Camp to
Kikelewa Caves
(Alternative finish:
Third Cave – Stage 2A)
Third Cave
Campsite
4000
Bread
Rock
3800
to Mawenzi
Tarn Hut
Kikelewa
Caves
Campsite
3600
Second
Cave
3400
Small
Cave
3200
Numerous streams
3000
2800
First Camp
(Simba Camp)
2600
2400
0
1
2
km
N

camp, the path reaches a **small cave**. Small and low-ceilinged, with a roof blackened from countless old campfires, it has previously used as a campsite despite a lack of an accessible water supply.

The path above the cave climbs up the valley between two ridges before scrambling onto the shoulder of one of them as it curves south-west across the track. Here the terrain becomes rockier and steeper. Several false summits offer false hope before you finally reach the top of the ridge. The path then crosses a flatter area, liberally dotted with heathers and wild flowers. Half an hour after passing the small cave, the path comes to the **Second Cave** (3480m), which is clearly signposted.

Second Cave is a much larger hollow, whose more substantial overhang provides some cover for those cooking or eating. This is often used as a lunch stop, and there is a long-drop toilet just in front of the cave.

From the rocky mouth of the cave you can see out across the northern flank of Kilimanjaro. The pudding bowl dome of Kibo and the Eastern Icefields on the crater rim are also visible to the west, as they have been in the approach to the cave.

From Second Cave the path splits. Those on the shorter five-day alternative route continue south (see Stage 2A below). Take the path heading south-east for Kikelewa Camp, directly towards Mawenzi. Having climbed over a small knoll, the path drops to cross a riverbed. It then rises again on the far side of this waterway, albeit on a gentler gradient since you are now essentially traversing the contours of the mountain; you only gain around a further 180m height in the final 3km section.

The path rises and falls repeatedly, skirting above a series of gullies and ravines and crossing two further, frequently dry streams. After the second of these, the track edges around a rocky promontory and around 2hrs from Second Cave drops into a valley that contains the **Kikelewa Camp** (3680m).

Kikelewa Camp is set just below the Saddle, in a valley full of *senecio*, and is an attractive spot to stay overnight with all of the usual facilities and further fine views. Kibo can be seen just above the ridge that hides the campsite from the Saddle.

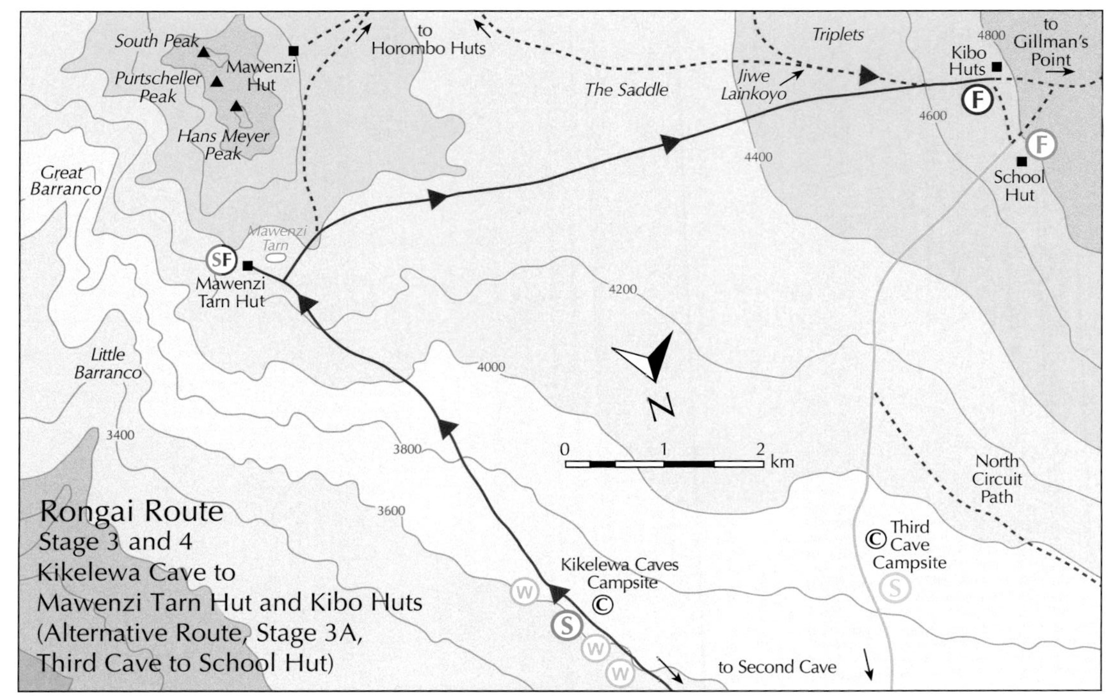

Rongai Route
Stage 3 and 4
Kikelewa Cave to
Mawenzi Tarn Hut and Kibo Huts
(Alternative Route, Stage 3A,
Third Cave to School Hut)

STAGE 3

Kikelewa Camp to Mawenzi Tarn Hut

Start	Kikelewa Camp (3680m)
Finish	Mawenzi Tarn Hut (4300m)
Distance	5km
Time	3–4hrs
Altitude gain	620m

This is a shortish day that elevates you quite quickly on a relatively steep trail. The effort is well rewarded by sumptuous views and an exceptional campsite beneath the jagged spires of Mawenzi that will leave you with a tangible sense of wilderness and isolation.

The path heads south from Kikelewa Camp and climbs steadily on a ridge through an area of *senecio*. On either side of you other ridges rise as well, making the whole place appear incredibly rugged. The path climbs fairly steeply and you ascend towards Mawenzi rapidly. After 1½hrs the gradient eases slightly. At this point the vegetation begins to alter as the heath plants give way to everlastings and hardier species.

Relentlessly the path continues to climb for a further half hour before it crests a false summit and temporarily levels. Beyond here the path climbs more steeply and negotiates a five-metre section of slope that you may have to use your hands to scramble up. Cresting a ridge, you enter the north-east valley on Mawenzi. The path eases around Mawenzi's edge, contouring across the mountain and hugging the rumpled lie of the land.

Dropping slightly, the path squelches across a boggy section bisected by a stream. As the trail gains height once more, the vegetation fades away and the area becomes more barren and exposed, seeming to only support everlastings. The trail rounds a rock outcrop to suddenly reveal Mawenzi Tarn set beneath the blasted, shattered slopes of Kilimanjaro's second summit. Allegedly the tarn never runs dry, although it can shrink considerably during periods of sustained dry weather. On the far side of the tarn are a small, corrugated tin shack and a signpost announcing the site of the **Mawenzi Tarn Hut** (4300m).

Since this a fairly **short stage**, you ought to arrive here with much of the afternoon spare. Use this time to rest and rehydrate, and after that to explore, climbing before dropping to sleep at a lower elevation, thereby aiding your acclimatisation. Clamber up onto Mawenzi's foothills, scour the cirque and

Camp below Mawenzi (photo: Mountaintreks/Shutterstock.com)

marvel at the sheer edifices and damaged rock slopes that make Mawenzi such a challenge to climb. Be careful while doing so though, as the slopes here are unstable and can be prone to rock falls.

MAWENZI TARN HUT

This is one of the most dramatic campsites on the mountain. Less heavily used than others, it is a relatively quiet, ethereal place to stay overnight, one where 'Dark and threatening the shattered bulwarks of Mawenzi rise sternly into the upper air' (Hans Meyer). The tarn and campsite are set in a cirque at the foot of Mawenzi and the walls immediately above the campsite have the appearance of an organ vault. On either side of the valley containing the tarn are serrated ridges. The one to the west barely conceals Kibo, which can be seen from some vantage points peering over the crest.

To the east is a further ridge, beyond which is a scooped slope that leads to a sudden, dramatic drop. Further east are the stunning, chilling gouges in the mountainside that comprise the Little and Great Barrancos, two abyss-like river gorges that fall away from the summit. These two features have been described as being 'Himalayan' in scale and are too deep to see into. Hans Meyer recorded his impressions of the gorge from high on Mawenzi: 'On this its eastern side, from an altitude of about 16,830ft, the mountain sinks sheer downward into a gigantic cauldron, the sides of which are scarred with innumerable, rugged ravines. As we gazed from our dizzy height upon the hills and valleys, the streams and bushes, the endless proliferation of gullies and gorges 6000 or 7000 feet below, it seemed as if we had a birds-eye view of earth from a balloon.'

The sunrise from Mawenzi Tarn Hut is also spectacular. As the sun creeps up behind the jagged, silhouetted spires, the shadows shorten before the light bursts from behind the peaks and floods the rest of the mountain. From vantage points above the campsite it is just possible to see over the western ridge to the sparkling snows on the summit of Kibo.

STAGE 4

Mawenzi Tarn Hut to Kibo Huts

Start	Mawenzi Tarn Hut (4300m)
Finish	Kibo Huts (4710m)
Distance	9km
Time	3–4hrs
Altitude gain	410m

This is a simple day that culminates with you being in a position to tackle the summit. Little additional height is gained as you forge across the lunar-like Saddle landscape between Mawenzi and Kibo, allowing you to prepare physically and psychologically for the challenge ahead. If the weather is bad or the winds are high, this very exposed section of the mountain can become tough.

See the map in Stage 3 for this part of the route. Initially, retrace your steps from the previous day, passing back past Mawenzi Tarn. Then ascend the scree and lava ridge to the north-west of the campsite. After 15–30mins the path crests the ridge to reveal extraordinary views of the Saddle and Kibo.

The **views** from this outstanding vantage point are particularly potent if poor weather or afternoon cloud obscured them on the previous day. Kibo's squat dome and eternal snows are clearly visible across the vast, spreading Saddle. The strong morning light picks out a myriad of colours and creates a truly beautiful picture. Even at this early time of day, cloud is often boiling up the lower slopes and preparing to storm the Saddle. The wisps and tendrils of cloud make the object of the day's walk seem even more remote and grand

View of Kibo massif above cloud band from Mawenzi's North West Ridge

than previously imagined. Make sure that you don't break camp too late in the morning otherwise the view may already be hidden from you.

The path descends from the ridge, slip-sliding down the loose lava pebbles for half an hour. At the foot of the descent the path passes a junction with a trail that leads to Kikelewa Camp. Follow the left-hand fork and veer west towards the Kibo massif.

The path climbs sharply for 30–45mins, regaining the lost height, passing past heathers and everlastings until it plateaus out at the start of the Saddle. It continues to rise on a slow, steady incline as it progresses across this featureless moonscape.

The **terrain** is flat and barren, supporting little life as it is so exposed. Small outcrops of hardy grasses and everlastings can be spotted sheltering under orange-red lava bombs and rock fragments. In the distance Middle Red Hill and the Triplets, some of Kilimanjaro's parasitic cones, can be made out to the south-west – they appear to remain distant but you inch closer.

The narrow path snakes ahead. The journey across the northern section of the Saddle seemingly takes an age since there are few landmarks to gauge your progress by. This is particularly true if the cloud has swamped the Saddle or the weather is bad, in which case visibility can be dramatically reduced. The constant buffeting by the wind and the searing cold can take their toll: make sure that you are properly dressed in warm clothes.

Eventually Kibo Huts comes into view, settled on a rise at the foot of the Kibo crater wall. The path continues to ascend towards this point. Adjacent to the Triplets, at a point known as **Jiwe Lainkoyo**, an old local hunters' campsite, the path intersects with the Marangu Route ascending from Horombo Huts and then makes the final push. Rising past a rocky outcrop, the path arrives at the stone outhouses at the **Kibo Huts** (4710m).

At **Kibo Huts**, the huts are only for trekkers on the Marangu Route; cleared tent pitches surround the basic buildings for trekkers on other routes. There is no water so you must make sure that everything you'll need for the night and the following day's climb to the summit is carried with you to this point. The views back across the Saddle towards Mawenzi are dramatic, especially at dusk, when the blue and violet colours in the sky and the sinisterly shadowed silhouette of the second summit are most striking.

Continuing on from the Rongai Route

You are now poised for the final climb to the peak. The Normal/Marangu Route (Route I) starts from behind Kibo Huts and climbs to Gillman's Point, from where it is possible to access Uhuru Peak, ideally in time to witness the sunrise over Africa.

STAGE 2A

First Camp to Third Cave

Start	First Camp (2635m)
Finish	Third Cave (3935m)
Distance	9km
Time	4–5hrs
Altitude gain	1300m

This shorter, alternative five-day Rongai Route diverts from the more leisurely Rongai Route, offering a faster and more direct route to Kibo. Having ascended to First Camp on the same path as those following the normal Rongai Route, this second stage begins in the same fashion for both branches of the Rongai Route. It isn't until Second Cave, the usual lunch stop, that the paths split and is where the route description for the Alternative Rongai Route begins. See the map for Rongai Route, Stage 2 when following this route.

See Stage 1 and Stage 2 route descriptions in the Rongai Route for instructions as to how to reach this point. Just above the Second Cave the path splits. For Third Cave follow the right-hand fork as it leads straight ahead on a southerly bearing. The path ascends steeply and steadily, crossing several dry streams amid increasingly rocky terrain. A number of clearly visible cairns highlight the way ahead and help you to negotiate the tributary streams of the Nare Moru River. As you near Third Cave, the trail passes a large, distinctive **Bread Rock** on the left-hand side.

Bread Rock is about 12m high and is often adorned with a sizeable cairn, a tradition that has seen other cairns and stacks of stones spring up in the vicinity. Other large rocks now become apparent around the trail, sheltering everlastings.

The path crosses a broad river bed 1½hrs after leaving Second Cave, and brings you to the large, shallow cave that the site is named after at **Third Cave** (3935m). There are long-drop toilets here. The small stream just below the campsite is the last water point on this particular ascent route.

STAGE 3A

Third Cave to School Hut

Start	Third Cave (3935m)
Finish	School Hut (4715m)
Distance	5km
Time	3hrs
Altitude gain	780m

This brief section leads you up a steady incline of increasingly loose scree to either School Hut or Kibo Huts, from where the summit attempt will be launched. Please see the map for Rongai Route, Stage 3 when following this route.

The path leads south-west from Third Cave, climbing steadily all the while. The trail is fairly obvious and clearly marked by cairns. Half an hour after leaving the camp, the track reaches an indistinct crossroad. The path heading roughly north-south is the Northern Circuit Path. Ignore this and continue straight ahead, climbing south-west slowly through the increasingly desolate landscape where everlastings and red lichen provide the only colour relief from the interminable browns and greys of the rock and lava.

After an hour of snaking through this barren place the path crests a false summit. It then descends briefly in a series of zigzags, crossing a number of solidified lava tracks. All too soon it begins to climb again and proceeds to do so for the next hour, becoming even steeper in the immediate approach to **School Hut** (4715m).

School Hut is a large, shabby metal uniport with a wooden floor, set beneath a large rocky outcrop. There are long-drop toilets adjacent to the hut, but no water source. There is a trail from School Hut to Kibo Huts, which heads south from behind one of the toilet shacks for 45mins before arriving at the Kibo Huts site.

CONTINUING FROM THE ALTERNATIVE RONGAI ROUTE

The final ascent from School Hut begins by scrambling west of the hut on a faint trail marked by cairns. The path then follows a south-westerly direction over solidified lava flows, before it zigzags up the loose scree that follows. Rather than heading to the crater rim, however, the path merges with the Normal/Maranagu Route from Kibo Huts after 2km. The two paths meet between William's Point (5130m) and Hans Meyer Cave (5260m). The junction comes after a slight descent, 2hrs from School Hut. You are then faced with a 15min climb to Hans Meyer Cave, which is marked by a memorial plaque for Count Teleki and a subsequent 2½hrs of slogging up loose scree on a series of seemingly endless switchbacks to Gillman's Point and the chance to climb to Uhuru Peak. See Summit ascent routes, Normal/Marangu, Route I, for details.

CIRCUIT PATHS

One of the least used routes on Kilimanjaro is the Circuit Path that surrounds the base of Kibo and circumnavigates the crater mound. Although sections of its southern half are frequently used in conjunction with the Shira, Lemosho, Machame and Umbwe Routes, very few people access the northern part of the loop or indeed complete a full circuit of Kilimanjaro.

The first full circuit of Kibo was completed in 1912 by Oehler and Klute, who spent 10 days in September 1912 carrying out a photogrammetric survey as they skirted the massif. The second full circuit was then not completed until 1969, when a party circumnavigated Kibo in 3½ days. With the further development of the Southern Circuit Path, the route can now readily be completed in just three days. However, a compromise, taking five or six days is much more realistic and enjoyable. The full circuit amounts to nothing more than a stiff walk and although it rises to 4600m, it is not unduly taxing, particularly if additional days are built into your itinerary. If you're interested, you will need to plan it well in advance, find an outfit that can arrange it and possibly secure permission from KINAPA for such an unusual outing on the mountain

The path is largely clear and eminently walkable, particularly on the southern half. The main difficulty is the lack of water on some sections. To counter this, sufficient supplies must be carried to prevent you becoming dehydrated at any point.

Camp amid the lava below Kibo on the Southern Circuit Path (photo: Callum MacNab/Shutterstock.com)

Typical track signposts, seen here showing junction of Southern Circuit Path and Marangu Route

All overnight accommodation is in tents as the battered old uniports that can be found on some stretches of the circuit are unappealing and unsuitable places to sleep. Along some parts of the circuit, even uniports haven't been constructed. At each campsite there are long-drop toilets.

The Circuit Path can be accessed from any number of points, mostly along the southern section. It can then be tackled using a variety of combinations, depending on how long you intend to spend on the mountain. For the sake of simplicity and to reflect the disparity in numbers using each half of the circuit, it is described here in two parts, beginning with the more popular Southern Circuit Path, followed by the less frequented Northern Circuit Path.

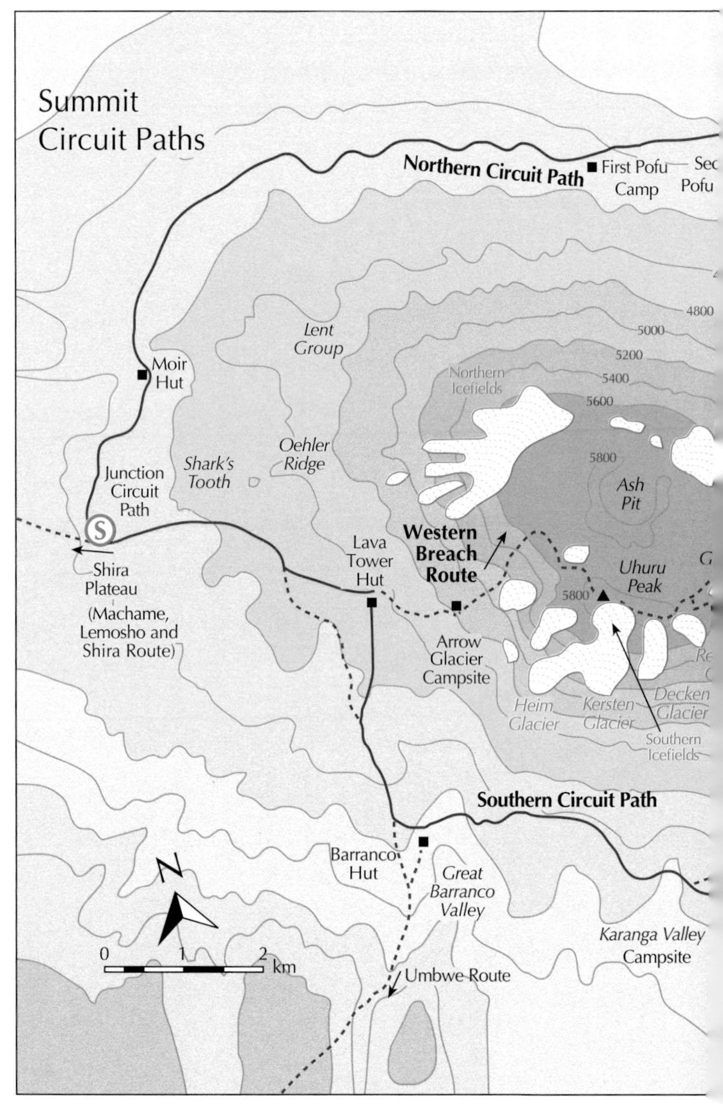
Summit
Circuit Paths
Northern Circuit Path
First Pofu
Camp
Pofu
4800
5000
5200
5400
5600
5800
Lent
Group
Moir
Hut
Northern
Icefields
Oehler
Ridge
Shark's
Tooth
Junction
Circuit
Path
Ash
Pit
S
Western
Breach
Route
Lava
Tower
Hut
Shira
Plateau
(Machame,
Lemosho and
Shira Route)
Uhuru
Peak
5800
Arrow
Glacier
Campsite
Heim
Glacier
Kersten
Glacier
Decken
Glacier
Southern
Icefields
Southern Circuit Path
Barranco
Hut
Great
Barranco
Valley
N
Karanga Valley
Campsite
0
1
2
km
Umbwe Route

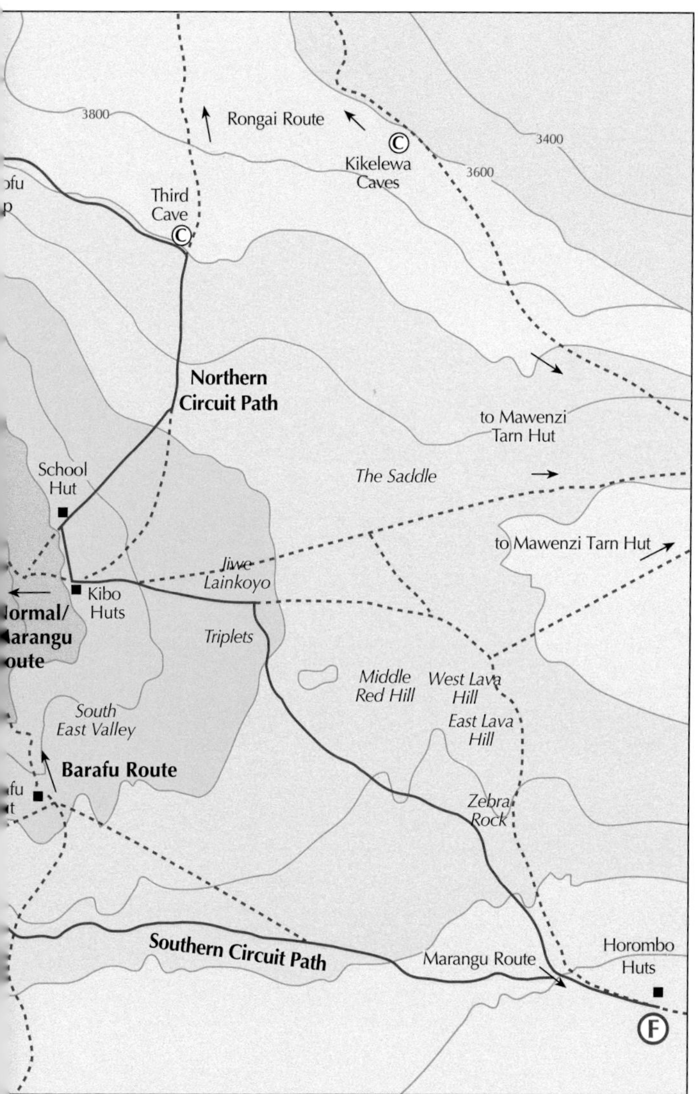

3800
Rongai Route
Kikelewa
Caves
3400
3600
Third
Cave
Northern
Circuit Path
to Mawenzi
Tarn Hut
School
Hut
The Saddle
to Mawenzi Tarn Hut
Jiwe
Lainkoyo
Kibo
Huts
Triplets
Middle
Red Hill
West Lava
Hill
East Lava
Hill
South
East Valley
Barafu Route
Zebra
Rock
Southern Circuit Path
Marangu Route
Horombo
Huts
F

ROUTE G

Southern Circuit Path

Start	Shira Plateau
Finish	Horombo Huts

If you tackle Kilimanjaro by any route other than the Marangu or Rongai Route, you will inevitably end up using part of the Southern Circuit Path to complete your ascent. The path circumnavigates the southern section of Kibo, passing beneath the glorious icefalls of the Heim, Kersten and Decken Glaciers.

At its western end, the path connects to the Machame Route above Shira Hut. This point can also be reached from the Shira and Lemosho routes. The Southern Circuit Path then runs around Kibo, linking the Shira, Lava Tower and Barranco Hut before connecting to the Marangu Route above Horombo Huts at its eastern end. Along its length it is joined by the Umbwe Route and in turn gives rise to the Western Breach and Barafu routes to the crater rim and the Mweka descent route.

Most groups will travel the Southern Circuit Path from west to east, and as such it is described below.

From the Shira Plateau to the Barranco Hut

The beginning of the circuit above the Shira Plateau is indistinct and not at all well marked. The path officially begins just east of the junction of the Shira Route and the Northern Circuit Path. This junction is marked by a splash of red paint on a rock and a sign that points north towards Moir Hut on the Northern Circuit Path. After this point and unbeknown to most walkers, they are traversing the Southern Circuit Path.

At the beginning of the circuit, above the Shira Plateau, the path heads east, aiming directly for Kibo. It undulates towards the massif before curving right and bearing south. Arriving at a distinctive black wedge-shaped rock outcrop, the path splits. The left-hand fork climbs to the foot of the Lava Tower, from where you can access the Arrow Glacier and scale the Western Breach. Most groups take the left-hand fork as it climbs a little higher and aids acclimatisation. It is also privy to some of the most outstanding scenery and views of the Lava Tower and the impressive Western Breach. The right-hand fork winds down a rocky slope and passes to the south of the Lava Tower; after 1km the paths re-join.

From here the route continues to undulate, gradually losing height as it approaches the Barranco Hut (3985m). It takes 2¼hrs to amble from the **Lava Tower** to Barranco

View of the Western Breach and summit amid cloud

Hut, passing a clearly signposted junction that leads directly to **Arrow Glacier** after an hour. **Barranco Hut** is idyllically situated on the western side of the Great Barranco Valley and is a very attractive campsite.

From the Barranco Hut to the Barafu Hut

From the Barranco Hut, the Southern Circuit Path continues east, dropping into the **Great Barranco Valley** and weaving between giant groundsel and *lobelia*. It crosses the Umbwe River tributary at the bottom of the valley and passes a giant boulder at the foot of the Barranco Wall. The 300m high Barranco Wall is a rough, craggy volcanic cliff. Although visually imposing, it isn't too difficult to negotiate. A series of tight switchbacks clamber up the steep face for 30mins and lead to a level area at the top of the Wall. The views from here are simply breathtaking.

Having crested the Barranco Wall, the Southern Circuit Path enters an area of high alpine desert. It continues to skirt Kibo, contouring around the mountain, rising and falling as it negotiates the valleys and ravines that are scratched into the mountainside. The path descends into the picturesque **Karanga Valley** where a stream runs between ferns and heathers. This is the last water for many kilometres and you should take advantage of this to collect as much as possible. The valley is narrow and steep-sided, and is a pleasant place to camp.

A steep zigzag path brings you to the top of the eastern side of the valley. From here the path undulates beneath the looming slopes and Southern Icefields of Kibo. The Heim, Kersten, Decken and Rebmann glaciers bear silent witness to your passing as you struggle onwards.

The Southern Circuit Path reaches a crossroads atop a ridge 7km after leaving the Barranco Hut. The left-hand trail rises steeply through an exceptionally bleak landscape to the Barafu Hut (4660m) on the edge of the South East Valley. The right-hand fork drops smoothly and swiftly off the mountain along the Mweka Route.

From the crossroads to the Horombo Huts

From the crossroads below the Barafu Hut, the Southern Circuit Path itself continues straight on, rippling across the vast expanse of moorland that lies beneath the Saddle.

From here it descends gently across rumpled slopes until it joins the **Marangu Route**, at its eastern end. The Southern Circuit Path–Marangu Route junction is poorly marked and unclear. The faint Southern Circuit Path simply fades into the larger Marangu Route 1km above and to the north-west of the Horombo Huts (3720m).

ROUTE H

Northern Circuit Path

Start	Shira Plateau
Finish	Horombo Huts

Kilimanjaro's Northern Circuit Path is one of the loneliest, least used stretches of track on the entire mountain. To walk this section of path is to be truly isolated and to enjoy the mountain undisturbed. Although you miss out on some of the Southern Circuit highlights and iconic views, you will instead get to enjoy some unusual views of the peaks and be able to appreciate a different aspect of the mountain. You will also be able to look out and over Kenya, in particular the savannah and wild spaces of Amboseli National Park. The route has great, untapped potential, some of which is slowly being realised by people who are combining the Lemosho Route with the Northern Circuit Path and an ascent to the summit from Third Cave Camp on the Rongai Route.

The Northern Circuit Path stretches from the Shira Plateau in the west around Kibo, beneath the massed steps of the Northern Icefields, to the Saddle. The path is relatively straightforward to follow, although it is rocky, uneven and, because it doesn't feature as a part of any of the official routes to the summit, untended and so indistinct in places.

A SEVENTH WAY

The Northern Circuit Path has a raised profile in recent years due to some trekkers and outfitters opting to climb Kilimanjaro starting on the Lemosho Route, then passing on to the Northern Circuit Path and tackling an ascent to the summit from Third Cave Camp on the Rongai Route, via School Hut. Names for this nine-day, 70km hybrid trek vary, but look out for 'Alternative Lemosho', 'TK Lemosho Route' or increasingly outfitters simply offering the 'Northern Circuit Route' and check the details of the itinerary before committing. In taking this route, you avoid the busiest areas on the mountain by staying clear of the Southern Circuit Path used by other routes, can experience the remote northern slopes with their wild scenery and get to see Kilimanjaro from almost all angles. The extra few days this requires allows trekkers to acclimatise better as well. Of course, the extra time and length adds to the cost of the trip, and it is also worth bearing in mind that the route's isolation makes it much harder to escape from in the event of an accident or injury.

From the Shira Plateau to the Moir Hut

At its western extreme, the path begins above the Shira Plateau. While trekking on the Lemosho or Shira Route, east of Simba Cave Camp, you'll see a red splash of paint daubed on a rock and a signpost angled north and inscribed 'Moir Hut', which are the indications that the Northern Circuit Path is about to begin. The path contours around the north-western side of Kibo, averaging around 4100m but peaking at just over 4400m. It begins by climbing slowly for an hour to the west of the Oehler Ridge rock projection that stretches out from beneath the Credner, Drygalski and Pengalski glaciers. Some 3km and around 2hrs after the Moir Hut signpost, the path enters the sheer Lent Valley and reaches the **Moir Hut** (4150m).

Moir Hut itself is a dirty, damaged uniport, but there are tent pitches adjacent and long-drop toilets nearby, all set in an attractive location with good views over the Shira Ridge. Water is available in the vicinity, from a stream about 100 metres below the hut.

Some 2km west lie a number of parasitic cones that collectively form the Lent Group. During the afternoon, following arrival at the Hut, trekkers can climb a nearby ridge to a waterfall fringed with alpine plants.

From the Moir Hut to the Pofu Camps

From the Moir Hut, the path continues to circumnavigate Kibo, climbing steeply out of the valley to the highest point of the day at around 4400m before descending again and contouring clockwise across numerous gullies, rocky lava ribs and gashes in the northern slopes. The path is uneven and littered with rubble and fragments of lava that make the going slow and exhausting. The views up to the peak are good, while downslope you have expansive panoramas first of heathland and forest then of the Kenyan savannah and Amboseli National Park. Keep your eyes peeled and you may also notice buffalo and eland tracks crisscrossing the trail.

There is no other hut or obvious campsite on the remaining section of the Northern Circuit Path. There have long been plans to construct one on the north-eastern side of Kibo, but as yet nothing has come to fruition. Instead, there are three rudimentary sites stood on ridges between valleys at heights between 4000m and 4100m. They all share the same name and are known as the **First, Second and Third Pofu Camps**.

Out of the **Pofu Camps**, typically, the Second Pofu Camp (4030m) is the one operators target on this stretch. None has facilities, not even toilet blocks. Water is also scarce on this section, although the path does stumble across a number of small streams during its traverse of the northern slopes. Unfortunately, at certain times of year these may well be dry.

From the Pofu Camps onwards

Beyond whichever site you camp at, on the eastern side of Kibo, the path continues the following day in the same vein, rising and falling before it eventually climbs up towards the Saddle. A ridge opens onto views of Mawenzi for the first time on this side of the mountain before the path undulates eastwards to intersect with the Rongai Route's direct ascent to School Hut, at the campsite at **Third Cave** (3935m). See Stage 3A and Route I for details of the route from here to the summit.

With the evolution of the latest route on the mountain, the Northern Circuit Path now focusses on climbing from Third Cave to School Hut and to complete a circuit of Kibo you'll need to climb to School Hut, cross to Kibo Huts and then descend via the Marangu Route to Horombo Huts. However, if you are with a guide who knows the way, there are faint tracks beyond the campsite at Third Cave, which allow the original Northern Circuit Path to stumble on south, climbing onto the back of **the Saddle**. Once on the Saddle, it crosses the other branch of the Rongai Route as it tracks from Mawenzi Tarn Hut to Kibo Huts. Cutting across the austere landscape between Mawenzi and Kibo, the Northern Circuit Path descends from the Saddle past West Lava Hill, East Lava Hill and Zebra Rock to meet the junction with the Southern Circuit Path just to the north of Horombo Huts (3720m).

SUMMIT ASCENT ROUTES

Gillman's Point sign and Eastern Icefields in the background

There are three ways that walkers can access the crater rim on Kibo from the high huts on the lower approach routes. Those people who have climbed via the Marangu or Rongai routes will make their summit bid via the Normal/Marangu Route and access the crater rim at Gillman's Point. If instead you climbed either the Umbwe, Machame, Lemosho or Shira routes, you will have been asked to make a choice ahead of your departure as to which final ascent route you would like to tackle. Most people will have opted for the longer but substantially easier Barafu Route, which accesses the crater rim at Stella Point. Those more experienced, fitter and better-acclimatised groups that chose to tackle the alternative route will access the crater via the Western Breach.

The summit day is a long and arduous one, regardless of the route that you take. This is because not only will you make the climb to the crater rim from your top hut or camp, but you will then ascend to the actual summit, before you have to descend again. The descent though takes you not just to the top hut or camp but further off the mountain, to an overnight stop much lower down. You will walk not just the summit ascent route described here but also the first stage of the subsequent descent route: a total of between 15.5 and 22km, over a period of 9–14 hours, with much of this time spent at high altitude.

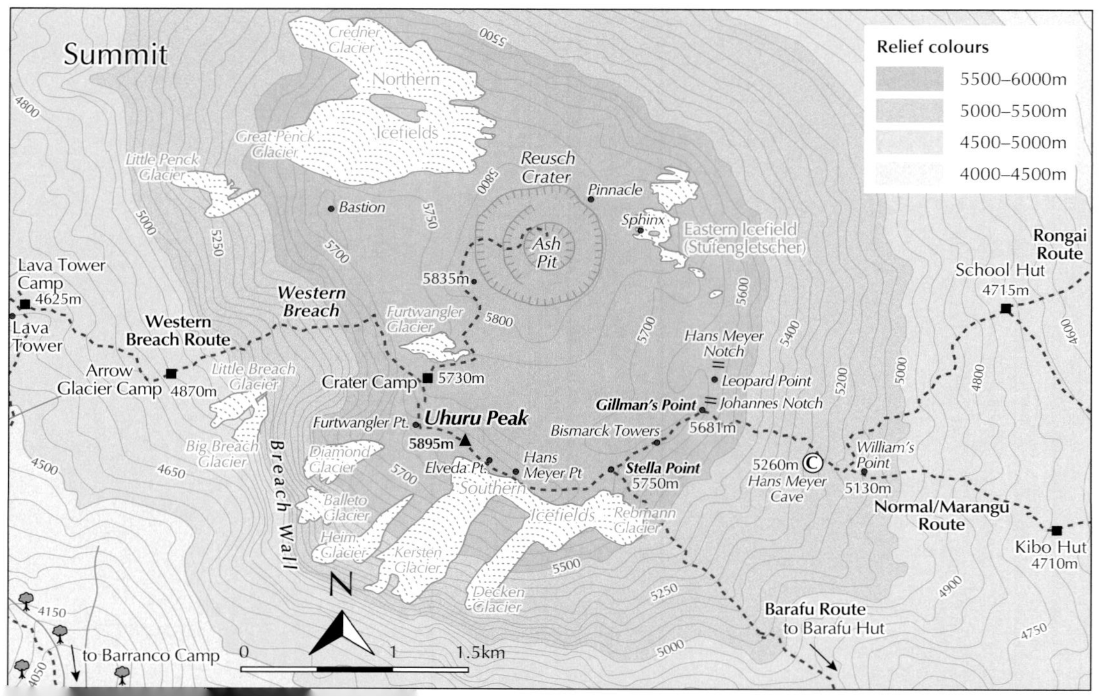
Summit
Relief colours
5500–6000m
5000–5500m
4500–5000m
4000–4500m
Credner Glacier
Northern Icefields
Great Penck Glacier
Little Penck Glacier
Reusch Crater
Pinnacle
Sphinx
Eastern Icefield (Stufengletscher)
Bastion
Ash Pit
Rongai Route
School Hut 4715m
Lava Tower Camp 4625m
Lava Tower
5835m
Western Breach
Western Breach Route
Furtwangler Glacier
Hans Meyer Notch
Leopard Point
Arrow Glacier Camp 4870m
Little Breach Glacier
Crater Camp 5730m
Gillman's Point
Johannes Notch
5681m
Furtwangler Pt.
Uhuru Peak
5895m
Bismarck Towers
Big Breach Glacier
Breach Wall
Diamond Glacier
Elveda Pt.
Hans Meyer Pt
Stella Point 5750m
5260m
Hans Meyer Cave
William's Point 5130m
Southern Icefields
Rebmann Glacier
Balleto Glacier
Heim Glacier
Kersten Glacier
Decken Glacier
Normal/Marangu Route
Kibo Hut 4710m
Barafu Route to Barafu Hut
N
to Barranco Camp
0
1
1.5km
5500
4800
5800
5750
5000
5250
5700
5600
5800
5700
5400
5200
5000
4800
4600
4500
4650
5700
5500
5250
5000
4900
4750
4150
4050

ROUTE I

Normal/Marangu Route

Start	Kibo Huts (4710m)
Finish	Uhuru Peak (5895m)
Distance	6km
Time	6–8hrs
Altitude gain	1185m
Descent route	Marangu Route
Note	This stage describes only the first part of your day: on reaching Uhuru Peak, you will then walk a further 16km to descend, following the first stage of the Marangu descent route (Route L), to overnight at Horombo Huts. A headlamp is vital for this long day and walking poles may also make your progress easier on the unstable, shifting surface.

This is the standard ascent route for the majority of climbers on Kilimanjaro. First climbed by Lange and Weigele on 6 July 1909, it is essentially a continuation of the Marangu Route. As such, it is frequently known as the Marangu Route to the summit. The push to the crater rim from Kibo Huts is a steep, endless slog on loose scree that frequently gets the better of aspiring summit groups. In fact, the success rate on this route is surprisingly low, in part because of the steep and loose surface and partly because this ascent route crests the crater rim at the furthest point from the summit, leaving you the longest trek round the rim to the actual highest point of the mountain. The ascent to Gillman's Point takes around four-and-half to six hours and the push to Uhuru Peak takes a further one-and-half to two hours. If the weather is bad, this final section may take much longer or even be impractical to attempt.

Your day is not over when you reach the summit. After celebrating your achievement, you will then walk the first stage of the Marangu descent route (Route L) to reach Horombo Huts.

What time to set off? Most groups will aim to leave at around midnight–1.00am in order to maximise their chances of being on the summit for sunrise just after 6.00am, depending on the time of year. Furthermore, by setting off in the dark, the scree is more likely to be frozen, making passage easier. You will also be unable to see the sheer scale of the task ahead! Besides, sleep for any length of time at this altitude is hard to come by. However, try not to arrive on the crater rim too early as you may have to wait in very cold, windy conditions for the sunrise to take place, and there is no shelter on the summit of a mountain.

Slower moving groups may well arrive on the summit long after the sun is in the sky. Do keep an eye on the time, however, since the summit marks only the halfway point for your day's exertions – you must also descend to Kibo Huts and most usually beyond, to Horombo Huts, the same day.

Having been shaken from your fitful sleep, try to drink something before setting off. The path to the summit lies directly behind Kibo Huts. Follow your guide as the track winds away from the huts and begins to scale the slopes. The early sections are uneven and rocky and care should be taken as you find a suitable, comfortable rhythm. A slow, steady pace is less tiring than taking a lot of short breaks and moving too quickly between them. It is imperative that you stick to the Kilimanjaro mantra, and ascend 'pole pole', slowly, slowly.

After 2hrs the trail climbs to Williams Point (5130m) and then on for 30mins to Hans Meyer Cave (5260m), which marks the approximate halfway point in time spent climbing, although you have gained less than half the requisite height by this stage. The cave is much less grand than its name suggests and is a rather shallow hollow, marked by a plaque that commemorates the Hungarian Samuel Teleki's stay here in 1887.

After the cave, the trail steepens considerably as it begins a series of demoralising switchbacks over small scree and gravel. This is by far the hardest part of the climb. The zigzags tighten as you gain altitude and pass between two rocky ridges. You are now required to focus on the endless and enormous task of stepping into the footprints of the walker ahead of you. Set yourself small goals and continue to march on. Use trekking poles for balance and support, especially if the wind picks up on this very exposed section. Small kick steps will reduce the likelihood of scree slipping back and carrying you down the slope. The pure drudgery will dull even the most resilient spirit and the sheer exertion means that there is very little spare energy for talking. Equally, there is nothing in the repetitive nature of the climb to hold your attention, bump your thoughts from snippets of song on heavy rotation or disturb the incessant reiteration of snatches of conversation in your head.

Although the looming ridge seems to refuse to get any closer, your progress up the slope is fairly rapid. Just below the crater rim, some 2½hrs from Hans Meyer Cave, the switchbacks and scree give way to larger boulders and jumbled rocks. The path here becomes even less distinct and you may have to scramble the last section onto the crater rim. Gaining the rim, you arrive at a small, level area, signposted Gillman's Point (5681m).

From **Gillman's Point** (named after a celebrated climber and prominent early member of the Mountain Club of East Africa) you can see down into the crater, across to the massive, stacked Eastern Icefields and out across the Saddle

THE TORTUOUS TRUTH

The photojournalist John Reader made a series of chilling calculations regarding the ascent from Kibo Huts to Gillman's Point. In his book, *Kilimanjaro,* he wrote: 'Gillman's Point is 980 metres above Kibo Huts, that is almost the equivalent of three Empire State Buildings standing one on top of another. The horizontal distance between Kibo Huts and Gillman's Point is roughly 3000 metres, so the gradient averages about 1:3.3 and the distance covered on the way up is about 3300 metres – the equivalent of nine Empire State Buildings laid end to end up the incline. The climb is not difficult in mountaineering terms; you could say it is equivalent to scrambling up a staircase rather more than three kilometres long. Or you could say it is equivalent to clambering up the side of nine Empire State Buildings laid end to end at about sixteen degrees. But then at 4710 metres, where the final ascent of Kilimanjaro begins, there is little more than half the density of oxygen which occurs on Manhattan or at the foot of most staircases. So in effect, the aspiring climber attempts the equivalent of those feats with the equivalent of only one lung.' He goes on to conclude 'The result is agonizing, there is no other word for it.'

to the silhouetted outline of Mawenzi. Gillman's Point is a small access point and it isn't really possible to loiter here for long. Unless unable to carry on, you ought to move on fairly swiftly in order to make space for other climbers coming up behind you. However, do take a moment to catch your breath and marvel at the sheer beauty of the place.

If you arrive at the crater rim and there is no signpost, you are most likely to be just to the right of Gillman's Point, at Johannes Notch. This spot is named after the then District Officer in Moshi, who reached here in 1898. Catch your breath and clamber left for 5mins, along the rim of the crater, until you arrive at the appropriate place.

From Gillman's Point, walk left along the crater rim, teetering between the steep drop into the crater itself and the outer slopes as they fall away smoothly. The views in every direction are exceptional and as the sunrise unravels then bursts from behind Mawenzi, you will be privy to one of the most spectacular, moving sights in Africa.

The haul from Gillman's Point to Uhuru Peak typically takes 1½–2hrs and is riddled with false summits that test your stamina and commitment to conquering Uhuru Peak. Although not especially steep, it is exceptionally draining and you may need to rest regularly before you arrive at the signpost that marks the highest point in Africa, hopefully in time to see the sunrise.

To discover what lies on the summit, see the Summit section of this guide. Once you're ready to descend, it will again be on the Marangu Route, as you retrace your footsteps as you retreat, see Route L.

ROUTE J

Barafu Route

Start	Barafu Hut (4660m)
Finish	Uhuru Peak (5895m)
Distance	4.5km
Time	6–8hrs
Altitude gain	1235m
Descent route	Mweka Route
Note	This stage describes only the first part of your day: on reaching Uhuru Peak, you will then walk a further 11.5km to descend, following the first stage of the Mweka descent route (Route M), to overnight at Mweka Hut. A headlamp is vital for this long day and walking poles may also make your progress easier on the unstable, shifting surface.

A version of the Barafu Route was first used in the opening half of the 20th century to access Kibo's crater rim. Today it is usually tackled in association with the Machame Route, although it can also be accessed from the Umbwe, Lemosho and Shira routes. Regardless of the approach route, this is the most strenuous part of the climb. The climb to Stella Point on the crater rim usually takes around four-and-half to six hours and the push to Uhuru Peak takes a further one-and-half to two hours.

The Barafu Route is a steep, tough ascent on loose scree and small rocks that crests the crater rim alongside the Rebmann Glacier at Stella Point. The climb is only a stiff walk, except in the aftermath of heavy snow when it may become much more of an effort. During the driest months from December to March the whole route is usually free from snow. In the remainder of the year you may encounter snow as low as 4600m. However, the altitude and cold add to the overall hardship on the climb.

Your day is not over when you reach the summit. After celebrating your achievement, you will then walk the first stage of the Mweka descent route (Route M) to reach Mweka Hut.

> **What time to set off?** As on all of the final ascent routes, the climb to the crater rim begins shortly after midnight in order to take advantage of the frozen scree and ensure that you arrive on the crater rim or at the summit in time for sunrise. By setting off early, you will also guarantee that you have sufficient time to descend from the mountain to the Mweka Hut, the overnight campsite on the way down the mountain from here.

From the Barafu Hut the path winds up the western side of the South East Valley. The path scales two short, rocky cliffs to the north of Barafu Hut before levelling as it approaches the final steep climb to Stella Point. The path bends left and begins to zig-zag up the slope on a series of tight switchbacks. These switchbacks persist for the next 3hrs. The climb is in no way technical, but the tedious slog on loose and enervating scree and shale is disheartening. Kick your feet into the scree and plant your walking poles firmly into the slope to help you edge your way up the slope and prevent yourself from slipping unduly.

The gradient increases yet further as you arrive at the final incline. The switchbacks peter out and the final 30min direct ascent is done on fine, loose gravel. As you approach the snout of the Rebmann Glacier, the path jigs right to climb between this and the remains of the Ratzel Glacier. Follow the gap up until the gradient relents and you gain the crater rim at Stella Point (5750m).

> **Stella Point** is named after the wife of Kingsley Latham, a member of the Mountain Club of South Africa. They both reached this point in 1925. By this stage the sun is probably set to rise from behind Mawenzi and the thin band of red and gold on the horizon is likely to be expanding rapidly. Pause at Stella Point and revel in your achievement as the light fills the sky and

Silhouette of Mawenzi from Stella Point at sunrise

Rebmann Glacier lit by the rising sun, as seen from Stella Point

the sun bursts from behind the horizon, illuminating the glacial snows and the blanket of clouds lying far below you. Behind you, to the north, is the crater. The view across the inner Reusch Crater to the Northern Icefields is similarly powerful.

The route from Stella Point to Uhuru Peak is the same as that from Gillman's Point (the access point on the crater rim from the Marangu and Rongai routes). Gillman's Point lies 30–45mins to the right of Stella Point. For the summit, turn left and head west around the crater edge, passing above the stepped Rebmann Glacier, ascending slowly for 1–1½hrs until you arrive at the celebrated signpost on the 'Roof of Africa' at Uhuru Peak.

To discover what lies on the summit, see the Summit section. Once you are ready to descend, those climbers that ascended via the Machame Route or Lemosho, Shira and Umbwe routes will take the Mweka Route back down, see Route M.

ROUTE K

Western Breach Route

Start	Lava Tower (4625m)
Finish	Uhuru Peak (5895m)
Distance	6.5km
Descent	Mweka Route
Time	6–7½hrs (usually walked over 2 days, with an overnight at Arrow Glacier)
Altitude gain	1270m
Note	A headlamp is vital and walking poles may also make your progress easier on the unstable, shifting surface; if there has been a heavy snowfall you may require an ice axe and crampons.

The Western Breach can be accessed from the Machame, Umbwe, Lemosho and Shira routes, most usually via an overnight stop at Lava Tower. The descent from the summit after this route is traditionally done along the Mweka Route. It is the hardest, most impressive non-technical route to the crater rim. The Western Breach is a rugged gash in Kibo's flank, which disturbs the uniform shape of the summit. Created by a massive landslip around 100,000 years ago, the gradient here is marginally less steep than the sheer cliffs that surround the route. The climbers Oehler and Klute first descended the route in 1912. The date of the first ascent is not recorded, but it is known that the Sheffield University scientific survey party ascended the Western Breach in August–September 1953.

The views are breathtaking and the fact that the route is so much less popular than either the Normal/Marangu Route or the Barafu Route means that you will have a far greater sense of isolation and wildness. The reason for this lack of popularity is readily apparent. Although there is no technical climbing involved, this is a classic scramble route involving some very steep sections and some quite exposed areas. Exertion is high and the route should only be contemplated by fit and highly acclimatised groups.

The route has a reputation for toughness and has also been associated with tragedy. In January 2006 three American climbers were killed by rockfall and a further five were injured as a glacial deposit collapsed and sent stones hurtling 150m down the cliffside and onto the climbing party close to Arrow Glacier. In the aftermath the route was closed for a year while experts assessed the slope and looked into the incident. When it did reopen, climbers were required to wear helmets during the ascent and to sign a waiver clearing the operators of liability. A number of operators have dropped it from their portfolios as the route has remained unchanged and still navigates a section where rockfall is possible. Still, the route remains a non-technical climb on an average gradient of around 25 degrees, with some stiffer sections along its length. As far as is known, it has been free from incident since the 2006 tragedy.

The Western Breach is in some respects a one-way ticket, since there is little option of retreat once you have started up the face. A little after your departure, the porters will strike camp and race around the bulk of Kibo in order to meet you in time to pitch camp at Mweka Hut. Thus, if you turn back, there will be no shelter, food or water at Arrow Glacier. Your only real option is to then descend all the way to Mweka Hut yourself, in pursuit of your porters. That is, of course, unless you are camping in the crater, a rarely taken but exciting overnight option, which sees your climbing team ascend with you to set up tents at Crater Camp, from where you can explore the Reusch Crater and Ash Pit before ascending to Uhuru Peak.

STAGE 1

Lava Tower to Arrow Glacier

Start	Lava Tower (4625m)
Finish	Arrow Glacier (4870m)
Distance	2.5km
Time	1–1½hrs
Altitude gain	245m

The Western Breach is best tackled in two stages. The first stage sees you ascend from Lava Tower to Arrow Glacier, from where you are ideally poised to begin the final ascent. The ascent is very short but the additional 245m height gained and the extra 24-hour exposure to altitude is invaluable.

REACHING LAVA TOWER

Those arriving via the Lemosho Route or the Shira Route will end their ascent routes at Shira 2 Camp/Shira Hut. From there, you will follow the path from the campsite and ascend over 5km to join the Southern Circuit Path, where you will veer left to reach Lava Tower Camp. Those who followed the Machame Route will divert to Lava Tower Camp rather than continue on the more popular route to Barranco Hut. From the Umbwe Route, the trail joins the Southern Circuit Path, where you head north-west for 3.5km to reach the Lava Tower. If coming from the Umbwe Route or via the Southern Circuit Path, there is the option to skip Lava Tower and progress

Campsite at foot of Lava Tower

straight to Arrow Glacier. Unless you are exceptionally fit and well acclimatised, this is not recommended. Use the additional half day and time at Lava Tower to prepare yourself physically and psychologically for the challenge ahead.

From the campsite in the shadow of the orange-black volcanic plug of the Lava Tower, the path is clearly visible, winding across a set of desolate ridges. The track descends slightly and crosses a small stream of meltwater before beginning to climb on fine loose gravel. A series of small tight switchbacks carry you to the top of the first ridge after 20–30mins. From the top of this ridge there are great views of the Lava Tower and across the northern flank of Kilimanjaro towards the Shira Plateau.

The path dips briefly in order to descend into a small valley and ford a further meltwater stream. It quickly picks up and rises again, crossing slightly larger obstacles as it regains the lost height. Use walking poles and carefully placed steps to keep your balance here. After 30mins the path crests the ridge and enters a small, level area at the foot of a vast, natural amphitheatre. This is the Arrow Glacier Campsite (4870m).

ARROW GLACIER CAMPSITE

Arrow Glacier itself is visible east of the campsite on the far side of a creased plateau. The imperious glacier is in retreat and what was once a significant mass of ice is now a rather grubby shadow of its former self. Arrow Glacier Hut was destroyed by a rock fall in the mid 1980s and hasn't been rebuilt since.

There are few obvious tent pitches here, but, when selecting a site, try to place yourself in the lee of the rocky prow that rises on the western side of the plateau and affords some small shelter from the raging winds that hustle across the plateau. In the midst of the plateau are rather exposed long-drop toilets, some of which have been destroyed by rockfall. Water is usually fetched from meltwater streams flowing from the Arrow Glacier, 200 metres east of the camp.

The campsite is a particularly inhospitable, barren place to camp. However, the views are sensational. The camp is set right at the foot of the Western Breach. Ahead of you an enormous amphitheatre rises from the boulders and scree. To the east of the Western Breach itself stands the massive, sheer cliffs of the Breach Wall. This 1400m cliff features some of the hardest technical mountaineering on Kilimanjaro and indeed the whole of Africa. Legendary mountaineer Reinhold Messner, and Konrad Renzler first climbed the direct route on the Breach Wall, which includes an improbable ascent of a 90m icicle that links two glaciers, on 31 January 1978. The route has been likened to the north face of the Eiger in terms of technical difficulty.

There are several sobering reminders of the severity of the climbing in the area. While exploring the immediate slopes you may well come across a brass plaque commemorating the death of a young American climber in 1972 from AMS. However, it's worth remembering that it's not just climbers that must beware here, trekkers too are at risk and the 2006 tragedy serves to reinforce the need for caution in this area at all times.

The wind often picks up later in the day and can be heard whipping across the summit. Cloud will often mount up in the afternoon as well, obscuring the way ahead. Having explored the area, retreat to the relative comfort of your tent to eat and sleep, and await the early morning summons to tackle the climb to the summit.

STAGE 2

Arrow Glacier to Uhuru Peak

Start	Arrow Glacier (4870m)
Finish	Uhuru Peak (5895m)
Distance	4km
Time	5–6hrs
Altitude gain	1025m
Note	This stage describes only the first part of your day: on reaching Uhuru Peak, you will then walk a further 11.5km to descend, following the first stage of the Mweka descent route (Route M), to overnight at Mweka Hut.

This final approach to the crater rim and on to Uhuru Peak is the toughest non-technical climb on Kilimanjaro. In less than ideal conditions, the Western Breach has epic potential. The ascent is steep and exposed, requiring you to use both hands to scramble upwards in places. On the plus side, the climb is exhilarating and the sense of achievement enormous. The ascent is akin to a series of steep stairs with sections of ladder thrown in for good measure. Once you begin the ascent proper, the climb is free of the scree and loose material that characterises the climb to the crater rim on either the Normal/Marangu Route or the Barafu Route. The Western Breach ought to be clear and viable most of the year round. Although this is a non-technical trekking route, if there has been heavy snowfall then it may become impassable without the aid of an ice axe and crampons.

Your day is not over when you reach the summit. After celebrating your achievement, you will then walk the first stage of the Mweka descent route (Route M) to reach Mweka Hut.

What time to set off? Most groups depart from Arrow Glacier Campsite at around 1.00am, allowing themselves to climb through the night and take advantage of the frozen scree and more stable underfoot conditions. In turn, this should ensure that you arrive on the summit in time for sunrise.

If you are lucky and the night sky is clear, then you will begin by picking your way across the lower scree slopes beneath a star-studded, black obsidian sky. Use a head-light to illuminate a path over the rocks as you begin to ascend east on the small talus and scree hill above Arrow Glacier Campsite past overhanging cliffs and pale patches of snow and ice. Above this is a rock rib. Skirt this, climbing alongside it for 500 metres until the path arrives at the foot of the wall ahead. Here the path cuts right onto the rocky rib and becomes steeper. A section of abrupt scrambling follows, which will require you to stow your walking poles in order to be able to use both hands to stabilise and balance yourself. The Arrow Glacier Campsite shrinks far below you as you gain height, edging between the patches of residual snow and ice.

Unlike the other two walking ascents to the crater rim, you can not simply drift up the slope in a trance. On the Western Breach you must focus and concentrate closely on what you are doing. There is little margin for error and a fall here could be very serious indeed. Nonetheless, the haul to Uhuru is a sensational skywalk.

You will have unprecedented **views** over the Shira Plateau and western flank, providing the moon is full or even if the night is clear, allowing you to gauge the sheer physical size of the mountain and get a real feel for its enormity.

View of the sheer Breach Wall

The final climb to the crater rim takes 4–5hrs and is via a series of steep cliffs and intricate buttresses above airy drops, which require you to take large vertical steps and hold yourself in place with both hands. Having zigzagged from one cliff to another, you will arrive at a depression in the crater rim, occasionally referred to as the Great West Notch (5730m).

Once inside the crater, you will be faced by the Furtwangler Glacier at the western foot of the central ash cone. The glacier is named after a climber who summited in 1912 and then became the first man to descend Kilimanjaro on skis. To the right the crater rim rises approximately 250m and away to the south-east Uhuru Peak is visible. The path is indistinct, but circumvents the crater floor between the Furtwangler Glacier and the edge of the Western Breach.

Approach the peppermint snout of the glacier. Keep the glacier on your left as you crunch across the level interior of the crater. As you pass by the glacier, feel the icy chill that hums off the white-blue wall like electricity. On the far side of the crater, some 2km away, Stella Point is visible. Some 10mins from the crater rim is Crater Camp.

Crater Camp is the overnight stop for people sleeping in the crater itself. Bear in mind that this is an exceptional place to camp with extraordinary costs associated with it as your climbing team must all ascend to the crater with you. From here, there is a faint trail that snakes north, around the Furtwangler Glacier to arrive 45mins later at the Reusch Crater and the climb to a viewpoint that lets you gaze down into the Ash Pit itself.

South of the camp is a path that brings you to the foot of a steep gully. A clear track zigzags up the slope to the left of a prominent buttress. As you gain height on the switchbacks, pause and look back over the Furtwangler Glacier to the Reusch Crater and beyond to the massed steps of the Northern Icefields.

After 1hr of ascending these strenuous final switchbacks, the path bends left one more time and climbs onto the edge of the crater rim. Away to the west, Mount Meru is often hazily visible. From here the path follows the edge of the crater rim south for 15–30mins, climbing slightly to reach Uhuru Peak (5895m). As you approach the signpost that marks the summit, Mawenzi will be silhouetted across the crater and the sun will rise from behind its jagged peaks to signify the beginning of another glorious day.

For more detail on what lies on the summit see the next section. Those climbers that ascend the Western Breach will then drop off the summit via the Mweka Route, see Route M.

THE SUMMIT

'Kilimanjaro is a snow covered mountain 19,710ft high, and is said to be the highest mountain in Africa. Its western summit is called "Ngaje Ngai", the House of God.'

Ernest Hemmingway, The Snows of Kilimanjaro

Southern Icefields seen from the crater rim on the final push to Uhuru from Stella Point

The summit of Kilimanjaro is a remarkable, otherworldly place. The crown of Kibo is a vast crater that contains an inner crater and an ash pit – upon cresting the crater rim you finally get to see that what you've been climbing isn't a mountain but in fact a volcano. The blasted rock and shattered slopes give it a harsh air, while the improbable icefields and glaciers decorate the rim and upper slopes. The landscape here is akin to a still raw wound, redolent of the earth's violent and explosive past.

The highest point on the crater rim is Uhuru Peak (5895m). This is unsurprisingly the focus for the majority of walkers. However, whether they make it to the summit is still open to question since the peak is some distance from any of the crater access points. HW Tilman observed: 'Between the point at which the crater wall is first reached and this highest point, a distance of perhaps 600 or 700 yards, are three other peaks, points, or bumps of varying heights, all slightly lower than Kaiser Wilhelm Spitze [now Uhuru Peak] itself. These several points were always the cause of much heart burning.'

For many people simply gaining the crater rim is sufficient reward. Gillman's Point is the lowest point on the southern rim, just 25m above the crater floor. Accessed from the Normal/Marangu Route, it is still 1.5km from Uhuru Peak. The summit is a further 210m higher than this Gillman's Point and the arduous approach to Stella Point and onwards past Rebmann Glacier, Decken Glacier and the Southern Icefield, comprising Kersten Glacier and Heim Glacier, is often too daunting for exhausted walkers. Tilman himself, and his companion Eric Shipton, failed to reach Uhuru Peak on his first attempt in 1930, admitting that beyond Stella Point 'Yet another top loomed vaguely through the mists some distance ahead, but I am obliged to confess that its challenge aroused little interest in us, and, after debate, we turned in our tracks.'

Those that do have the strength to push on to the summit will be richly rewarded. The view from Uhuru is utterly breathtaking. The whole summit looks unfinished. In the thin and freezing air every line and every colour is sharp. Everything is jagged. There are no curves, no fading, no blurring. It is beautiful. From the summit you will be able to see across the outer crater and over the resurgent inner cone to the remarkable Northern Icefields and beyond to the sun-blushed clouds below. Inside the inner cone is the Reusch Crater and the 360-metres-wide, 120m-deep Ash Pit, reputed to be one of the finest examples of its type in the world.

For those wishing to access the Reusch Crater and see into the heart of the volcano, there is a trail that leads from the top of the Western Breach to Crater Camp (5730m). For this reason, it is mostly people tackling the Western Breach that go on to explore the Reusch Crater. Beyond the campsite, a faint trail makes its way around the southern edge of the much reduced Furtwangler Glacier before heading roughly northwards to the foot of the Reusch Crater and upwards to the top of the cone, where you'll smell sulphur and be able to see yellow deposits and fumaroles that still occasionally smoke, all clues confirming the fact that Kilimanjaro is only dormant and not extinct. The climb itself is relatively simple, allowing for the fact that you are at extreme altitude, and takes 45mins to an hour to complete from Crater Camp. If you ascend via the other summit routes it is still possible to drop into the crater, via Gillman's Point or, more usually, Stella Point, from where an indistinct trail picks its way gently downhill towards Crater Camp and then joins the route that climbs to the foot of the cone. The path is virtually invisible, but your guide should be able to find his way.

Sunrise from Uhuru Peak (FrdoGn/Shutterstock.com)

Make sure that you arrange the trip to the Reusch Crater well in advance of your climb. This remains a fairly unusual addition to any ascent of the mountain and will require additional preparation and will certainly incur extra cost. Similarly, if you intend to camp in the crater, which is only recommended for very well acclimatised climbers, bear in mind that this is unusual and as an exceptional overnight stay it will be exorbitantly expensive as your guide and porter team will have to ascend to the crater and camp there with you. But it's hard to beat for bragging rights.

KILIMANJARO'S FABLED HIDDEN TREASURE

A well-known legend alludes to the burial place of Menelik I, the great emperor of Ethiopia and the son of Solomon and Sheba, on the summit of Kilimanjaro. A popular and successful monarch, Menelik I expanded his territories to include the lands to the south of Ethiopia, as far as Kilimanjaro. As the elderly king journeyed home after these conquests, he passed over the Saddle and determined to die on the mountain. Gathering a number of his warlords and his personal slaves, Menelik I collected his finest treasures and set off up the slopes. The warlords later returned unaccompanied and reported that the king and his slaves had descended into the crater in order to sleep forever. The legend maintains that an heir to the throne will climb Kilimanjaro and discover the fabled treasures along with the Seal of Solomon, the mystical ring responsible for his great wisdom. Armed with this discovery, the heir would then claim the throne and help Ethiopia to reclaim her exulted status.

Jubilant celebrations at the summit

DESCENT ROUTES

Dendrosenecio in front of Kibo (photo: Avatar/Shutterstock.com)

In order to reduce the potential damage to the mountain and to channel people descending off the summit, there are several dedicated descent routes on Kilimanjaro. Having ascended slowly to the summit over the course of several days, you will drop off the mountain quickly, taking a fraction of the time to return to a lower elevation.

National park regulations stipulate that particular ascent routes are affiliated with particular descent routes. Those people who climb the Marangu or Rongai routes will be required to descend along the Marangu Route. Those who used the other ascent routes will have to come off the mountain on the Mweka Route.

ROUTE L

Marangu Route

Start	Kibo Huts (4710m)
Finish	Marangu Gate (1905m)
Distance	29km (35km from Uhuru Peak)
Time	2 days
Altitude loss	2805m (3990m from Uhuru Peak)

Having ascended via the Normal/Marangu Route, whether in conjunction with the Marangu Route or the Rongai Route, you will descend the mountain along the Marangu Route. For those who used the Marangu Route on the ascent this is an unfortunate retracing of your steps that is one of the drawbacks to using this particular climb. For those who approached Kibo from the north along the Rongai Route, this is a chance to see an entirely different aspect of the mountain and to enjoy some of the forest sections that have been cleared on the lower northern slopes.

STAGE 1

Kibo Huts to Horombo Huts

Start	Kibo Huts (4710m)
Finish	Horombo Huts (3720m)
Distance	10km (16km from Uhuru Peak)
Time	3–4hrs (5–6hrs from Uhuru Peak)
Altitude loss	990m (2175m from Uhuru Peak)

If you've climbed Kilimanjaro on the Marangu Route you will have most likely ascended from Horombo Huts onto the Saddle via the Southern Path. In which case, persuade your guide to take you back via the Northern Path, which will prevent you from simply seeing the same features again and instead give you access to some incredible panoramas and some interesting hollows populated with giant groundsels. This is the path that is described below.

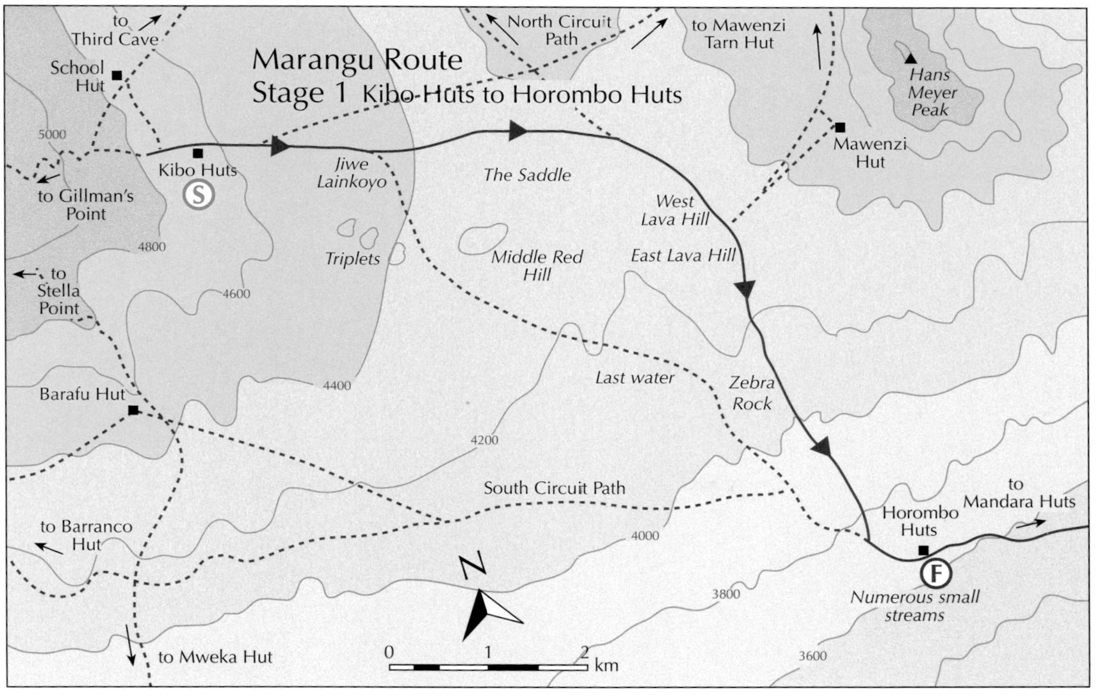
Marangu Route
Stage 1 Kibo-Huts to Horombo Huts
to Third Cave
School Hut
North Circuit Path
to Mawenzi Tarn Hut
Hans Meyer Peak
Mawenzi Hut
5000
Kibo Huts
S
to Gillman's Point
Jiwe Lainkoyo
The Saddle
West Lava Hill
4800
Triplets
Middle Red Hill
East Lava Hill
to Stella Point
4600
Last water
Zebra Rock
4400
Barafu Hut
4200
South Circuit Path
to Mandara Huts
Horombo Huts
to Barranco Hut
4000
F
N
3800
Numerous small streams
to Mweka Hut
0
1
2
km
3600

From Uhuru Peak to Kibo Huts

Having loitered on the summit, revelled in your achievement and taken the obligatory photographs, turn back and begin to retreat from Uhuru Peak around the crater rim to Gillman's Point. The return journey is equally slow and tiring due to the altitude. After an hour of shuffling and stopping, the path arrives at **Gillman's Point**.

> It is essential to be back at **Gillman's Point** around 3hrs after sunrise, since the top layer of snow is by now beginning to become wet and slippery, complicating your descent. Equally, the rising sun is very strong and can be harsh to spend too much time under.

From Gillman's Point, lower yourself over the large rocky outcrops until you reach the beginning of the scree slope. By now you can see just how large and horrific this gravel slope is. It is likely that it is also no longer frozen, making the surface much less stable. Every step will be accompanied by a sink and slide, making the descent to Kibo Huts almost as tough as the original climb. Many of the zigzags are indistinguishable, but try to avoid simply running down the scree, as this can cause large amounts of disturbance to the mountainside, forcing tons of rock down the slopes. It also causes a lot of fine, irritating dust to be kicked up and will increase your chances of having a potentially dangerous fall.

The descent to Kibo Huts takes 2hrs, although it will feel much longer since the huts are visible from high on the mountainside and don't appear to get any closer despite your exhausted, sleep-deprived body's best efforts in steadily rising temperatures.

Eventually the path careers past Hans Meyer Cave and Williams Point before coiling across the foothills and back to Kibo Huts, where, dusty and sweat-streaked, you'll receive your congratulations or commiserations. Try to rest here for 1–2hrs, drinking and rehydrating your body.

Leave **Kibo Huts** as you arrived and drop back down to the Saddle. Beneath the prominent rocky outcrop at the entrance to the Kibo Huts area is a fork in the path. Ignore the path to the left, which traverses the Saddle on its way to Third Cave Camp on the Rongai Route, and follow the larger, clearer track on the right-hand side of **the Saddle**.

Descend through the vast, featureless alpine desert for 45mins to an hour to **Jiwe Lainkoyo**. Beyond here, the standard Marangu Route branches right and then makes its way downhill, past the Triplets and Middle Red Hill, towards Horombo Huts. A fainter trail continues east towards Mawenzi from Jiwe Lainkoyo which makes a good alternative if you have already ascended the Marangu Route. Some 20mins later the trail passes a sign indicating the intersection with the Northern Circuit Path, although this new route is almost invisible in the soil of the Saddle, so faint it is. Ignore the sign and continue east, undulating as you work your way across Mawenzi's lower slopes.

An hour beyond the junction you reach the highest point on this section of path and are afforded excellent views by looking back across the expanse of the Saddle towards Kibo's eastern face. The path then drops due south gently past a series of low cliffs towards **Zebra Rock**. Once past this distinctive, unusually stripped cliff face, the path reconnects with the standard Marangu Route path and then descends briefly between rocky outcrops, boulders and groundsel to arrive at **Horombo Huts** (3720m), some 2½hrs after leaving Jiwe Lainkoyo. Here trekkers from the Marangu ascent will stay in the huts and people from the Rongai ascent will camp.

STAGE 2

Horombo Huts to Marangu Gate

Start	Horombo Huts (3720m)
Finish	Marangu Gate (1905m)
Distance	20km
Time	4–4½hrs
Altitude loss	1815m

This final section is a very satisfying end to your Kilimanjaro experience. The descent is gentle and steady and passes through some very pleasant stretches of scenery. If you ascended via the Rongai Route, on the other side of the mountain, this will be the first opportunity you have to really explore this forest zone and the flora found here. Walk slowly, enjoy the downhill gradient and look at the minutiae along the trail. You'll also be able to see both Kibo and Mawenzi slip away from you.

Retrace your steps across the heath/moorland through the tussock grasses and heathers. Inevitably, a multi-coloured tide of humanity flowing uphill will pass you on its way towards Kibo's ramparts. The path re-enters the forest and drops swiftly to **Mandara Huts**, arriving here after 2½–3hrs. This is usually used as the last lunch stop on the mountain.

Having finished your snacks, continue walking by joining the path as it snakes through the forest. Make the most of your final moments on this monolith, since the Marangu Gate is reached after only a further 1½hrs. To avoid having to retrace your footsteps all the way back to the gate, consider taking the signposted route onto the Marangu Nature Trail. This heavily overgrown path isn't often trekked so can be a bit wild but it gives you a good forest experience as you come off the mountain and is only marginally longer than the standard route. At the end of the path, it ascends some steps to join the main path, with the gate ahead of you. Pass under an archway and finish before the National Park Offices, where you conclude your trip by registering your success and collecting your certificate.

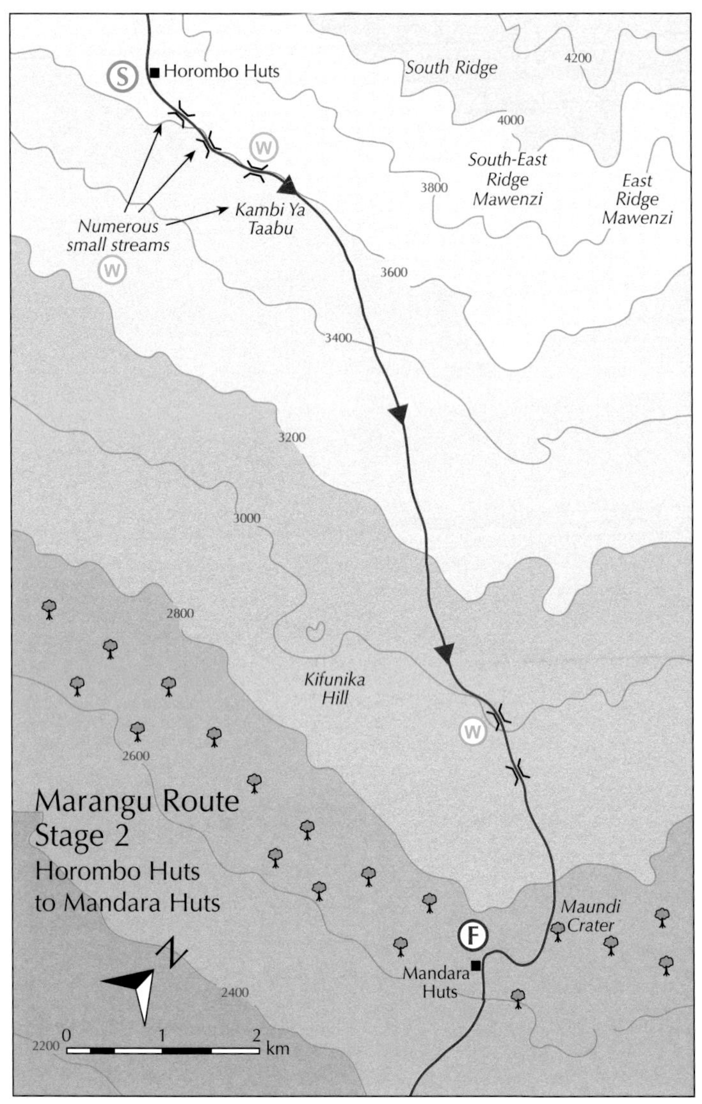
Horombo Huts
South Ridge
4200
4000
South-East Ridge Mawenzi
3800
East Ridge Mawenzi
Kambi Ya Taabu
Numerous small streams
3600
3400
3200
3000
2800
Kifunika Hill
2600
Marangu Route Stage 2
Horombo Huts to Mandara Huts
Maundi Crater
Mandara Huts
2400
2200
0
1
2
km

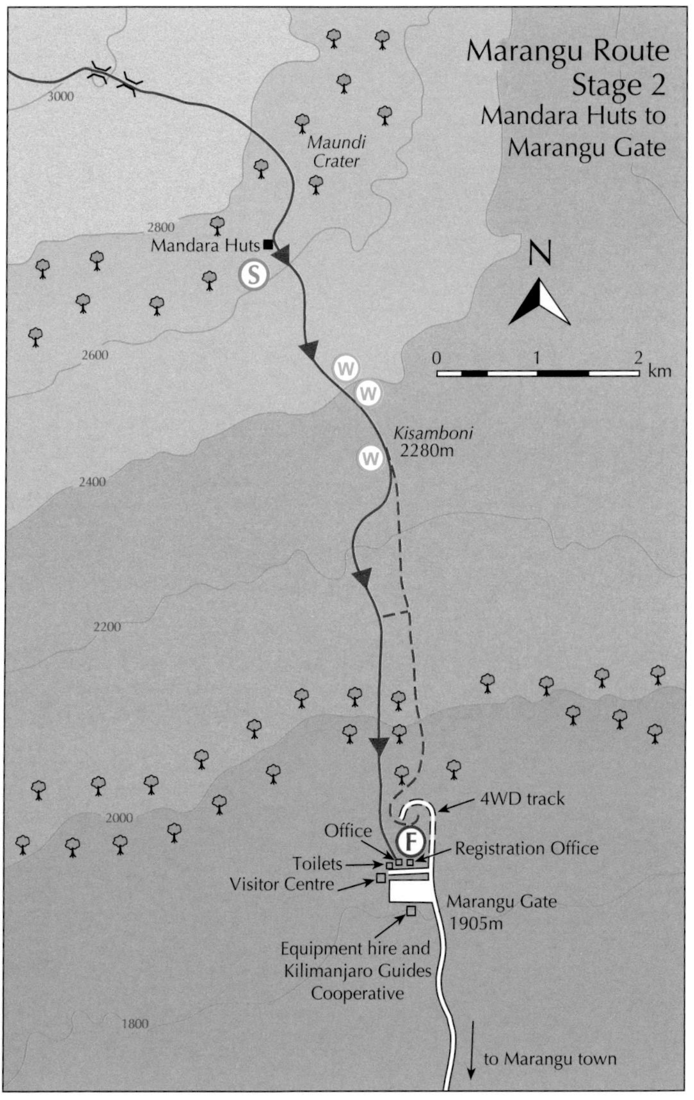
Marangu Route
Stage 2
Mandara Huts to
Marangu Gate
3000
Maundi
Crater
2800
Mandara Huts
S
N
2600
W
W
0
1
2
km
Kisamboni
2280m
W
2400
2200
2000
4WD track
Office
F
Registration Office
Toilets
Visitor Centre
Marangu Gate
1905m
Equipment hire and
Kilimanjaro Guides
Cooperative
1800
to Marangu town

ROUTE M

Mweka Route

Start	Barafu Hut (4640m)
Finish	Mweka Gate (1630m)
Distance	17km (20.5km from Uhuru Peak)
Time	2 days
Altitude loss	3010m (4265m from Uhuru Peak)

The successful attainment of the summit is only the first part of what will seem like an endless day. Having reached Uhuru Peak, or even just the crater rim, you will still need to descend. What's more, you must drop not only to Barafu Hut, but then also onto Mweka Hut for the overnight camp. The descent is steep and you lose height rapidly. It is consequently very tough. The slopes leading from the crater rim are unstable and the slipsliding descent means that your knees will take a pounding.

The Mweka Route is the stipulated descent route for the Umbwe, Machame, Lemosho and Shira ascent routes. It is used having climbed to the crater rim via either the Barafu or Western Breach routes. First opened in 1965, the Mweka Route is the easternmost route on the western flank and provides a very fast, direct descent from the mountain.

Originally, park regulations only permitted a small number of people to use the various forest and moorland ascent routes, which meant that the authorities could control and regulate the number of people descending on the Mweka Route. Thereby they were able to restrict the damage that was being done to the mountain. With the removal of the cap on the numbers of people walking the various routes and the general increase in popularity of the Machame Route, it was inevitable that the extra wear on the path would result in massive track damage. The Mweka Route as it was simply couldn't cope with the additional volume of traffic. Consequently, the route was closed for a while in August 2001 so that essential track maintenance could be carried out and the surrounding environment could recover and regenerate. Following extensive restoration, the Mweka Route was reopened at the end of 2002 and once more became the nominated descent route for the western and southern approach routes.

STAGE 1

Barafu Hut to Mweka Hut

Start	Barafu Hut (4660m)
Finish	Mweka Hut (3105m)
Distance	7km (11.5km from Uhuru Peak)
Time	2½hrs (5–6hrs from Uhuru Peak)
Altitude loss	1555m (2790m from Uhuru Peak)

From Uhuru Peak to Barafu Hut

From Uhuru Peak, initially follow the crater rim south and then east, passing above the Southern Icefields, until you reach **Stella Point**. The circumnavigation of the crater takes an hour. From here drop off the side of the crater and zigzag down the Barafu Route to the summit, retracing your steps if you climbed to the crater this way or experiencing the scree slope for the first time if you arrived at Uhuru Peak via the Western Breach. By this stage of the day, the scree will have unfrozen and the ground underfoot will be even less stable than it was during the ascent to the top. Retain your balance by using trekking poles and by not rushing. Do not feel pressured into descending too quickly as there is a real risk of a serious fall here. You might witness the more energetic or nimble climbers coming off the mountain and cutting between the switchbacks, scree running on the descent as a quicker alternative to actually following the path as it snakes back and forth. While this is undoubtedly a faster way to get down and can be exhilarating, it's also dangerous to dash headlong down Kibo on loose scree and the damage that you do displacing the scree in this way is harmful to the structure of the mountain, so please stick to the path to minimize disruption and reduce the risk of a fall.

At the foot of the scree slope the path regains more solid ground. It winds across a flatter stretch before descending two short, steep, stepped cliff sections to arrive at Barafu Hut after 1½–2hrs. Rest and recuperate briefly on the barren, lava-strewn ridge here, taking the time to rehydrate and reflect on the earlier mornings achievements.

From **Barafu Hut**, the path drops south and then south-west for 45mins along a prominent ridge above **South-East Valley**, through a thoroughly bleak and benighted landscape. The path tumbles out of the desolate, highland desert and into the moorland, where it arrives at a crossroads that marks the intersection of the descent route with the **Southern Circuit Path**. The crossroads is well signposted, with directions to the Karanga Valley and Barranco or Horombo Huts via the Southern Circuit Path and to the Mweka Hut, your overnight campsite. Continue straight ahead, descending in a roughly southerly direction. Vegetation begins to reassert itself as you drop lower and heathers and grasses reappear alongside the path as you enter the moorland.

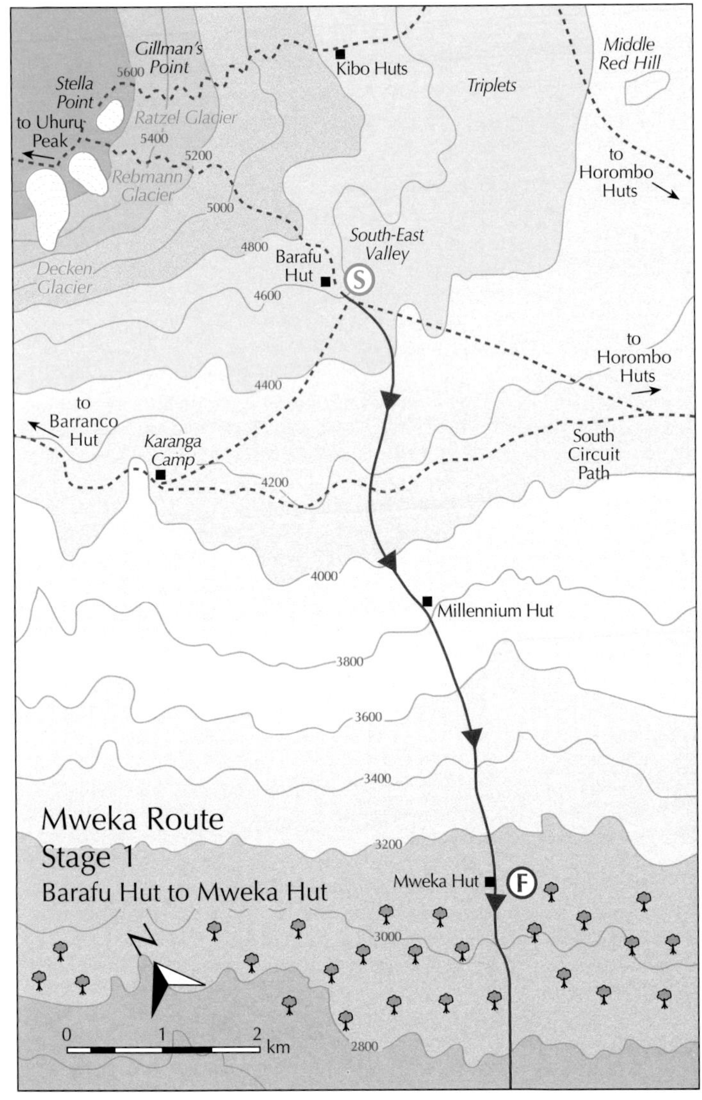

Gillman's Point
5600
Stella Point
to Uhuru Peak
Ratzel Glacier
5400
5200
Rebmann Glacier
5000
Kibo Huts
Triplets
Middle Red Hill
to Horombo Huts
4800
Barafu Hut
South-East Valley
S
Decken Glacier
4600
to Horombo Huts
4400
to Barranco Hut
Karanga Camp
South Circuit Path
4200
4000
Millennium Hut
3800
3600
3400
Mweka Route
Stage 1
Barafu Hut to Mweka Hut
3200
Mweka Hut
F
3000
0
1
2
km
2800

Shortly after the crossroads you will be able to make out the roof of a uniport in the distance amid a grove of trees. Some 30–40mins after the crossroads, the path drops through light forest to this hut and high campsite, now known as **Millennium Hut** (3830m).

The **Millennium Hut** was named after its usage during the celebratory climb to mark the millennium but previously referred to as High Camp or Rescue Hut. For most people, it is a deceptive vision: although the hut has a relatively quiet campsite next to it, it has traditionally only been used by those descending late or too slowly to make the Mweka Hut. As the Mweka hut site becomes more and more busy, however, with swelling numbers on the mountain, so Millennium Hut is increasing in popularity. It's an attractive spot too, with toilets and a good water supply, which makes it an appealing alternative if the lower camp is busy or, as sometimes happens after heavy rain, flooded.

The path continues to descend steadily south through giant heathers and patchy grasses. Other plants begin to reappear as you get lower, including *Protea* and *Erica* bushes.

A great deal of work has been done to improve the quality of the track here, and many of the worst sections have been re-laid and levelled. Steps have been built to ease the slope and drainage channels have been cut alongside the track to prevent the soil from washing away during heavy rains. However, in some places the stones laid

Kibo looming above the forest as seen from the Mweka Hut

to level the track are unbalancing and awkward to walk on and the path has begun to deteriorate as a consequence of the heavy traffic it has to endure.

The path broadens and runs to the west of a wide, shallow valley, through an area rich in *Protea* and *Erica*. After an hour the trees gain height and the understorey becomes thicker. Some 15mins later the path dips steeply before veering right and climbing through a series of S-bends to emerge in a large clearing adjacent to **Mweka Hut** (3105m).

Mweka Hut consists of two large uniports set amid a series of clearings. There are a large number of tent pitches straggling alongside the path leading south-west from the huts. There are also toilets. Mweka Hut is frequently dry, so water must be carried from the high campsite or retrieved from a stream 30mins further down the mountain. Although it's a pretty plain campsite, there are good views to be had looking north over the treetops towards the glistening snowfields atop Kibo.

STAGE 2

Mweka Hut to Mweka Gate

Start	Mweka Hut (3105m)
Finish	Mweka Gate (1630m)
Distance	9km
Time	2½–3¼hrs
Altitude loss	1475m

This is a short, relatively swift final day that sees you descend the remaining distance through the forest to Mweka Gate. The forest section is lush and extremely picturesque. The track here used to be very narrow and after rainfall would degenerate rapidly into a slippery trench. A lot of work was done to improve this section of track and much of it has been graded and levelled, although the passing of so many feet is inevitably taking its toll. Steps have been cut into the steeper sections and water channels line the path to prevent or at least slow its future deterioration.

The path from Mweka Hut passes south-west through a copse of skinny trees and giant heathers before dropping quite suddenly into much denser cloudforest. The path passes along the crest of a narrow ridge with steep-sided valleys to either side. After half an

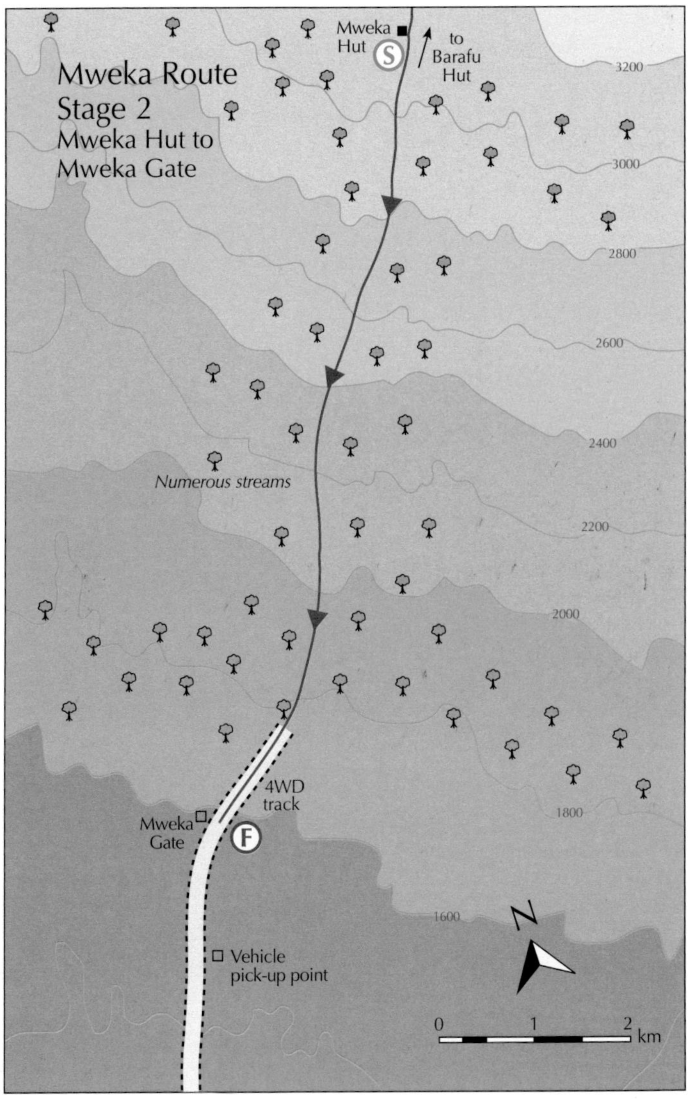
Mweka Route
Stage 2
Mweka Hut to
Mweka Gate
Mweka
Hut
S
to
Barafu
Hut
3200
3000
2800
2600
2400
Numerous streams
2200
2000
4WD
track
Mweka
Gate
F
1800
1600
N
Vehicle
pick-up point
0
1
2
km

The track through the forest below the Mweka Hut

hour there is a signpost that indicates the indistinct track that winds down through the vegetation to the left of the path, to reach the stream at the bottom of the valley.

The path snakes through the forest and in places crosses the old route. The old path is set up to over half a metre deep in the ground as a result of heavy erosion and had been worn smooth to resemble a dry irrigation channel. In wet weather it resembled a muddy stream. Blissfully, this has been replaced with a better, more graded path that descends alongside and sometimes crosses over the original, in one place via a small bridge.

As you continue to descend steeply, be aware of teams of porters rushing past you. Step to one side and allow the faster moving people to pass. Don't rush. Walk slowly and take in the tall forest trees, dense tangled patches and sunlit glades where mosses and lichens glow rich and green in the sunlight. Watch too for the reappearance of *Impatiens kilimanjari*.

After 1½–2hrs the path broadens into a dusty 4WD track, which used to be used as a logging road. The forest opens up as you near the Mweka Gate until 30–45mins later you emerge amid a bustle of people and Land Rovers at the **Mweka Gate**. Register at the hut here to complete your climb.

Unfortunately, most outfitters will not have a **vehicle** here to collect you, so you must gird yourself and walk a further 15mins downhill through banana plantations to arrive at the road end, where you will find a host of curio shops and the Tobit Kilimanjaro View Centre, which is ostensibly a bar full of exhausted, exhilarated climbers.

Alternative Mweka Route

During the time that the Mweka Route was closed for rehabilitation, from the end of 2001 to late 2002, the park authorities opened a new descent route along similar lines. Descending from Stella Point along the Barafu Route, the Alternative Mweka Route diverged from the traditional Mweka Route just beyond Barafu Hut. It then dropped steeply just to the east of the original route and ended at the Kidia Gate. The route was sometimes referred to as the Kidia Route as a result and can still be seen on some maps. Some outfitters also knew it as the Rau Route, since it followed the course of the Rau River.

When, following renovation, the original Mweka Route was reopened, the Alternative Mweka Route was closed. It remains shut. Although having a second descent on this section of the mountain was a good idea as it reduced the pressure and foot traffic on the Mweka Route, the temporary track took a severe pounding and became badly eroded too. Therefore, despite the fact that Kilimanjaro is in need of another descent route, this is not considered to be the solution.

APPENDIX A

Accommodation

There is a wide variety of accommodation options at the foot of Kilimanjaro, in Moshi. Those listed here represent a spectrum of the options available and ought to cater for most budgets. The price ranges, given in US dollars, are: $ under $30, $$ 30–70 and $$$ over 70.

Bristol Cottages ($$–$$$)
98A Rindi Lane
tel 027 275 5083
www.bristolcottages.com

Pricier option that buys you a small, modern, immaculate cottage set in a tidy garden. Those closer to the road are US$10 cheaper, those with views of Kilimanjaro have a price hike of US$20. Restaurant on site.

Buffalo Hotel ($)
New St
tel 027 275 3736
email buffalocompanyltd@yahoo.com

Very popular three-storey hotel that represents good value for money, with single and double room rates. All rooms have a fan and mosquito nets, while some are en suite. Also has a restaurant on site.

Impala ($$$)
Lema Rd
tel 027 275 3443
www.kilimanjaro.impalahotel.com

Welcoming and attractive place to stay, with its own pool and en suite rooms. Single and double rooms, with breakfast included in the room rate.

Key's Hotel ($$$)
Uru Rd
tel 027 275 2250
www.keys-hotel-tours.com

Quiet, comfortable and long-standing venue that has a superb reputation. Rooms in the main building are better than the cottages at the back. Pool, restaurant and bar on site. Single and doubles, with a/c an additional US$20. Camping is possible in the grounds.

Kilimanjaro Backpackers ($)
Mawenzi/Double Rd
tel 027 275 5159
www.kilimanjarobackpackers.com

Despite being pretty basic, this is a popular place – in large part due to the reasonable rates. Dorms, single and double rooms are available, half board and full board packages also.

Kilimanjaro Crane Hotel ($$–$$$)
Kaunda Rd
tel 027 275 1114
www.kilimanjarocranehotel.com

Large, modern, plain hotel with reasonable amenities. Single/double/triple rooms are available with a/c costing US$10 more. Bar and restaurant on site.

Kindoroko Hotel ($–$$)
Mawenzi Rd
tel 275 4054
www.kindorokohotels.com

Small but long-established place to stay that has a good reputation and is reasonably priced. Single, double and family rooms. Rooftop bar and restaurant on site.

Moshi Leopard Hotel ($$–$$$)
Market St
tel 027 275 0884
www.leopardhotel.com

Large, modern hotel in a busy part of town, that is perennially popular. Good amenities in single and double rooms, including fridge and TV, with a restaurant on site and a popular terrace bar.

Mountain Inn ($–$$)
Marangu Rd
tel 027 275 2370
www.kilimanjaro-shah.com

Run by Shah Tours and located 4km east of town, this is an attractive, comfy place with single, double and deluxe rooms. Restaurant and pool on site. Discounts available for those taking Shah Tours' treks.

New Coffee Tree Hotel ($)
Next to clock tower
tel 0752 388311

Single and double rooms, some with en suite, are basic but essentially clean and secure.

Nyumbani Hotel ($$$)
Rengua Rd
tel 027 275 4432
www.nyumbanihotels.com

Smart property offering private single and double B&B rooms with satellite TV and Wi-Fi.

Park View Inn ($$–$$$)
Aga Khan Rd
tel 027 275 0711
www.pvim.com

Large but smart place to stay. Reasonably priced singles, doubles and suites with most mod cons and friendly service.

Springlands Hotel ($$)
tel 027 275 3105
http://zara.co.tz/springlands/

Run by Zara. Located 1.5km south of town, this is a decent hotel with first-rate amenities. There is a pool, small shop, restaurant and bar on site. Unfortunately, you are only likely to stay here if you book a climb with Zara, in which case you will receive a free night's accommodation before and after your trip.

YMCA ($–$$)
Taifa Rd
tel 027 275 1754
email tzymca@africaonline.co.tz

Over priced, but safe and clean, if a bit run down. Very popular with backpackers. Good views of Kilimanjaro from some rooms. Pool and restaurant on site.

Zebra Hotel ($$)
tel 0766 998648

Large, centrally located hotel with rather plain en suite singles, doubles and triples, with a/c, at reasonable rates.

APPENDIX B

Useful contacts

Kilimanjaro National Park Headquarters is situated at Marangu Gate, 6km north of the Marangu village (accessible by tarmac road), 48km from Moshi and about 90km from Kilimanjaro International Airport.

Kilimanjaro Senior Park Warden
PO Box 96, Marangu, Tanzania

Kilimanjaro Porters Assistance Project (KPAP)
tel 0754 817 615
https://kiliporters.org
Hill St, Moshi, behind a coffee shop

Outfitters

There are a large number of outfitters in Moshi who will volunteer to organise and equip a climb of Kilimanjaro for you. Many of these are professional, reliable outfits, but there are some charlatans about. The outfitters listed below represent the most recognised, established groups. Contact each outfitter direct to obtain an up-to-date list of the services they provide, the routes that they cover and the rates that they charge.

African Scenic Safaris
Hostel Hoff
tel 0783 080239
www.africanscenicsafaris.com

Budget outfit offering just a handful of basic treks at very reasonable rates.

Ahsante Tours
Karanga Drive
tel 027 275 0248
www.ahsantetours.com

The Kilimanjaro outfitter for several overseas travel companies. Solid service.

Akaro
Old Moshi Rd
tel 027 275 2986
www.akarotours.com

Friendly outfit with some mixed feedback, offering a surprisingly cheap climb.

Bryson Adventures
Mankinga Rd
tel 0754 318033
www.brysonadventures.com

More recently established outfit with good rates and reasonable approach to porters.

Dotcom Safaris
Kaunda St
tel 027 275 4104
www.dotcomsafaris.com

Long-standing but relatively little-used budget outfitters providing basic treks at low rates.

Gladys Adventure
Hill St
tel 0787 111881
www.gladysadventure.com

Successful and popular outfit with strong service record offering three levels of budget trek, depending on which hotel you stay at before and after the climb.

Key's
Uru Rd
tel 027 275 2250
http://keys-hotel-tours.com

Long-standing outfitter who provides solid, professional packages for most routes. Reasonably priced, without being cheap.

Moshi Expedition and Mountaineering
Kaunda St
tel 027 275 4234
www.memafrica.com

There are three standards of decent trek offered by MEM Tours at varying rates and levels of luxury that include nights in one of Moshi's hotels (hotel dependent on standard picked).

Pristine Trails
Boma Rd
tel 0717 100 788
www.pristinetrails.com

Comprehensive outfit offering three levels of trek (standard, luxury and exclusive) all at reasonable rates, with a good reputation for service and porter welfare.

Shah Tours
Mawenzi Rd
tel 027 275 2370
www.shah-tours.com

Very well established family-run outfitter with a superb reputation for offering excellent climbs. Reasonable rates for most routes that also include a night's accommodation in the Mountain Inn.

Snow Cap Mountain Climbing Camp
Taifa Rd
tel 027 275 4826
www.snowcap.co.tz

Rongai Route specialists that dabble elsewhere on the mountain but deliver quality treks on their focus route.

Summit Expeditions and Nomadic Experience
tel 027 275 3233
www.nomadicexperience.com

Focus on the Lemosho Route and Western Breach, and include several nights' stay at the owner's farm. A member of the KPAP Partner's scheme, it has a very good reputation for taking care of its porters and staff and receives rave reviews.

Trans-Kibo Travels
YMCA Building
Kilimanjaro Rd
tel 0754 287618
www.transkibo.com

Reasonable travel agency organising tours and trips with fair prices.

Trek2kili
tel 0788 360715
www.trek2kili.com

Fairly priced budget trekking outfit with solid service record, good success rate and a positive approach to supporting porters.

ZARA
Rindi Lane
tel 0784 451000
www.zaratours.com

Very well established, reliable, professional institution. Slightly more expensive, but provides an outstanding service on all routes, with accommodation before and after at their Springlands Hotel.

Trekking clubs

Mountain Club of Kenya
Wilson Airport
Nairobi
tel 020 501 747
www.mck.or.ke

Meets weekly. Members can participate in treks and climbs around the country.

Kilimanjaro Mountain Club
PO Box 77
Moshi
www.kiliweb.com/kmc

Less of a club and more of an information service, this voluntary group also organises monthly meetings, excursions and camping trips.

Airlines

Air Tanzania
www.airtanzania.co.tz

British Airways
tel 08457 733 377
www.britishairways.com

Egyptair
tel 020 7734 2343
www.egyptair.com

Emirates
tel 0870 243 2222
www.emirates.com

Ethiopian Airlines
tel 020 8987 7000
www.ethiopianairlines.com

Gulf Air
tel 0870 777 1717
www.gulfair.com

Kenya Airways
tel 01784 888 222
www.kenya-airways.com

KLM
www.klm.com

Precision Air
www.precisionairtz.com

Qatar Airways
www.qatarairways.com

South African Airways
tel 020 7312 5000
www.flysaa.com

Swissair
tel 0845 601 0956
www.swissair.com

Turkish Airlines
www.turkishairlines.com

Private bus services between Nairobi and Arusha and Moshi

Impala

www.impalashuttles.com

Nairobi address:
Silver Springs Hotel
Hurlingham Roundabout
tel 020 271 7373

Arusha address:
Impala Hotel
tel 0784 550012
email impala@impalahotel.com

Moshi address:
Opposite KNCU Building
Moshi
tel 0754 360658
email impala@kilinet.com

Riverside

www.riverside-shuttle.com
tel 0754 270089/0757 091120

Nairobi address:
1st Floor, Lagos House
Monrovia St
tel 0725 999121

Arusha address:
Sokoine Road and desk at the Novotel Mount Meru Hotel
tel 027 250 2639

Moshi address:
Room 122
1st Floor
Voda House
Boma Road
tel 027 275 0093

Other companies

AA Luxury Shuttle Bus
www.aashuttles.com

East Africa Shuttles
www.eastafricashuttles.com

Nairobi Arusha Shuttle Transport
www.nairobiarushashuttle.com

Regional Luxury Shuttle
www.regionalluxuryshuttle.com

Foreign embassies

UK

Tanzania High Commission
3 Stratford Place
London
W1C 1AS
tel 020 7569 1470
fax 020 7491 9321
http://tanzaniahighcomm.co.uk

Kenya High Commission
45 Portland Place
London
W1B 1AS
tel 020 7636 2371
http://kenyahighcom.org.uk

Kenya

Tanzanian High Commission
9th Floor
Reinsurance Plaza
Taifa Rd
PO Box 47790
Nairobi
tel 020 331 2027
www.tanzaniahc.or.ke

British High Commission
Upper Hill Rd
Nairobi
tel 020 284 4000
email Nairobi.Enquiries@fco.gov.uk
www.gov.uk/government/world/kenya

US Embassy
United Nations Ave
PO Box 606
Village Market
Nairobi
tel 020 363 6000
https://ke.usembassy.gov

Australian Embassy
ICIPE House
Riverside Drive
Nairobi
tel 020 427 7100
http://kenya.embassy.gov.au

Canadian High Commission
Limuru Rd
Gigiri
PO Box 1013
Nairobi
tel 020 366 3000
www.canadainternational.gc.ca/kenya/

Irish Embassy
4th Floor
Delta Office Suites
Waiyaki Way
Muthangari
Nairobi
tel 0729 000 353
www.dfa.ie/irish-embassy/kenya

French Embassy
Barclays Plaza
Loita St
PO Box 41784
Nairobi
tel 020277 8000
https://ke.ambafrance.org

German Embassy
Riverside Drive 113
PO Box 30180
Nairobi
tel 020 426 2100
www.nairobi.diplo.de

Tanzania

Kenya High Commission
Ali Hassan Mwinyi/Kaunda Drive
Junction
Oysterbay
PO Box 5231
Dar es Salaam
tel 022 266 8285

British High Commission
Umoja House
Hamburg Av
PO Box 9200
Dar es Salaam
tel 022 229 0000
www.gov.uk/government/world/
tanzania

USA Embassy
686 Old Bagamoyo
Msasani
Dar es Salaam
tel 022 229 4000
https://tz.usembassy.gov

Australia
There is no Australian embassy or high commission in Dar es Salaam. Australian citizens are advised to contact the Canadian High Commission, who will offer consular assistance.

Canadian High Commission
38 Mirambo St
Garden Ave
Dar es Salaam
tel 022 216 3300
www.canadainternational.gc.ca/
tanzania-tanzanie

Irish Embassy
353 Toure Drive
PO Box 9612
Dar es Salaam
tel 022 260 2355
www.dfa.ie/irish-embassy/tanzania/

French Embassy
Ali Hassan Mwyini Rd
Kinodoni
PO Box 2349
Dar es Salaam
tel 022 219 8800
https://tz.ambafrance.org

German Embassy
Umoja House
Mirambo St/Garden Ave
PO Box 9541
Dar es Salaam
tel 022 211 7409
www.daressalam.diplo.de

Netherlands Embassy
Umoja House
Garden Ave
Dar es Salaam
tel 022 219 4000
www.netherlandsworldwide.nl/countries/tanzania

South African High Commission
Plot 218/50
Corner of Garden Ave and Shabani Robert Rd
PO Box 10723
Ilala Distict
Dar-es-Salaam
tel 022 221 18500

Information on health

See www.nomadtravel.co.uk for information and details of their stores.

APPENDIX C

Further reading

Interest books

There has been a great deal written about Kilimanjaro over the years, from early explorers' accounts of their expeditions to contemporary glossy, coffee-table style accounts of trips up the mountain.

Perhaps the best-known book is Ernest Hemmingway's celebrated short story, *The Snows of Kilimanjaro* (first published by Jonathan Cape in 1939 and reproduced in 1994 by Arrow). Written in 1936, two years after Hemmingway returned from his first African safari, it tells the story of a wealthy writer on safari, who has contracted gangrene in his leg and is dying in the shadow of the great peak. The gangrene in his leg forces him to confront the fact that he has betrayed his vocation and frittered away his literary talent on a life of luxury. He realises that he will never produce anything as enduring or enchanting as the brilliance of the snow-capped summit nearby. The story celebrates, and made famous, the leopard found frozen on the summit. The leopard's upward exploration, while not explained, stands for artistic endeavour and its frozen carcass remains as a testament.

The book was made into a film in 1952 starring Gregory Peck, Susan Hayward and Ava Gardner, and featuring a giant painting of Kilimanjaro as a backdrop. Rewritten in order to guarantee a happy ending, whereby the protagonist recovered from gangrene and resolved to not let his literary talent go to waste, the film outraged Hemmingway who railed at this version of his vision.

Interestingly, Hemmingway never actually climbed Kilimanjaro, and only came close to the mountain when flying to Arusha.

The following books provide a broad commentary on Kilimanjaro. Some of them, particularly the older expedition accounts, are out of print and can only be found in second-hand bookshops or the British Library:

Peter Beard, *The End of the Game* (Thames and Hudson, 1988). Pointed photographic and narrative account of the decimation of African wildlife and the African landscape.

Stephen Carmichael, *Climbing Mount Kilimanjaro* (Medi-Ed Press, 2002). Plenty of pre-departure guidelines and advice as to what to take, but contains no details relating to the mountain or the routes on it.

Richard and Nicholas Crane, *Bicycles Up Kilimanjaro* (Oxford Illustrated Press, 1985). An account of mountain biking to the summit of Kilimanjaro in order to raise money for a charity project looking to build windmills to pump water in East Africa.

Daniel Dorr, *Kissing Kilimanjaro – Leaving it all on Top of Africa* (Mountaineers Books, 2010). A solid step-by-step account of failing to summit via the Machame Route and a return trip to tackle the Rongai Route.

Charles Dundas, *Kilimanjaro and Its People* (H, F and G Witherby, 1924; Frank Cass and Co, 1968). Very authoritative, fascinating description of the Chagga people, their daily lives and rituals.

Rolf Edberg, *The Dream of Kilimanjaro* (Pantheon, 1976). Recounts his pilgrimage to the Rift Valley and contains a digression on the development and evolution of mankind in Africa.

MG Edwards, *Kilimanjaro – One Man's Quest to go over the Hill* (CreateSpace, 2012). At 40 years old and on the verge of a mid-life crisis, the author decided to make a dramatic life change by climbing a mountain. This is his account of the Marangu Route and facing life's challenges at middle age.

Phil Gray, *Kilimanjaro via the Marangu Route: 'Tourist Route' My Ass* (iUniverse Inc, 2006). Light-hearted, throwaway account of a climb via the oft-punted 'Tourist Route' demonstrating that there's no such thing as an easy ascent.

HH Johnston, *The Kilima-njaro Expedition* (Kegan Paul, 1886). A record of scientific exploration by the explorer and administrator who was to effect a series of treaties with local chiefs and pre-empt the founding of the British East Africa protectorate. Contains some fanciful details but also good descriptions of the natural history, ethnology and the commercial prospects of the region.

Peter MacQueen, *In Wildest Africa* (LC Page, 1909). A record of his hunting and exploration expedition in East Africa at the time of the German occupation. Includes an account of his ill-fated ascent to the snowfields on Kilimanjaro.

Hans Meyer, *Across East African Glaciers: The First Ascent of Kilimanjaro* (G Philip and son, 1891). A fantastically detailed, enlightening account of the first ascent of Kilimanjaro. Beautifully illustrated.

Charles New, *Life Wanderings and Labours in Eastern Africa* (Hodder and Stoughton, 1873). Interesting account of New's time on the slopes of Kilimanjaro and of his encounters with the Chagga.

David Pluth, *Kilimanjaro – The Great White Mountain of Africa* (Camerapix, 2001). Photographic book detailing the history and appeal of Kilimanjaro. Lyrical text and good photographs describe the main routes on the mountain in brief.

Johannes Rebmann, *Church Missionary Intelligencer Articles, Vol 1, May 1849* (Seeleys, 1850). First reports of Rebmann's three trips to the Kilimanjaro region and his assertion that there was indeed snow on the equator.

John Reader, *Kilimanjaro* (Elm Tree Books, 1982). Outstanding photographic guide to the mountain, that also contains detailed historical and geological sections.

Rick Ridgeway, *The Shadow of Kilimanjaro: On Foot Across East Africa* (Bloomsbury, 1998). An incredible journey that in the course of a month took him up and over Kilimanjaro, across the plains of Tsavo to the coast. Well written, it provides a good ground-level view of East Africa both past and present.

Geoffrey Salisbury, *The Road to Kilimanjaro* (Minerva, 1997). Contains an account of an expedition led by Salisbury that took a group of eight blind African children up Kilimanjaro along the Loitokitok Route.

Audrey Salkeld, *Kilimanjaro: To the Roof of Africa* (National Geographic Books, 2001). Sumptuous coffee-table book full of contemporary photographs. Text describes the history and background to the mountain as well as details an ascent of Kilimanjaro via the Machame Route in the company of an IMAX film crew.

Neville Shulman, *On Top of Africa: The Climbing of Kilimanjaro and Mount Kenya* (Element, 1993). Spiritual tinged trekker's tale of climbing Kilimanjaro.

Eva Stuart Watt, *Africa's Dome of Mystery* (Marshall, Morgan and Scott Ltd, 1930). An early descriptive account of the Wachagga people and of an ascent to Kibo's crater rim by a young colonial.

Rob Taylor, *The Breach: Kilimanjaro and the Conquest of Self* (Wildeyes, inc, 1981). An account of Taylor's 1978 attempt to climb the Breach Wall, which ended in disaster and resulted in Taylor making a daring escape from the mountain many days after his accident. Highly contentious at the time of publication, it provoked strong reactions and disagreements with his companion on the climb.

Wilfred Thesiger, *My Kenya Days* (Harper Collins, 1994). Autobiography detailing Thesiger's 30 years in Kenya. Includes an account of his ascent of Kilimanjaro.

HW Tilman, *Snow on the Equator* (Bell and Son Books, 1937). Reproduced in Seven Mountain Travel Books (Baton Wicks, 2003). Rumbustious account of Tilman's failed ascent of Kilimanjaro with Eric Shipton in 1930 and his later solo success in 1933.

Tim Ward, *Zombies on Kilimanjaro* (Changemakers Books, 2012). Subtitled 'A Father/Son Journey above the Clouds', this is an intensely personal account of a bonding trek that spends rather more time on the familial relationship than it does on the mountain.

Wildlife and birds

David Hosking, *Wildlife of East Africa* (Harper Collins, 2002). Straightforward, illustrated checklist of the animals most frequently encountered on a trip to East Africa.

Ber Van Perlo, *Birds of Eastern Africa* (Harper Collins, 1995). Useful introduction and checklist for bird spotting in the region.

Dale Zimmerman, *Birds of Kenya and Northern Tanzania* (Christopher Helm, 2001). High quality, illustrated guide to the bird species found in this region.

Websites

A simple search on any Internet search engine for references to Kilimanjaro will turn up a myriad list of sites. A vast number of these are personal accounts of trips or advertisements by trekking outfitters.

Many of the trekking outfitters that offer climbs on Kilimanjaro have websites that outline the itineraries available on the various routes. These sites often also have a smattering of background information relating to the mountain.

For general information, try www.tanzania.go.tz, the official site of the Tanzanian government, or www.africatravelresource.com, which has a printable fact file.

Otherwise, you may wish to look at the official Tanzanian Tourist Board website, www.tanzaniatourism.com, which has a section dedicated to Kilimanjaro. Alternatively, try www.kilimanjaro.com or www.kiliweb.com, both of which have trekking details and interesting links.

APPENDIX D

Language glossary

While it would be entirely possible to climb Kilimanjaro without ever speaking a word of Swahili, a little effort and the simplest of phrases can elicit a very positive response. While trekking with a guide and porters plenty of opportunities to practise a few words and sentences will arise and any attempt to speak the language will be appreciated.

The following glossary lists a handful of words that may be useful on the trail. There are also a number of small, pocket-sized phrasebooks and dictionaries available that may be worth consulting.

English	Swahili
hello	jambo
How are you?	Habari (response: good – nzuri, fine – salama)
How's things?	Mambo? (response: cool – poa)
welcome	karibu
Do you speak English?	Unasema Kiingereza?
I don't speak Swahili	Sijui Kiswahili
goodbye	kwa heri
please	tafadhali
thank you	asante
thank you very much	asante sana
you're welcome	karibu sana
no problem	hakuna matata
yes	ndiyo
no	hapana
I want to go to …	Nataka kwenda …
I'm looking for …	Natafuta …
How many hours to …?	Masaa mangapi …?
Is it far?	Ni mbali?
How many kilometres from here?	Ni kilomita ngapi kutoka hapa?

English	Swahili
left	kushoto
right	kulia
straight ahead	moja kwa moja
east	mashariki
west	magharibi
north	kaskazini
south	kusini
mountain	mlima
guide	mwongozi
porter	mchukuzi
map	ramani
path	njia
stone	jiwe
summit	kilele
scree	mawe kidogo
cliff	mlima mdogo
valley	bonde
let's go!	twendai!
slowly, slowly	pole, pole
hotel	gesti/hoteli (hoteli also means restaurant)
campsite	kambi
tent	hema

English	Swahili
hot water	maji ya moto
toilet	choo
bath	bafu
telephone	simu
fan	feni
key	ufunguo
hungry	njaa
thirsty	kiu
meat	nyama
chicken	nyama kuku
beef	nyama ng'ombe
fish	samaki
milk	maziwa
vegetable	mboga
potato	kiazi ulaya
bread	mkate
coffee	kahawa
tea	chai
drinking water	magi ya kunywa
ice	barafu
beer	bia (order by brand name)
wine	mvinyo
What's the weather like?	Hali ya hewa ikoje?
It's cold	Ni baridi
It's hot	Ni joto
It's raining	Mvua inanyesha
It's sunny	Kuna jua
It's windy	Kuna upepo
snow	theluj
cloud	mawingu
Danger!	Hatari!
Help!	Nisaidie!/Saidia!
I need help	Naomba msaada

English	Swahili
I'm lost	Nimepotea
I'm ill	Ninaumwa
I feel dizzy	Nasikia kizunguzungu
I feel nauseous	Nataka kutapika
I feel weak	Najisikia mnyofu
I've been vomiting	Nina tapika
Is the water good to drink?	Maji haya ni safi ya kunywa?
0	sifuri
1	moja
2	mbili
3	tatu
4	nne
5	tano
6	sita
7	saba
8	nane
9	tisa
10	kumi
11	kumi na moja
12	kumi na mbili
20	ishirini
30	thelathini
40	arobaini
50	hamsini
60	sitini
70	sabini
80	themanini
90	tisini
100	mia/mia moja
200	mia mbili
1000	elfu
2000	elfu mbili

NOTES

LISTING OF CICERONE GUIDES

SCOTLAND

Backpacker's Britain: Northern Scotland
Ben Nevis and Glen Coe
Cycling in the Hebrides
Great Mountain Days in Scotland
Mountain Biking in Southern and Central Scotland
Mountain Biking in West and North West Scotland
Not the West Highland Way
Scotland
Scotland's Best Small Mountains
Scotland's Far West
Scotland's Mountain Ridges
Scrambles in Lochaber
The Ayrshire and Arran Coastal Paths
The Border Country
The Cape Wrath Trail
The Great Glen Way
The Great Glen Way Map Booklet
The Hebridean Way
The Hebrides
The Isle of Mull
The Isle of Skye
The Skye Trail
The Southern Upland Way
The Speyside Way
The Speyside Way Map Booklet
The West Highland Way
Walking Highland Perthshire
Walking in Scotland's Far North
Walking in the Angus Glens
Walking in the Cairngorms
Walking in the Ochils, Campsie Fells and Lomond Hills
Walking in the Pentland Hills
Walking in the Southern Uplands
Walking in Torridon
Walking Loch Lomond and the Trossachs
Walking on Arran
Walking on Harris and Lewis
Walking on Jura, Islay and Colonsay
Walking on Rum and the Small Isles
Walking on the Orkney and Shetland Isles
Walking on Uist and Barra
Walking the Corbetts Vol 1
Walking the Corbetts Vol 2
Walking the Galloway Hills
Walking the Munros Vol 1
Walking the Munros Vol 2
West Highland Way Map Booklet
Winter Climbs Ben Nevis and Glen Coe
Winter Climbs in the Cairngorms

NORTHERN ENGLAND TRAILS

Hadrian's Wall Path
Hadrian's Wall Path Map Booklet
Pennine Way Map Booklet
The Coast to Coast Walk
The Coast to Coast Map Booklet
The Dales Way
The Pennine Way

LAKE DISTRICT

Cycling in the Lake District
Great Mountain Days in the Lake District
Lake District Winter Climbs
Lake District: High Level and Fell Walks
Lake District: Low Level and Lake Walks
Lakeland Fellranger
Mountain Biking in the Lake District
Scafell Pike
Scrambles in the Lake District – North
Scrambles in the Lake District – South
Short Walks in Lakeland Book 1: South Lakeland
Short Walks in Lakeland Book 2: North Lakeland
Short Walks in Lakeland Book 3: West Lakeland
Tour of the Lake District
Trail and Fell Running in the Lake District

NORTH WEST ENGLAND AND THE ISLE OF MAN

Cycling the Pennine Bridleway
Isle of Man Coastal Path
The Lancashire Cycleway
The Lune Valley and Howgills
The Ribble Way
Walking in Cumbria's Eden Valley
Walking in Lancashire
Walking in the Forest of Bowland and Pendle
Walking on the Isle of Man
Walking on the West Pennine Moors
Walks in Lancashire Witch Country
Walks in Ribble Country
Walks in Silverdale and Arnside

NORTH EAST ENGLAND, YORKSHIRE DALES AND PENNINES

Cycling in the Yorkshire Dales
Great Mountain Days in the Pennines
Historic Walks in North Yorkshire
Mountain Biking in the Yorkshire Dales
South Pennine Walks
St Oswald's Way and St Cuthbert's Way
The Cleveland Way and the Yorkshire Wolds Way
The Cleveland Way Map Booklet
The North York Moors
The Reivers Way
The Teesdale Way
Walking in County Durham
Walking in Northumberland
Walking in the North Pennines
Walking in the Yorkshire Dales: North and East
Walking in the Yorkshire Dales: South and West
Walks in Dales Country
Walks in the Yorkshire Dales

WALES AND WELSH BORDERS

Glyndwr's Way
Great Mountain Days in Snowdonia
Hillwalking in Shropshire
Hillwalking in Wales – Vol 1
Hillwalking in Wales – Vol 2
Mountain Walking in Snowdonia
Offa's Dyke Path
Offa's Dyke Map Booklet
Pembrokeshire Coast Path Map Booklet
Ridges of Snowdonia
Scrambles in Snowdonia
The Ascent of Snowdon
The Ceredigion and Snowdonia Coast Paths
The Pembrokeshire Coast Path
The Severn Way
The Snowdonia Way
The Wales Coast Path
The Wye Valley Walk
Walking in Carmarthenshire
Walking in Pembrokeshire
Walking in the Forest of Dean
Walking in the South Wales Valleys
Walking in the Wye Valley
Walking on the Brecon Beacons

Walking on the Gower
Welsh Winter Climbs

DERBYSHIRE, PEAK DISTRICT AND MIDLANDS

Cycling in the Peak District
Dark Peak Walks
Scrambles in the Dark Peak
Walking in Derbyshire
White Peak Walks: The Northern Dales
White Peak Walks: The Southern Dales

SOUTHERN ENGLAND

20 Classic Sportive Rides in South East England
20 Classic Sportive Rides in South West England
Cycling in the Cotswolds
Mountain Biking on the North Downs
Mountain Biking on the South Downs
North Downs Way Map Booklet
South West Coast Path Map Booklet – Minehead to St Ives
South West Coast Path Map Booklet – Plymouth to Poole
South West Coast Path Map Booklet – St Ives to Plymouth
Suffolk Coast and Heath Walks
The Cotswold Way
The Cotswold Way Map Booklet
The Great Stones Way
The Kennet and Avon Canal
The Lea Valley Walk
The North Downs Way
The Peddars Way and Norfolk Coast Path
The Pilgrims' Way
The Ridgeway Map Booklet
The Ridgeway National Trail
The South Downs Way
The South Downs Way Map Booklet
The South West Coast Path
The Thames Path
The Thames Path Map Booklet
The Two Moors Way
Walking in Cornwall
Walking in Essex
Walking in Kent
Walking in London
Walking in Norfolk
Walking in Sussex
Walking in the Chilterns
Walking in the Cotswolds
Walking in the Isles of Scilly
Walking in the New Forest
Walking in the North Wessex Downs
Walking in the Thames Valley
Walking on Dartmoor
Walking on Guernsey
Walking on Jersey
Walking on the Isle of Wight
Walking the Jurassic Coast
Walks in the South Downs National Park

BRITISH ISLES CHALLENGES, COLLECTIONS AND ACTIVITIES

The Book of the Bivvy
The Book of the Bothy
The C2C Cycle Route
The End to End Cycle Route
The End to End Trail
The Mountains of England and Wales: Vol 1 Wales
The Mountains of England and Wales: Vol 2 England
The National Trails
The UK's County Tops
Three Peaks, Ten Tors

ALPS CROSS-BORDER ROUTES

100 Hut Walks in the Alps
Across the Eastern Alps: E5
Alpine Ski Mountaineering Vol 1 – Western Alps
Alpine Ski Mountaineering Vol 2 – Central and Eastern Alps
Chamonix to Zermatt
The Tour of the Bernina
Tour of Mont Blanc
Tour of Monte Rosa
Tour of the Matterhorn
Trail Running – Chamonix and the Mont Blanc region
Trekking in the Alps
Trekking in the Silvretta and Rätikon Alps
Trekking Munich to Venice
Walking in the Alps

PYRENEES AND FRANCE/SPAIN CROSS-BORDER ROUTES

The GR10 Trail
The GR11 Trail – La Senda
The Pyrenean Haute Route
The Pyrenees
The Way of St James – France
The Way of St James – Spain
Walks and Climbs in the Pyrenees

AUSTRIA

The Adlerweg
Trekking in Austria's Hohe Tauern
Trekking in the Stubai Alps
Trekking in the Zillertal Alps
Walking in Austria

SWITZERLAND

Cycle Touring in Switzerland
The Swiss Alpine Pass Route – Via Alpina Route 1
The Swiss Alps
Tour of the Jungfrau Region
Walking in the Bernese Oberland
Walking in the Valais
Walks in the Engadine – Switzerland

FRANCE

Chamonix Mountain Adventures
Cycle Touring in France
Cycling the Canal du Midi
Écrins National Park
Mont Blanc Walks
Mountain Adventures in the Maurienne
The Cathar Way
The GR20 Corsica
The GR5 Trail
The GR5 Trail – Vosges and Jura
The Grand Traverse of the Massif Central
The Loire Cycle Route
The Moselle Cycle Route
The River Rhone Cycle Route
The Robert Louis Stevenson Trail
The Way of St James – Le Puy to the Pyrenees
Tour of the Oisans: The GR54
Tour of the Queyras
Tour of the Vanoise
Vanoise Ski Touring
Via Ferratas of the French Alps
Walking in Corsica
Walking in Provence – East
Walking in Provence – West
Walking in the Auvergne
Walking in the Cevennes
Walking in the Dordogne
Walking in the Haute Savoie: North
Walking in the Haute Savoie: South
Walks in the Cathar Region
Walking in the Ardennes

GERMANY

Hiking and Biking in the Black Forest
The Danube Cycleway Volume 1
The Rhine Cycle Route
The Westweg

ICELAND AND GREENLAND

Trekking in Greenland
Walking and Trekking in Iceland

IRELAND

The Irish Coast to Coast Walk
The Mountains of Ireland

ITALY

Italy's Sibillini National Park
Shorter Walks in the Dolomites
Ski Touring and Snowshoeing in the Dolomites
The Way of St Francis
Through the Italian Alps
Trekking in the Apennines
Trekking in the Dolomites
Via Ferratas of the Italian Dolomites Volume 1
Via Ferratas of the Italian Dolomites: Vol 2
Walking and Trekking in the Gran Paradiso
Walking in Abruzzo
Walking in Italy's Stelvio National Park
Walking in Sardinia
Walking in Sicily
Walking in the Dolomites
Walking in Tuscany
Walking in Umbria
Walking on the Amalfi Coast
Walking the Italian Lakes
Walks and Treks in the Maritime Alps

SCANDINAVIA

Walking in Norway

EASTERN EUROPE AND THE BALKANS

The Danube Cycleway Volume 2
The High Tatras
The Mountains of Romania
Walking in Bulgaria's National Parks
Walking in Hungary
Mountain Biking in Slovenia
The Islands of Croatia
The Julian Alps of Slovenia
The Mountains of Montenegro
The Peaks of the Balkans Trail
Trekking in Slovenia
Walking in Croatia
Walking in Slovenia: The Karavanke

SPAIN

Coastal Walks in Andalucia
Cycle Touring in Spain
Mountain Walking in Southern Catalunya
Spain's Sendero Histórico: The GR1
The Mountains of Nerja
The Mountains of Ronda and Grazalema
The Northern Caminos
The Sierras of Extremadura
The Way of St James Cyclist Guide
Trekking in Mallorca
Walking and Trekking in the Sierra Nevada
Walking in Andalucia
Walking in Menorca
Walking in the Cordillera Cantabrica
Walking on Gran Canaria
Walking on La Gomera and El Hierro
Walking on La Palma
Walking on Lanzarote and Fuerteventura
Walking on Tenerife
Walking on the Costa Blanca
Walking the GR7 in Andalucia

PORTUGAL

Walking in Madeira
Walking in Portugal
Walking in the Algarve

GREECE, CYPRUS AND MALTA

The High Mountains of Crete
Trekking in Greece
Walking and Trekking on Corfu
Walking in Cyprus
Walking on Malta

INTERNATIONAL CHALLENGES, COLLECTIONS AND ACTIVITIES

Canyoning in the Alps
The Via Francigena Canterbury to Rome – Part 1
The Via Francigena Canterbury to Rome – Part 2

AFRICA

Climbing in the Moroccan Anti-Atlas
Kilimanjaro
Mountaineering in the Moroccan High Atlas
The High Atlas
Trekking in the Atlas Mountains
Walking in the Drakensberg

JORDAN

Jordan – Walks, Treks, Caves, Climbs and Canyons
Treks and Climbs in Wadi Rum, Jordan

ASIA

Annapurna
Everest: A Trekker's Guide
Trekking in the Himalaya
Bhutan
Trekking in Ladakh
The Mount Kailash Trek

NORTH AMERICA

British Columbia
The John Muir Trail
The Pacific Crest Trail

SOUTH AMERICA

Aconcagua and the Southern Andes
Hiking and Biking Peru's Inca Trails
Torres del Paine

TECHNIQUES

Geocaching in the UK
Indoor Climbing
Lightweight Camping
Map and Compass
Outdoor Photography
Polar Exploration
Rock Climbing
Sport Climbing
The Hillwalker's Manual

MINI GUIDES

Alpine Flowers
Avalanche!
Navigation
Pocket First Aid and Wilderness Medicine
Snow

MOUNTAIN LITERATURE

8000 metres
A Walk in the Clouds
Abode of the Gods
The Pennine Way – the Path, the People, the Journey
Unjustifiable Risk?

CICERONE

Juniper House, Murley Moss, Oxenholme Road, Kendal, Cumbria LA9 7RL
Tel: 015395 62069 info@cicerone.co.uk
www.cicerone.co.uk and **www.cicerone-extra.com**